H 4035

Studies in Renaissance Literature

Volume 3

THE SONG OF SONGS IN ENGLISH RENAISSANCE LITERATURE

KISSES OF THEIR MOUTHS

Many English Renaissance poets offer readings of the Song of Songs, including Shakespeare, Spenser and Milton. Although it is treated in a variety of ways, all versions strike a balance between oral and written, carnal and spiritual. Flinker aims for a greater understanding of how this balance operates by introducing a Rabbinic model for juxtaposing orality and textuality in Canticles. He uses this to demonstrate how, in recovering approaches to these seventeenth-century texts, a balance is achieved between an open, oral and sexual understanding of the erotic biblical text and a more closed textual and spiritual reading.

NOAM FLINKER lectures in English at the University of Haifa.

Studies in Renaissance Literature

ISSN 1465–6310

Founding editor
John T. Shawcross

General Editor
Graham Parry

Editorial board
Helen E. Wilcox
John N. King
Graham Parry

Volume 1: *The Theology of John Donne*
Jeffrey Johnson

Volume 2: *Doctrine and Devotion in Seventeenth-Century Poetry
Studies in Donne, Herbert, Crashaw and Vaughan*
R. V. Young

Studies in Renaissance Literature offers investigations of topics both spanning the sixteenth and seventeenth centuries and growing out of medieval concerns, up to the Restoration period. Particularly encouraged are new examinations of the interplay between the literature of the English Renaissance and its cultural history.

Proposals or queries may be sent directly to the editors at the addresses given below; all submissions receive prompt and informed consideration.

Professor Graham Parry, Department of English, University of York, Heslington, York YO1 5DD, UK

Professor Helen E. Wilcox, Rijksuniversiteit Groningen, Broerstraat 5, POB 72, 9700 AB, Groningen, The Netherlands

Dr John N. King, Department of English, the Ohio State University, Columbus, Ohio 43210, USA

THE SONG OF SONGS IN ENGLISH RENAISSANCE LITERATURE

KISSES OF THEIR MOUTHS

Noam Flinker

D. S. BREWER

© Noam Flinker 2000

All Rights Reserved. Except as permitted under current legislation no part of this work may be photocopied, stored in a retrieval system, published, performed in public, adapted, broadcast, transmitted, recorded or reproduced in any form or by any means, without the prior permission of the copyright owner

First published 2000
D. S. Brewer, Cambridge

ISBN 0 85991 586 7

D. S. Brewer is an imprint of Boydell & Brewer Ltd
PO Box 9, Woodbridge, Suffolk IP12 3DF, UK
and of Boydell & Brewer Inc.
PO Box 41026, Rochester, NY 14604–4126, USA
website: http://www.boydell.co.uk

A catalogue record for this book is available
from the British Library

Library of Congress Cataloging-in-Publication Data
Flinker, Noam, 1943–
  The Song of Songs in English renaissance literature: kisses of their mouths/Noam Flinker.
    p. cm.
  Includes bibliographical references (p.) and index.
  ISBN 0-85991-586-7 (alk. paper)
  1. English literature – Early modern, 1500–1700 – History and criticism. 2. Sex in literature. 3. Bible. O.T. Song of Solomon – Criticism, interpretation, etc. 4. Religion and literature – England – History – 16th century. 5. Religion and literature – England – History – 17th century. 6. Erotic literature, English – History and criticism. 7. Sex – Religious aspects. 8. Bible – In literature. 9. Sex in the Bible. 10. Intertextuality. I. Title.
PR428.S48 F58 2000
820.9′382239–dc21   00–022566

This publication is printed on acid-free paper

Typeset by Joshua Associates Ltd, Oxford
Printed in Great Britain by
St Edmundsbury Press Ltd, Bury St Edmunds, Suffolk

CONTENTS

Preface	vii
Acknowledgments	viii
Introduction	1
Chapter One William Baldwin's *The Canticles, or Balades of Salomon*: The Shaping of History, Sexuality and Subsequent English Poetry	31
Chapter Two Canticles, Baldwin and Spenser's *Amoretti*	66
Chapter Three Canticles as Erased Convention in *Venus and Adonis*	88
Chapter Four The Spenserian Canticles of Robert Aylett: The Protestant Tradition Continues	100
Chapter Five Ranter Sexual Politics: Canticles in the England of 1650	120
Chapter Six Adam's Revised Rant with Eve	140
Conclusion	160
List of Works Cited	161
Index	170

For my parents
Sylvia G. Flinker and Sanford Flinker

PREFACE

During the many years that I have worked on this project, the intellectual debts that I have incurred have become too numerous to be summarized here. There are, however, a limited number of people whose assistance and suggestions have been of such importance as to make it ungracious in the extreme to neglect to acknowledge them here. It goes without saying, of course, that the responsibility for understanding their help remains entirely my own. For many years the thoughts and comments of Marshall Grossman (University of Maryland) have been of considerable significance for me. In addition, I owe much to John T. Shawcross (University of Kentucky), David Lee Miller (University of Kentucky), Murray Roston (Bar Ilan University), Harold Fisch (Bar Ilan University) and Jacob L. Mey (Odense University, Denmark). My colleagues in the Dept of English Language and Literature at the University of Haifa have all been highly supportive, but I must single out the criticism and support of Bill Freedman and Elliott Simon. People who have helped by reading and commenting on my Introduction include Mark Geller (University of London), Menachem Kellner (University of Haifa), Me'ir Malul (University of Haifa), Ofra Meir (University of Haifa), Samuel T. Lachs (Bryn Mawr College) and Gil Nativ (University of Haifa). Without them, I would have committed a great many unfortunate blunders in my foraging in scholarly fields not ordinarily included in the study of English literature.

I have been most fortunate in receiving support and assistance from various libraries in the United States and Britain. The Folger Shakespeare Library (Washington, DC) provided a generous grant in 1994 which made it possible to work there during a sabbatical leave from the University of Haifa in 1994–95. In addition, I have been privileged to conduct research at other libraries including the Henry E. Huntington Library and Art Gallery (San Marino, CA), the William Andrews Clark Memorial Library (Los Angeles, CA), The Walter J. and Leonore Annenberg Rare Book & Manuscript Library at the University of Pennsylvania (Philadelphia, PA), the Magill Library of Haverford College (Haverford, PA), the Mariam Coffin Canaday Library of Bryn Mawr College (Bryn Mawr, PA) and the British Library in London. I owe a special debt to the library and its staff at the University of Haifa for ongoing support and acquisitions over a great many years.

Finally, I must try to acknowledge the years of support and encouragement that my wife Ilana and sons Ohad and Adeen have provided. Without them, I doubt that this book could have been completed.

ACKNOWLEDGMENTS

Chapter four is a revised and corrected version of 'Robert Aylett's Spenserian Canticles: Links to Milton', *Philological Quarterly* 69 (1990): 273–97.

Chapter five is revised from 'Ranter Sexual Politics: Canticles in the England of 1650', which appeared in Mark Gelber, ed., *Identity and Ethos: A Festschrift for Sol Liptzin on the Occasion of his 85th Birthday* (Bern: Peter Lang, 1986), 325–41.

Much material in the sixth chapter is revised from an earlier article, 'Milton and the Ranters on Canticles', in Mary Maleski, ed., *A Fine Tuning: Studies of the Religious Poetry of Herbert and Milton*, MRTS vol. 64 (Binghamton, NY), 273–90. Copyright Arizona Board of Regents for Arizona State University.

INTRODUCTION

OVERVIEW: RABBINIC BALANCE BETWEEN ORAL AND WRITTEN AS MODEL

THE tradition of the biblical Song of Songs is long and complex in diachronic terms, yet synchronically read, exhibits a remarkable stability over the past four or five thousand years. Although the most obvious elements of this synchrony include thematic tension between holy and profane, as well as a series of parallels in phrasing, situation and motif, there are two other kinds of tension that help establish and connect the various elements of the synchronic pattern. The first of these concerns the relationship between orality and textuality in the diachronic development of the themes and patterns we now recognize as related to the Canticles tradition. The second involves the tension between a reading that stresses the eternal now as opposed to one that implies some aspect of narrative closure or apocalypse.[1] These dichotomies need to be explored and connected in order to clarify their significance for the thematic, situational and rhetorical elements of the tradition.

The distinction between orality and textuality purports to account for material differences in the ways in which culturally specific literary practices communicate and record experience. The seminal work of Milman Parry and

---

[1] Cf. Marshall Grossman's discussion of the 'formal tension between lyric and narrative . . . Narrative indulges time as the medium in which the exigent contents of experience must be encountered, only to negate this medium in a moment of closure that converts the apparently contingent episodes to elements in an atemporal structure. Narrative is thus a formal rhetoric by which a sequence of diachronically unfolding events is joined to a synchronic design through an act of metaleptic anticipation . . . Lyric, on the other hand, resists this displacement forward by dwelling on the presence of a speaker in the time of the poem's enunciation. If the lyric voice generalizes from within its setting, the appeal to design, to law, to stable and timeless structure is more immediate, less likely to be deferred through a temporal sequence of discovery . . . By presenting itself as the repetition of a lived moment, lyric also represents the momentary escape of history from its narrative containment' (23–4). Although my interest in balance between these and other dichotomies owes much to Grossman's dense and brilliant work, it is only tangential to his primary concerns: 'As the world we confront changes, it provides numerous moments in which the rhetoric of the self in relation to its world and its actions in that world is multiple, fluid, subject to adjustment – moments in which two or more possibilities hold out a choice, and it is in such moments that the subject of history also becomes its agent. My project is to identify and follow such moments of change as they constitute literary historical events' (16).

Introduction

Albert Lord on Yugoslavian oral poetry has led to an important reassessment of the place of orality in Homer's epics.[2] We are now aware of the significant changes as a society becomes literate in the ways that the creating imagination conceives and organizes the world. Such accounts, however, often assume that a fairly simple transition takes place in any given culture once literacy is introduced. The rabbinic myth of two different kinds of Torah provides an alternative model for understanding the interaction of orality and textuality as each balances the other. The insights fostered by this myth of reading offer a means of describing details of the diachronic development of the Canticles tradition through history as well as a methodology for approaching the Renaissance English texts which are the basis of this study.

Some aspects of the myth can be viewed through midrashic texts which themselves were probably reports of oral communication designed to teach and interpret Scripture. A comparison between thematically similar parables in a comparatively late midrashic collection and in Matthew's Gospel indicates a parallel juxtaposition between oral and written modes. The midrashic parable thematizes this balance and situates it in a domesticized, this-worldly context that conceptualizes Torah and its dual modes as livable. This perspective provides an interesting contrast to the apocalyptic imagery in Matthew which seems designed to elicit a response of fearful zealousness. Although apocalypse eventually became part of the official Christian mode of reading in general (and of Canticles in particular), the ancient balance between the sexual and the holy, and likewise between orality and textuality, continued to play a significant role in the popular mind as well as in literary circles.

Walter J. Ong has worked out a complicated account of a movement toward what he views as the silencing of the written text in *Ramus: Method and the Decay of Dialogue* (1958). In a later article he points to the orality of classical rhetoric which 'included as one of its five parts *pronuntiatio* or delivery – which meant oral delivery – as well as memory' ('Oral Residue' 147). Here he goes so far as to recognize what he calls 'oral residue' in sixteenth-century English prose but sees this as part of an apparently irreversible shift from ancient and medieval orality to the silence of modern print culture.[3] One major problem with his point of view is that it reads primarily in terms of the research of Parry and Lord with Yugoslavian oral poets. Even when the object of his attention is Tudor prose, Ong focuses on Greek and Latin practices as he insists on the relevance of the 'epic singer' who 'is not a memorizer in our post-Gutenberg sense of the word, but a skilled collector' (149). There are, however, other models for cultural literacy aside from those

---

[2] Milman Parry's project of recording and analysing oral poetry in Yugoslavia was cut short by his tragic death in 1935. Lord developed his mentor's work in *The Singer of Tales*.
[3] For a critique of such a view of shift from orality and literacy, see Jonathan Boyarin's introduction to his *Ethnography of Reading* (1–4).

of classical Greek and Latin. Ong's notion of 'oral residue' could be understood as part of a more considerably reversible process of balance with textuality.[4]

THE RABBINIC MYTH OF THE TWO KINDS OF TORAH

Jacques Derrida views writing as much more than a technology of communication and in some sense as a state of culture that precedes the oral. His notion of Writing or 'Écriture'[5] could be taken as partially analogous to the unpointed Hebrew of the Torah scroll which has no sound or voice (for which vowels are necessary). One midrashic tradition regards this writing as God's blueprint for creation (Genesis Rabbah 1.1).[6] As such, it precedes the real world and must be reconstituted with voiced vowels and interpreted before it can communicate. The polysemy that such a balanced view of textuality and orality necessitates makes the midrashic Torah-centric world quite different from that of logocentrism. In the discussion that follows I propose to examine the approach to reading of classical rabbinic sages in order to show how these practices and strategies provide a consciously formulated principle of balance which accounts for similar practices in

---

[4] In a later book, *Orality and Literacy*, Ong does refer to the orality of textual cultures before Gutenberg. For example, he shows that 'manuscript cultures remained largely oral–aural even in retrieval of material preserved in texts. Manuscripts were not easy to read, by later typographic standards, and what readers found in manuscripts they tended to commit at least somewhat to memory' (119). Nonetheless, he goes on to insist that 'eventually, however, print replaced the lingering hearing-dominance in the world of thought and expression with the sight-dominance which had its beginnings with writing but could not flourish with the support of writing alone' (121). He continues to conceive of orality in a textual world as temporary 'oral residue' rather than as part of a stereoscopic balance between oral and written. It is noteworthy that in his intellectual history of the Babylonian Talmud, David Kraemer cites Ong's statement and claims that it 'obviously pertains to Babylonian rabbinic culture. Written documents within such a culture – as, I have suggested, the Bavli [Hebrew for Babylonian Talmud] was – nevertheless retained powerful "oral residues". For this reason, written texts, in many of their features, *looked* oral' (116). Earlier in his book, Kraemer cites claims for the orality of rabbinic discourse based on 'a class of "professional" repeaters' (21) but is cautious about accepting them as reliable. It is beyond the scope of my study (and competence) to venture a critique of Kraemer's views of rabbinic discourse. It is enough for me to indicate that a text which looks oral conveys the values and attitudes toward orality with which this study is concerned. Kraemer may be correct in his claims for the written origin of rabbinic discourse, but a text that presents itself as an oral record is very different from a written text with no such appearance.

[5] Susan Handelman suggests that 'it would be better to translate Derrida's key term, *Écriture*, as *Scripture*, which it can also mean in French' (164).

[6] 'The Torah declares: "I was the working tool of the Holy One, blessed be He." In human practice, when a mortal king builds a palace, he builds it not with his own skill, but with the skill of an architect. The architect, moreover, does not build it out of his head; but employs plans and diagrams to know how to arrange the chambers and the wicket doors. Thus God consulted the Torah and created the world' (*Midrash Rabbah*, 1.1).

Introduction

Christian readings of Canticles and love poetry. The rabbinic articulation of the principle of balance need not have been consciously adopted by the poets under consideration here. In practice, however, this principle helps to account for the ancient synchronic pattern that balances the many dichotomies invoked by the tradition of Canticles.

It is important to distinguish between the related kinds of orality implicit in a variety of textual practices. On one level, the written letter in most ancient and modern languages conveys one or more sounds, which enables readers to pronounce and thus hear the sound of a written text. On a different plane, the messages conveyed in the intertextual responses of interpreters of such a text can be viewed as part of its oral aspect. Rabbinic tradition, for example, distinguishes between the written law of Moses which must be preserved without changing even a decorative 'tail' on a single letter, and its oral interpretation which is ongoing and always subject to new development. It appears that early rabbinic traditions resisted the writing down of the oral law, ostensibly to guard against allowing it to change the written face of the received text. Whatever the original reasons for the practice, however, one of its effects was to allow oral flexibility to balance the traditional commitment to an unchanging written document.

The underlying principle is similar on levels of pronunciation and interpretation. In each case the written text is silent and incomplete until it is pronounced and interpreted by means of the oral tradition. The need to mix or balance the written and the oral is reflected in synagogue ritual where the Torah scroll must be chanted publicly by a reader who voices the silent consonantal text in the scroll by memorizing the proper vowel sounds that make it possible to pronounce the text. Today this is done by means of a printed 'pointed' text (i.e. one with the dots and dashes that constitute vowels in Hebrew), but these points have assisted readers of Hebrew for little more than a thousand years (since the ninth century). Before that time, one had to commit these sounds to memory in what was a long and arduous educational process that combined the visual text with oral memory in order to produce the proper sounds. Synagogue practice thus re-enacts the ancient need to read by combining oral and written in such a way as to compose the combined Torah text in a temporal world in which the sound is a momentary experience which must always be recreated by balancing written and oral.[7]

---

[7] José Faur's *Golden Doves* provides a much more detailed account of the ways in which the different levels of orality and textuality were treated by the classical rabbis and their medieval successors (100–108, 135–8). His treatment of the written Torah as an 'oraculum' shows that 'precisely because the original *oraculum* cannot be reduced to articulation and can never be exhausted, it may be expressed in countless variations. Eternity of the Tora – a fundamental premise in Hebrew thought – thus takes on a dynamic aspect: fresh and hitherto unknown significations may always be discovered . . . The oral Law is grounded on the irreducible tension between the *oraculum* and articulation. Rather than suppress that tension, or pursue

4

Introduction

On the level of interpretation, study of the Torah was traditionally practiced in academies at which renowned authorities would discuss and dispute the meaning of the written law. The oral law thus consisted of the sayings of the various rabbis which were rehearsed in the memories of their students and only committed to writing after hundreds of years. Even at the point that the various talmudic interpretations were codified in writing, however, they continued to maintain much of their original orality. Despite the obvious fact that the oral law was ongoing and developing, the rabbis insisted that it had all been revealed to Moses on Mt Sinai along with the written Torah.

This myth of the two kinds of Torah, written and oral, is reflected in various rabbinic sources. One midrash recounts that on Sinai, God told Moses everything that was to be said about the written Torah, 'Even what a faithful student was someday to ask his teacher.'[8] For example, a talmudic story (*Menahot* 29b) tells of a meeting during which God has Moses witness the oral teaching of R. Akiba (first to second century CE). Moses meets God in heaven as He is attaching 'crownlets' to some of the letters of the Torah. When he asks about their significance he is told that in the future Akiba will base legal decisions on these markings. He asks to hear the teaching but understands nothing until the sage explains to his students that the source of his statements is what God told Moses on Sinai. The point seems to be that even the significance of the scribal flourish on a letter of the Torah had been explained to Moses on Sinai. Nonetheless, the narrative remains deliberately paradoxical as the confused, humbled Moses is peremptorily silenced by God when he asks why the brilliant Akiba was not chosen to receive the Torah in his place. This tone is maintained as Moses witnesses Akiba's 'reward': death by Roman torture.

This story is itself a model for the complex interaction between orality and textuality in the rabbinic world view. Like most of the Talmud, it is part of the oral Torah even as it deals with the formal appearance of the Torah's written text. It ascribes meaning to the scribal flourishes which were supposedly attached to the letters by God in anticipation of an oral interpretation of their meaning that would only be expounded many years in the future. On one

---

the insane game in search of the "absent book" (which eventually could reduce the *oraculum* to articulation), the oral Law accepts the tension (and the absence of the book) as a constant. Its object is to formulate the tension and explain the absence; that is to be a commentary (*pirush*) ... There is a symmetrical relationship between the written and the oral Law. This can best be understood by considering their respective levels of textuality. On the one hand, the written Law has a purely consonantal text which defies enunciation; and has scriptural value; on the other hand, the oral Law has a vocal text which is unwritable, and therefore has no scriptural value. There is *writing* without the possibility of enunciation, and *enunciation* without the possibility of writing. The point of contact between these mutually exclusive levels is the vocal version transmitted by the oral tradition of "reading" (*qeri'a*) the Scripture, the written Law' (132–3).

[8] Exodus Rabbah 47.1 as translated in Bialik and Ravnitsky, 441.

Introduction

level the narrative juxtaposes the domestic humility of Moses against the intellectual sophistication of Akiba which is apparently connected to the apocalyptic violence of his 'reward'. On another plane entirely, it reflects the rabbinic balance between orality and textuality: the entire oral interpretation of the Torah was presented to Israel at the same time as the written version. The silent written text is interpreted by oral commentary.[9] Proper reading requires a balance between the written text and its oral aspect in order to pronounce *and* understand it.

The strategy of reading known as 'Midrash' guaranteed a theoretical commitment to polysemy with regard to the biblical text and, one might argue, midrashic elements in the New Testament extended this approach to reading into Christian discourse.[10] By the first century, midrashic readings had introduced a series of dualities into biblical interpretation that juxtaposed orality with textuality, lyricism with apocalypticism, literal carnality

---

[9] It is, perhaps, significant that the narrative in *Menahot* 29b also focuses upon the balance between textuality and orality on the level of the interaction between God and man. Once Moses has heard Akiba teach, he questions his own role as Torah giver: '"Lord of the Universe, Thou hast such a man and Thou givest the Torah by me!" He replied, "Be silent, for such is My decree!"' The silence that God imposes on this oral colloquy rejects the self doubt expressed by the humility of Moses. This is likewise the case when Moses implies that Akiba's death or 'reward' was unfair or excessive: '"Lord of the Universe," cried Moses, "such Torah, and such a reward!" He replied, "Be silent, for such is My decree"' (*Babylonian Talmud* 190). God imposes silence on Moses only at the point that the man's humility prompts him to deny his own role as Torah giver. Akiba's way seems to be closely connected to his violent death and the political struggle against Rome that led up to it. The balance between oral and textual is apparently framed, in this narrative at least, to privilege the domestic simplicity of Moses over Akiba's apocalyptic messianism.

[10] Gerald Bruns provides a working definition of the term: 'In general "midrash" is simply the ancient Hebrew word for interpretation. It is the word for the relationship of Judaism to its sacred texts (Torah), and one could say that it covers the relationship of one sacred text to another as well. Midrash is a rabbinical concept, or practice, but it is certainly as old as writing itself. The word derives from *darash*, meaning "to study" or "to tread", as if interpretation had as much to do with walking as with reading. Hence "midrash" also includes the sense of "to search", "to investigate", "to go in quest of"' (190). Daniel Boyarin sees the 'central defining characteristic' of midrash as 'the creative reading of the ways in which scripture reads its own writing, earlier texts the later and later the earlier, what the midrash itself refers to as "stringing [like beads or pearls DB] the words of Torah together and from the Torah to the Prophets and from the Prophets to the Writings"' (217). Boyarin claims that the 'reading method is . . . not allegorical – relating signifier to signified – but intertextual – relating signifier to signifier'. He acknowledges, however, that 'it is indeed possible for midrashic – intertextual readings to be substantially the same thematically as allegorical readings, since the Torah-texts to which the Song of Songs was understood to refer describe the relationship of Israel to God. Thus the very same thematic material could be transposed, as it were, from the midrashic mode of the earlier Rabbis to the allegorical mode of the later ones' (226). Boyarin's important project connecting midrash and intertextuality is, however, only partially relevant to my concern here which is to focus on the ways in which rabbinic reading practices (early and late) can be used to better understand western Christianity in general and Renaissance England in particular.

Introduction

with allegorical spirituality. Each of these sets of terms contributes a slightly different perspective to the general picture and focuses attention on divergent aspects of a similar problem. Taken together they help to establish a basis for grasping issues of historical moment in terms of literary and interpretive practice. The struggle to maintain polysemic openness in the interpretive process can be traced back through history despite the conscious attempts of religious authorities to limit and control the modes of reading.

There is no full agreement among scholars as to the historical development of the text of the oral law in general or that of the Midrash in particular. During the early centuries of the Christian era there was an ongoing conflict within the rabbinic community about the extent to which the oral law could be preserved in written form. The various codifications which were preserved in writing (Mishnah c. 210 CE; Jerusalem Talmud c. 400 CE; Babylonian Talmud c. 600 CE)[11] do not include all of the oral law. Evidently oral traditions continued to develop and grow by word of mouth long after these collections had been 'published'. Rabbinic discourse is generally couched in an oral context whether or not this, in fact, represents what actually happened in the technical preservation of the tradition. Many statements are presented as the 'sayings' of one or more sages. Although talmudic scholars continue to sift these materials in an effort to work out an accurate account of their textual history, it seems clear that the earliest written records reflect a significantly earlier oral account.

Although consideration of the oral roots of classical Jewish and Christian texts is seriously hampered by the ephemeral nature of the mode, it is still possible to indicate a general outline of these oral formulations. In contrast, then, to scholarship that considers the history of specific rabbinic sayings on the one hand and that of the New Testament on the other, attention to the orality that these sources share breaks down the distinctions between them. Thus it is a commonplace of New Testament scholarship to observe that Jesus was a Pharisaic teacher whose oral discourses were not written down for many years. Few New Testament scholars date any of the Gospels earlier than

---

[11] These dates are approximations and the subject of considerable academic debate. Although scholars agree more or less about the codification of the Mishnah and the Jerusalem Talmud, there has been much discussion of the possible date of the compilation of the Babylonian Talmud. David Goodblatt summarizes the 'traditional theory' that 'it was completed and "sealed" by the end of the fifth century' (311 [2.174]). He then goes on to discuss the way in which more recent twentieth-century scholars have worked out what he calls '"two source" theories' (314–18 [2.177–81]) which extend the redaction to the seventh century. The different versions of this position are the work of a number of scholars who have been publishing on the Talmud since 1925. Richard Kalmin extends the foundations for this theory which distinguishes between earlier materials from before the sixth century and later 'unattributed discourse'. He concludes that 'given the present fragmentary state of our knowledge concerning the formation of the Talmud and the history of the rabbinic period, we have no choice but to acknowledge our ignorance regarding the critical issue of the transition from attributed to unattributed discourse' (94).

Introduction

60 CE. There is, therefore, much uncertainty about the specific tone, texture and ultimate purpose of most of the 'sayings' of Jesus. We know what the Gospel writers report him to have said but that is ultimately just proof of what these specific writers understood these texts to signify. The original oral discourse was almost certainly somewhat different.

This is exactly the case of rabbinic discourse in general. Talmudic scholars have their hands full trying to determine just what the received written texts mean. Any attempt to determine the exact time of composition is hopeless because of various problems including the orality which characterizes the entire rabbinic project. It is thus quite possible that a text first written down as late as the early Middle Ages could reflect an oral tradition with a pedigree of hundreds of years.

Such could be the case of a Midrash which first appears in writing in a collection entitled *Tanna DeBe Eliyyahu* (*The Lore of the School of Elijah*, hereafter referred to as *Tanna*). Although recent assessments assign this work to the ninth century, earlier scholars have placed it as far back as the third century and as late as the tenth.[12] Authorities such as Ephraim Urbach (183–4) and David Stern (213–14) refer to the distinctive Hebrew style of the work as opposed to the less individualized quality of earlier collections. Such analysis, however, concentrates attention upon the personal style of the unknown compiler or editor. From an oral perspective, *Tanna* is a written version of material that purports to have been handed down from generation to generation in a culture that did not privilege writing over speech or seeing over hearing. On this level, the tradition which first received definite written shape in the ninth century may very well contain material that was orally available in the first.

The second section of *Tanna* (Eliyyahu Zuta) includes a midrashic parable thematically similar to Matthew's parable of the Talents which has not been noticed by the various studies of rabbinic sources of the Gospels:[13]

> One time, as I was walking along a road, a man accosted me. He came at me aggressively with the sort of argument that leads to heresy. It turned out that the man had Scripture but no Mishnah. He asserted: Scripture was given us from Mount Sinai. Mishnah was not given us from Mount Sinai. I replied: My son, were not both Scripture and Mishnah given by the Almighty? Does the fact that they are different from each other mean that both cannot have been given by Him? By what parable may the question be answered? By the one of a mortal king who had two servants whom he loved with utter love. To one he gave a measure of wheat and to the other he gave a measure of wheat, to one he gave a bundle of flax and to the other a bundle of flax. What did the clever one of the

---

[12] A full discussion of the various theories as to the period in which this work was first written down is to be found in Braude and Kapstein's introduction to their translation of *Tanna*, especially pp. 5–9.

[13] I have found no reference to this midrash in any of the various studies of the rabbinic background of the New Testament, including the exhaustive Strack and Billerbeck.

two do? He took the flax and wove it into a tablecloth. He took the wheat and made it into fine flour by sifting the grain first and grinding it. Then he kneaded the dough and baked it, set the loaf upon the table, spread the tablecloth over it, and kept it to await the coming of the king.

But the foolish one of the two did not do anything at all.

After a while the king came into his house and said to the two servants: My sons, bring me what I gave you. One brought out the table with ⟨the loaf baked of⟩ fine flour on it, and with the tablecloth spread over it. And the other brought out his wheat in a basket with the bundle of flax over the wheat grains.

What a shame! What a disgrace! Need it be asked which of the two servants was the more beloved? He of course, who laid out the table with ⟨the loaf baked of⟩ fine flour upon it.

. . . when the Holy One gave the Torah to Israel, He gave it to them as wheat out of which the fine flour of Mishnah was to be produced and as flax out of which the fine linen cloth of Mishnah was to be produced. (*Tanna* 407–9)

This midrashic parable is remarkably similar to that of Jesus in Matthew:

For the kingdom of heaven is as a man travelling into a far country, who called his own servants, and delivered unto them his goods. And unto one he gave five talents, to another two, and to another one; to every man according to his several ability; and straightway took his journey. Then he that had received the five talents went and traded with the same, and made them other five talents. And likewise he that had received two, he also gained other two. But he that had received one went and digged in the earth, and hid his lord's money. After a long time the lord of those servants cometh, and reckoneth with them. And so he that had received five talents came and brought other five talents, saying, Lord, thou deliveredst unto me five talents: behold, I have gained beside them five talents more. His lord said unto him, Well done, thou good and faithful servant: thou hast been faithful over a few things, I will make thee ruler over many things: enter thou into the joy of thy lord. He also that had received two talents came and said, Lord, thou deliveredst unto me two talents: behold, I have gained two other talents beside them. His lord said unto him, Well done, good and faithful servant; thou hast been faithful over a few things, I will make thee ruler over many things: enter thou into the joy of thy lord. Then he which had received the one talent came and said, Lord, I knew thee that thou art an hard man, reaping where thou has not sown, and gathering where thou hast not strawed: and I was afraid, and went and hid thy talent in the earth: lo, there thou hast that is thine. His lord answered and said unto him, Thou wicked and slothful servant, thou knewest that I reap where I sowed not, and gather where I have not strawed: thou oughtest therefore to have put my money to the exchangers, and then at my coming I should have received mine own with usury. Take therefore the talent from him, and give it unto him which hath ten talents. For unto every one that hath shall be given, and he shall have abundance: but from him that hath not shall be taken away even that which he hath. And cast ye the unprofitable servant into outer darkness: there shall be weeping and gnashing of teeth. (Matthew 25.14–30, Authorized Version)

Introduction

The mortal king in the Midrash is like the master in the Gospel, the wise servant like the two servants who trade with their talents, the foolish servant like the 'wicked and slothful servant' and so on. The divergences between the written versions of the parables are no less obvious. Aside from the different number of servants (likewise different in Luke's parable of the ten pounds [19.11–27]), the atmosphere and significance of the parables are distinct. In the Midrash, the domestic imagery of the Sabbath ritual is much more peaceful and less threatening than the capitalist world of trade, hell and apocalypse in Matthew and Luke. To some extent, these differences can be ascribed to the different interpretations provided for each parable. Thus, Jesus in the Gospels is concerned with apocalypse. In the light of the political tensions between Rome and Judea, the historical Jesus could have been addressing himself to a definite sense of closure in anticipation of some imminent set of catastrophic events. If so, judicious use of the talents would have had a great deal to do with the final end. This certainly seems to account somewhat for the violent intensity of the conclusion to the parable in Matthew: 'Cast ye the unprofitable servant into outer darkness . . .' In similar terms, the Midrash can be tied to the conflict between rabbinic Judaism and the Karaites in the early middle ages, since the 'heresy' of rejecting the oral Torah (here termed 'Mishnah'[14]) was a major Karaite tenet. On the other hand, this apocalyptic note need not be read into the parable, so that the use of the talents could be understood as a shoring up of the oral tradition in its struggle against textual closure. Balance between orality and textuality could be the point in an attempt to maintain and preserve a mode of understanding that would reject the inflexibilities of apocalypse in favour of the cyclic patterns of domesticity found in the midrashic text of *Tanna*.

Nevertheless, this sort of diachronic account of these parables in terms of the specific historic context in which the written text can be understood, ignores the thematic similarity between the stories in the Midrash and the New Testament. The rabbinic notion or myth of the written and oral kinds of Torah which were both promulgated at Sinai, if examined from the perspective of recent investigation of orality, can provide a different sort of explanation for the similar parables. The work of Parry and Lord on Serbo-Croatian oral epic postulates that poets cannot compose orally once they learn how to read (Lord 129–30). Such a view may be useful for dealing with oral epic like that of Homer and it certainly has the advantage of focusing attention upon the differences between modes of thinking before and after the introduction of writing in a given culture. It does not, however, have much to say about the more complex cultural arena in which both oral and written modes of thought operate simultaneously. Since the availability of both oral and written modes of communication characterizes almost by definition most of what we know of

---

[14] Jacob Neusner works out a highly detailed discussion of rabbinic orality in which he concludes that 'the Mishnah constitutes oral tradition' (148).

Introduction

human history, it is important to find a model for understanding how the two modes interrelate. The rabbinic myth of the two kinds of Torah can be understood as a thematization of its practices in just such a context.

Even the recent studies of the material in *Tanna* recognize the clear possibility that the author or compiler of the texts made a deliberate effort to make his work appear to seem traditional (*Tanna* 10; Stern 211). If we take this as a critical principle, it is possible to regard the particular midrashic parable about the linen and the wheat as an expression of the myth of the two kinds of Torah. The message of the parable stresses the importance of reading Torah in terms of Mishnah or its oral tradition. As a balancing of the modes of oral and written communication in order to work out a methodology of reading, the parable can be taken as an expression of the Pharisaic approach to the available technologies of communication.

The myth of the two kinds of Torah presents various facets in different contexts or situations. It is peaceful yet threatening, domestic but warlike. In one sense, the textual issue that determines the tone is connected to the way in which the balance is achieved. José Faur points out that 'the unreadable consonantal text was processed into the vocal text that Moses enunciated to the children of Israel. As with the first tablets, Moses "breaks" the consonantal text, thereby giving it articulation and meaning' (136). The violent level of the imagery here is noteworthy. Interpretation of the tablets is equivalent to breaking them upon discovering that the people were worshipping the golden calf (Exodus 32.15ff.). This is to situate the moment of reading almost exactly in the path of the destructive fury of Moses and the children of Levi (Exodus 32.25–35).

The relevance of this methodology to western textuality is likewise open ended. One could argue that in the rabbinic oral tradition, this particular parable was always associated with the balance between orality and textuality and that this is what Jesus originally meant by his parables of the pounds and talents. If so, the relation between orality and textuality in the context of apocalyptic expectation is less balanced than one sided. On other levels, however, the rabbinic myth is clearly related to similar polarities central to the Christian tradition. The implicit tension between Scripture on the one hand and the Logos or preaching of it on the other are of major importance for all branches of Christianity, but they are especially significant for Protestant thought and thus for the English literary scene. There is a movement within Christian thought that works toward a new Pauline synthesis that arises from the juxtaposition of Jesus as Logos or principle of spoken rationality and the word of God as written down in the Hebrew Scriptures. For Luther there is likewise a need to confront all of Scripture with constant attention to the spoken word of the preacher. In terms of the two kinds of communication, both Judaism and Christianity oscillate between a textual longing for apocalyptic closure and a less determined oral openness that is potentially available as a mode of

Introduction

interpretation. Instead of an abrupt shift from the exclusive orality of ancient epic poets to a supposedly pure textuality thereafter, we would do well to examine the balances and shiftings between these two different approaches to knowledge and understanding.

THE TRADITION OF CANTICLES

The pages that follow trace elements of a synchronic pattern that can be constructed in retrospect on the basis of a diachronic description of specific stages in the development of the Canticles tradition. At various stages of this very brief account of the growth of a literary motif, it will be useful to apply the principles of rabbinic balance in terms of theme (holy and profane), transmissional modes (oral and written) and time (present and future). The poetic examples from ancient and medieval poems and commentaries illustrate some of the ways in which the theme grew and extended itself as it took on oral and written modalities and reflected the tension between present and future, between the lyrical now and apocalyptic closure. The literary history which emerges is on one level enriched by the added perceptions provided by the consideration of orality. It is likewise darkened somewhat as the lyrics of the various cultures and civilizations are perceived to have been read as apocalyptic texts that thematize the end of all things.

Pagan Roots: Sumer and the Ancient Near East

Ancient Sumerian poems seem to be the earliest extant texts that exhibit the themes, situations and rhetoric which characterize the Song of Songs. In these texts, lyrical moments with explicitly sexual nuances appear in contexts that have been understood by some as mythic and religious and by others as merely secular. This dichotomy between holy and profane is only one of a number of theoretical tensions that complicate these texts. The very written nature of the lyric generally suggests a tension between its oral and textual modes. In these poems, the same cuneiform texts have often been rendered in conflicting ways as the experts differ about basic interpretation. Such diverse readings serve to support a distinction between specific diachronic readings as opposed to a synchronic pattern that is broad enough to include both poles of the dichotomies.

Thus, for example, scholars differ on such matters as the religious nature of the Sumerian texts. Are they holy or profane? In a recent translation of a poem that various scholars have connected with the Song of Songs,[15] Yitschak

---

[15] Kramer devotes an entire chapter to the parallels between Sumerian love poetry and the Song of Songs. Pope's voluminous commentary on the Song of Songs also points to similarities (569). Lambert shows that 'outside Mesopotamia the Hebrew Song of Songs is highly relevant, and clearly belongs to the same phraseological tradition as the Sumero-Babylonian

Introduction

Sefati claims that the love goddess 'Inanna makes [her consort] Dumuzi take an oath of premarital chastity, i.e., that he had not previously had sexual relations with another woman' ('An Oath of Chastity' 49). Not unlike Samuel N. Kramer's view of this poem,[16] Sefati's conclusion is that 'it is reasonable to assume that it was recited or chanted at one of the stages of the sacred marriage rite, which took place in Uruk or one of the other Sumerian cultic centers' ('An Oath of Chastity' 51). Sefati renders:

texts' (27). He points to a series of general parallels throughout his article (27, 29, 34). Sefati likewise refers to Canticles ('An Oath of Chastity' 54–5).

[16] According to Kramer, the poem in question presents 'the bitter end of the Dumuzi–Inanna love romance, which began in joyous bliss and ended in tragic death' (104):

O my *lubi*, my *lubi*, my *lubi*,
O *my labi*, my *labi*, my *labi*, my honey of the mother who bore her,
My . . . wine [?], my . . . honey, my comfort [?] of her mother,
Your eyes – their gaze delights me, come now my beloved sister,
Your mouth – its words of welcome delight me, my comfort [?] of her mother,
Your lips – their bosom-touch delights me, come now my beloved sister.
My sister, your grain – its beer is tasty, my comfort [?] of her mother,
Your herbs – their juice [?] is tasty, come my beloved sister,
In your house, your luxuriance delights me, my comfort [?] of her mother,
My sister, your riches delight me, come now my beloved sister,
Your house is a steadfast house . . . my comfort [?] of her mother.
. . .
Brother, on the outskirts of the city you will come to an end, you have been decreed an evil fate . . .
Your right hand you have placed on my vulva,
Your left, stroked my head,
You have touched your mouth to mine . . . (104–5)

Kramer quotes these lines at the conclusion of his chapter 'The Sacred Marriage and Solomon's Song of Songs' in which he tries to provide 'a true picture of the parallels between the biblical book and some of its probable cuneiform forerunners' (91). He interprets the poem as a narration of the myth commemorated by annual fertility rites in which the Sumerian king cohabits with the priestess of Inanna in order to make the land fertile. The colloquy here between male and female is an account of the love between Inanna, goddess of love, and Dumuzi, the shepherd king who is soon to die and then be resurrected. Dumuzi praises his goddess-lover, but she warns him of his 'evil fate' which will follow his sexual activity with her. Kramer concludes: 'But fortunately for mankind, Dumuzi's death was only temporary; he was saved from death eternal by the tender love of his sacrificing sister' (106). Sefati more or less agrees with Kramer's views: 'Kramer's grouping of all the Dumuzi–Inanna songs into three categories – songs of courtship, marriage songs and cultic love songs – is right in essence, although a classification here and there may be disputed' (*Love Songs* 21). His translation of 'The Women's Oath [DI B]' follows the spirit of Kramer's mythic understanding of the text. Nonetheless he rejects Kramer's reading 'Brother, on the outskirts of the city, you will come to an end, you have been decreed an evil fate' in favor of '"Brother" of the open country, you who gave me life, you will take an oath to me' (*Love Songs* 130). Sefati's avoidance of the motifs of death and resurrection here is based on the absence of conclusive evidence in the Sumerian texts. In a more detailed commentary on the poem in an earlier article he points out that the verb which Kramer took to mean 'to decree the fate' should here be rendered 'to swear' or 'to take an (assertory) oath' ('An Oath of Chastity' 48–9).

Introduction

> My 'dear', my 'dear', my 'dear',
> My 'darling', my 'darling', my honey of the mother who bore her,
> My sappy vine, my honey-sweet, my mellifluous mouth of her mother.
> Your eyes – their gaze delights me, *come* my beloved 'sister'!
> Your mouth – its utterance delights me, my mellifluous mouth of her mother.
> Your lips – their kiss delights me, *come* my beloved 'sister'!
> My 'sister', your barley – its beer is delicious, my mellifluous mouth of her mother,
> Your wort – its *liquor* is delicious, *come* my beloved 'sister'!
> In the house – your charms [*are irresistible*], my mellifluous mouth of her mother,
> Your charms, my 'sister', [*are irresistible*] . . . my beloved,
> Your house – the *storeho[use]* make . . . / m[y mellifluous] mouth of her mother,
> You, the *Princess* . . . my . . .
> (You) who gave me life, (you) who gave me life, you will take an oath for me,
> 'Brother' of the open country, (you) who gave me life, you will take an oath for me,
> You will take an oath for me that you did not lay hands on a strange *woman*,
> will take an oath for me that you did not [. . .] (your) head on a strange *woman*.
> . . .
> Your right hand on my nakedness should be placed,
> Your left on my head should be laid;
> When you have brought your mouth close to my mouth,
> When you have seized my lips in your mouth,
> By so (doing) you will take an oath to me,
> Thus is the 'oath of the women', oh my 'brother' of beautiful eyes!
> . . . (*Love Songs* 129–30 copyright Bar-Ilan UP, Ramat Gan, 1998)

Not all scholars, however, have been willing to accept Sefati's identification of the lovers as Inanna and Dumuzi in his mythic or religious reading of this and other Sumerian poems. Gwendolyn Leick summarizes the much more 'profane' reading of Sumeriologists such as Thorkild Jacobsen and Bendt Alster. Jacobsen has read the poem as 'a "crude low-life piece" in which "a stranger, after an evening in the ale-house, makes a play for the tapstress"' (Leick 126). Leick prefers to see the piece as 'the highly wrought artifice of seduction' but agrees that the poem is secular: 'it is quite the opposite of the neo-primitive "fertility rite" notion that the construct of the Sacred Marriage implies' (129). Her translation reflects this reading:

> O my *lubi*, my *lubi*, my *lubi*,
> O my *labi*, my la[*bi*, my *labi*], my honey of the mother who gave birth to her,
> My juicy grape, my honey sweet, my her-mother's honey-mouth,
> The glance of your eye delights me, come, my beloved sister,
> The words of your mouth delight me, come, my beloved sister,

Introduction

Kissing your lips delights me, come, my beloved sister!
O my sister, the beer of your grain is delicious, my her-mother's honey mouth,
The **gumeze** beer of your wort is delicious, come, my beloved sister,
In your house, your passion . . . , [come] my beloved sister,
Your house is . . . a storehouse, my her-mother's honey-mouth.
. . .
Brother, swear to me that, when you dwelt in the out-lying town,
Swear to me that a stranger did not touch (you) by the hand,
Swear to me that a stranger did not approach (?) (you) by mouth(?)!
My one who lifts the thin (?) gown off my vulva for me.
My beloved, man of my choice,
[for you(?)], let me prepare what belongs to the oath for you, my brother of fairest face.
My brother of fairest face, let me prepare what belongs to the oath for you:
May you put your right hand in my vulva,
With your left stretched towards my head,
When you have neared your mouth to my mouth,
When you have taken my lips into your mouth,
Thus you swear the oath to me . . . (127)

Together, these divergent renderings of the Sumerian text trace the synchronous pattern which recurs again and again in the history of western literature. The mythic or religious reading anticipates a conclusion that invokes sexual union as a means of ensuring the fertility of the land. This mythic text fashions a narrative of passion that makes the sexual activity with the goddess (or her representative) into a metaphor of cosmic unity. The secular or profane reading focuses on the present moment of love and makes the explicit sexual references part of a dialogue about jealousy and commitment. Taken together, these interpretations help to articulate different aspects of the original cuneiform text which itself remains silent and fragmented as it beckons to us from over the centuries so as to become an icon of its own irreducibility. Clay tablets onto which were inscribed lines and wedges to represent the spoken word can now be understood only by means of conflicting scholarly attempts to do justice to different aspects of their inscrutability.[17] Simultaneously holy and profane, oral and written, this and similar Sumerian texts are the first known versions of a pattern that eventually finds expression in some of the richest poems subsequent cultures would produce.

---

[17] The problems involved in treating the implicit polysemy of these texts are touched upon by Mark J. Geller in his introduction to a collection of essays on figurative language in the ancient Middle East. He points to the general neglect of literary theory and semiotics by Semitists 'because so much of the basic work of lexicography and the production of text editions remains to be done' (ix). His collection is intended 'to push back further the frontiers of reading, interpretation, and textual criticism into the world's oldest literature' (xiii). W. G. Lambert's contribution to the volume deals specifically with polysemy (e.g. 'double entendre . . . ambivalence' [28]) in these ancient texts.

Introduction

Love lyrics which often make use of the names of mythic deities in the context of the treatment of themes such as desire, passion, sexual union, longing and jealousy continued to be recorded during the thousands of years that intervened between the Sumerian civilization of 3000–2000 BCE and biblical culture of the first millennium BCE. Marvin Pope summarizes many of the Akkadian and Ugaritic parallels in the introduction to his monumental edition and commentary on the Song of Songs (cf. especially 69–85, 145–53, 210–29). Nonetheless, not all scholars are convinced of the relevance of these analogues. Michael V. Fox, for example, argues that the cultic Egyptian texts which seem to parallel the Song of Songs differ significantly from the biblical poems. Fox's interest is in the similarity between ancient Egyptian love songs and the Song of Songs. He argues that like the Egyptian poems which 'were, I believe entertainment' (244), 'Canticles too was probably entertainment, a song to be enjoyed on any occasion – including religious holidays – when song, dance, or other ordinary diversions were in order . . . Such secular love songs existed in Egypt and probably in Mesopotamia as well, although none of the latter are extant' (247). His secular reading of the entire genre is hard to ignore even as it eliminates a major element from the larger synchronic archetype.

The Song of Songs Secularizes Pagan Tradition

Hundreds of years later, someone composed or collected a group of Hebrew lyrics that celebrate love and sexuality in themes and phrases remarkably akin to the Mesopotamian and Egyptian texts. Tradition ascribes these poems to King Solomon and the biblical version is known as the Song of Songs,[18] Solomon's Song or Canticles. We can only speculate about the specific modes in which works from the earlier cultures made their way to ancient Israel. Fox, for example, makes a number of plausible suggestions about ways in which the Egyptian love songs could have reached the biblical world:

> Egypt controlled Palestine through a network of officials, many of whom were Egyptians trained in the scribal schools, where literary arts were cultivated alongside the professional skills needed by scribes. The scribes in these centers are one likely means of literary transmission . . . The path from Ramesside Egyptian love poetry to Canticles was a long one. Perhaps as much as a thousand years separate the Israelite love poem from its Egyptian counterparts. The love song genre certainly underwent many changes between its presumed Egyptian origins and the time when it reached Palestine, took root in Hebrew literature, grew in native forms, and blossomed as the Song of Songs. (191, 193).

---

[18] This is an accurate translation of the first two words in the Hebrew text, 'shir ha-shirim'. Pope's comment is, as usual, accurate and complete. Most relevant is the following: 'The construct connection of the same noun in the singular and plural . . . always indicates some sort of superlative sense . . . [here it] designates the absolutely superlative song, the very best, the sublime song' (294).

Introduction

Clearly Fox's point is quite relevant to an oral tradition in which singers rework that which they hear into songs of their own. In such an oral world, the poetic traditions of Egypt and Mesopotamia would have competed for the attention of Israelite singers. There need not have been a written text imported from abroad and read by a literate poet. If the foreign influences were oral, the Song of Songs may merely be the written record of one version of a long and complicated tradition which subsequently disappeared. In any case, it is important that we not impose the assumptions and prejudices of our own post-Gutenberg print culture as we examine ancient poetic texts that were probably sung in one way or another regardless of the extent to which its listeners were able to read and write. In a literary tradition that was at least as oral as it was written, the exclusively secular nature of the Song of Songs need not have been as culturally significant as Fox assumes. There may have been oral versions that were more religious in content and tone.

Nevertheless, it is most striking that in the Hebrew text of Canticles there is no explicit mention of God.[19] Thus, the biblical songs can be read as secularized reinscriptions of individual lyrics which may have had other levels of meaning in Mesopotamian and Canaanite culture. That is, one could regard the sexual desire of the biblical poems as deliberately presented without religious reference in order to distinguish them from the pagan contexts available elsewhere in the popular culture.

There are numerous parallels in the Song of Songs to a Sumerian lyric such as that rendered above by Se Fati, Kramer and Leick. One biblical passage provides such elements as the woman's desire for a man whom she calls brother, the association between love and sweet wine, and his hand on her head: 'O that thou wert as my brother, that sucked the breasts of my mother! when I should find thee without, I would kiss thee; yet I should not be despised. I would lead thee, and bring thee into my mother's house, who would instruct me: I would cause thee to drink of spiced wine of the juice of my pomegranate. His left hand should be under my head, and his right hand should embrace me' (Authorized Version, 8.1–3). While the Sumerian text remains open to interpretation that makes it either this worldly or mythic, the delicate yet secular biblical passage celebrates the lyrical moment of desire and love in terms that leave the transcendent level of the synchronous pattern unfulfilled.

---

[19] There is a single word toward the end of the Song of Songs (8.6) which concludes with two Hebrew letters that can be 'construed as the short form of the ineffable name of Israel's God' (Pope 670). This word, rendered in the Authorized Version 'coals of fire', is not ordinarily taken as a divine reference. Pope concludes 'To seize upon the final consonants *yh* as the sole reference to the God of Israel in the entire Canticle is to lean on very scanty and shaky support' (671).

Introduction

Allegorization

The allegorization of Canticles (during the early centuries of the Christian era) can be understood as reinstating the ancient pattern of the pagan tradition to the biblical materials that may have originated as secularized reductions of the Mesopotamian tradition. As allegory restores religious significance to the Song of Songs, it re-establishes the mythic transcendence of the pagan world, reinscribed as Jewish or Christian doctrine about God's love for mankind. It likewise provides narrative closure that is often presented as thematized apocalypse to a series of individual lyrics whose biblical context suggests only a timeless moment intertextually juxtaposed against the mythic cyclicity of the pagan world.

The decision to interpret the Song of Songs as allegory was historically inscribed by rabbinic sages as part of a communal project that eventually produced a canonized text for the Hebrew Bible. The ruling that this particular biblical book was to be understood only as allegory became part of an oral tradition which the rabbinic sages refused to commit to writing for many years. The hermeneutic status of the Song of Songs in general, however, was never quite settled. Jewish and Christian authorities traditionally read it allegorically, but the somewhat strident tone of many such readings suggests that they were in some sense responses to other interpretations that have not been preserved. Thus Rabbi Akiba's pronouncement that 'he who sings from the Song of Songs in a tremulous voice in a banquet hall and makes it into a kind of secular song, has no portion for the world to come'[20] seems to imply that he knew of such practices. Origen advised that 'if any man who lives only after the flesh should approach . . . this Scripture . . . he, not knowing how to hear love's language in purity and with chaste ears, will twist the whole manner of his hearing of it away from the inner spiritual man and on to the outward and carnal . . . and it will seem to be the Divine Scriptures that are thus urging and egging him on to fleshly lust'. He thus counsels that 'everyone who is not yet rid of the vexations of flesh and blood . . . refrain completely from reading this little book' (22–3). Presumably such readers were common enough to warrant the warning! It is significant that Origen refers to the 'hearing' of the 'man who lives only after the flesh'. Such a reader would have been more dependent upon orality than a more learned counterpart whose textually based spirituality would have been more fully developed. The point is that for both Akiba and Origen, there were oral contexts in which people could have heard Canticles that would have stimulated a carnal rather than spiritual interpretation of the Song. These contexts may have been silenced by

---

[20] My translation of the passage from Tosefta, *Sanhedrin* XII, 10 as cited by Samuel Tobias Lachs, 'Prolegomena to Canticles Rabba', *Jewish Quarterly Review* 55 (January 1965): 237, n. 12. Lachs points out that 'Akiba in his day was still defending Canticles as truly a holy book about which, according to him, there was never a controversy and that its true meaning was the allegorical one which had given it its place in the canon. Others of his generation were obviously not of the same opinion' (236).

the textual authority of official commentaries but they nevertheless continued to resound in the ears of the populace. The availability of both readings did, however, maintain the essential elements of the synchronic pattern.

Within the communities of Jewish and Christian biblical readers, there were many who read as their authorities directed, but there must have been others who chose to read like Origen's 'carnal man' and who ignored his various warnings against such a practice. Such interpretive choices were made theoretically conceivable by the same rabbinical reading procedures that began the historical process of allegorization. Although both the Rabbis and the Church Fathers seem to have had the same ideological commitment to their allegorized readings of Canticles, the rabbinical interpretive process carried with it an internalized resistance to closure that distinguished between different kinds of Torah.

The interrelation between orality and textuality carries with it the possibility for recovering an oral tradition for which we have only a limited series of traces. If we read written texts as if they contained vestiges of oral discourse that remain beneath the surface of writing and yet which reflect other attitudes towards the most important works of a culture, we may find that these classical 'frozen' texts take on new significance. This is especially true of western texts that are connected somehow to the biblical Song of Songs. On the surface, one might expect a medieval or Renaissance poet to make significant use of biblical lyrics that seem to celebrate passionate erotic play and desire. In practice, there are only a few 'vernacular' poems that pay much attention to the Bible in general or to the Song of Songs in particular. We can assume, however, that aside from the official readings of Canticles that were sanctioned by the Church there were other, more explicitly carnal, readings which grew out of oral reciting from the written text. These oral understandings rarely appear on the surfaces of written texts but when they do, these vestiges of a vanished culture tell us much about the complex balance that must have been palpable.

Chaucer's 'Januarie' heard such sounds[21] as did members of the seventeenth-century sect of Ranters whose carnal views of Canticles were part of what appear to have been heretical orgiastic practices.[22] I take these and other indications of carnal understandings of Canticles from the second through the seventeenth centuries as evidence of oral contexts that can be relevant to reading key poetic texts. Like the parables of the talents and of the wheat and flax, interpretations of Canticles move back and forth between the poles of apocalyptic closure and lyric and cyclic openness, between textual determination and oral tentativity, between allegorical spirituality and carnal celebration of the flesh. Although the official world of the Church loudly stipulated that the biblical text be read only as allegory, enough evidence has survived to indicate that other readings continued to remain available.

---

[21] Cf. Geoffrey Chaucer, 'Merchant's Tale', *Canterbury Tales*, IV (E) 2138–49.
[22] Cf. Chapter 5.

Introduction

MEDIEVAL DEVELOPMENTS

I am grateful for the variety of excellent scholarly accounts of the Canticles tradition during the Middle Ages which have allowed me to shorten what would have otherwise have been a long detour at this point. Peter Dronke's seminal volumes on *Medieval Latin* and *The Medieval Lyric* are of major importance. His article on Canticles and this tradition supplements material scattered through his books. E. Ann Matter traces the development of what she calls 'the genre of the Song of Songs' (10) from Origen through the twelfth century, with primary emphasis on Latin commentaries. Ann W. Astell provides an analysis of the Song of Songs in terms of the twelfth-century commentaries and their importance for later literature. Her book includes chapters on Middle English devotional works. Max Engammare's magisterial study of the Song of Songs in the Renaissance is an exhaustive account of translations and commentaries up through the sixteenth century. At the end of his highly detailed scholarly volume, he appends a long (182 pages) bibliography of texts and commentaries published during the fifteenth and sixteenth centuries. A convenient collection of ancient and medieval commentaries on the Song of Songs was prepared in the nineteenth century by Richard Frederick Littledale. Most of these scholars provide evidence about the way in which the medieval Church insisted on an allegorical reading of the Song. E. Ann Matter goes so far as to state that 'there is no "non-allegorical" Latin tradition of Song of Songs commentary' (4). Peter Dronke shows various ways in which poets nevertheless made use of language and motifs from Canticles in treating and developing erotic lyrics: 'Theologians, predictably, either ignored the erotic wellspring of such language or recognized it only in order to reject it. Yet inevitably this *fons hortorum* continued to flow in a poetic *hortus conclusus*, where mystical and sensual expressions and imagery grew together, a garden that was to be of lasting importance for the European imagination' ('Song' 242).

The Italian of Cavalcanti and Dante

One major source for evidence of this mixing of mystical and sensual appears in the work of Dante and his earlier contemporary, Guido Cavalcanti, toward the end of the thirteenth century. Theological support for their poetic expression can be found in twelfth-century biblical exegesis by men such as Hugh of St Victor, Bruno of Segni, Rupert of Deutz and others. Ann W. Astell sums up the emphasis on the historical letter of the Canticles text that these exegetes provided:

> Origen . . . values the Song primarily as an *allegoria* whose hidden meaning, once it has been discovered, has a didactic benefit that compensates for its potentially dangerous literal modality. He loves the Song for what it does not say, rather

Introduction

than for what it does. The twelfth-century exegetes, on the other hand, tend to value the Song for the affects it awakens, the example it sets, the images it provides for the communication of personal and communal experiences. Their commentaries prepared the way for, and actually initiated, the literary imitation of the Song by the Christian poets of the later Middle Ages. Indeed, from the twelfth century on, the *Canticum* stands as the most notable example of a biblical poem that exerted an incontestable formal and inspirational influence on contemporary literary composition, both profane and devotional. (22–3)

At the end of the thirteenth century, as practitioners of the *dolce stil nuovo* or sweet new style,[23] Dante and some of his associates developed a philosophy of love that extended what Maurice Valency terms the 'earthly perfection' (240) of the troubadours to a star or an angel with explicit spiritual powers associated with charity.[24] Guido Cavalcanti, one of the more famous of these poets, helped to set the characteristic tone of the *stil novisti* by writing to a lady who inspired him so intensely that in one well-known sonnet he sings of his love in terms of trembling and awe. Simultaneously angel and woman, the stilnovist's inspiration was thus responsible for poetry that analysed the ways in which the male poet desired yet feared his lady.

In his 'Chi è questa che uien'[25] Cavalcanti's speaker addresses a woman who causes the air to tremble and makes everyone sigh. For the stilnovist poet, the lady inspires awe and wonder as well as desire, and the lack of resolution in the sonnet reflects an underlying unwillingness to integrate what Maurice Valency has termed the 'supernatural radiance to the beauty of the lady' and 'the fever of the flesh' (230):

> Chi è questa che uien, ch'ogn'huom la mira;
> Che fa tremar di charitate l'a're?
> E mena seco Amor, si che parlare
> Null'huom ne puote; ma ciascun sospira? (di Guinta, *Rime* 64b)
>
> Who is she who comes, that everyone looks at her,
> Who makes the air tremble with clarity
> And brings Love with her, so that no one
> Can speak, though everyone sighs? (Cavalcanti, trans. Nelson 7)

Cavalcanti's lady appears in such a way as to remind Gianfranco Contini of the Song of Songs. Contini's anthology of thirteenth-century lyrics includes a commentary on this poem that points explicitly to Canticles and connects the allusion with the cult of Maria.[26] Cavalcanti's echo of Canticles has been

---

[23] For a discussion of Spenser and the stilnovist tradition (without reference to *Amoretti* 3), cf. O. B. Hardison's '*Amoretti* and the *Dolce Stil Novo*'.
[24] Valency's account of the stilnovists (205–55) provides a clear discussion of this movement. Cf. especially pp. 240–8.
[25] For a brilliant analysis of this sonnet, cf. Harrison 70–4.
[26] 'L'attacco è desunto dal Cantico dei Cantici, 6, 9: "Quae est ista quae progreditur?" ecc. (e cfr.

Introduction

recorded by others as well.[27] A verse from the biblical poem begins in the Vulgate in a manner that hauntingly suggests Cavalcanti's Italian:

> Quae est ista, quae progreditur quasi aurora consurgens, pulchra ut luna, electa ut sol, terribilis ut castrorum acies ordinata? (6.9)

The passages from Canticles have not, however, been analyzed in relation to thematic development within the biblical text. They trace a poetic account of the woman who is terrible as well as beautiful. First she emerges from the desert:

> Who is this that cometh out of the wilderness like pillars of smoke, perfumed with myrrh and frankincense, with all powders of the merchant? (3.6)

Later the biblical poet returns to her duality:

> Who is she that looketh forth as the morning, fair as the moon, clear as the sun, and terrible as an army with banners? (6.10)

The final occurrence of the motif stresses the lady's connections with her beloved:

> Who is this that cometh up from the wilderness, leaning upon her beloved? (8.5)

Together these biblical passages provided inspiration for later western poets interested in woman as a spiritual force with clear erotic desirability. She is the object of spiritual attraction and romantic longing, but nevertheless remains a terrible threat to the male consciousness. This aspect of love represents the core of a myth with biblical roots that was developed by the stilnovists in the form of the 'donna angelicata'. The lady whose loveliness is terrifying as she ascends from the desert and makes her way into the gardens is implicitly part of Cavalcanti's poem. The echoes of the biblical passage allude to a tradition that moves back and forth between carnal and spiritual, even as it plays oral against written in terms of the intertextual echoes of biblical texts that resound without being literally present.

The stilnovist tradition of a pure lady who inspires her lover from afar is at the root of Cavalcanti's poem. The question as to the nature of her identity opens his sonnet but is never answered. The conclusion of the final tercet is

---

3, 6; 8, 5 "Quae est ista quae ascendit?" ecc.); e poiché l'esegesi cristiana applicò questi passi a Maria, è evidente l'assimilazione al culto mariano' (Contini 495).

[27] Harrison refers to the editorial work of Contini and also cites Domenico De Robertis, *Il libro della 'Vita Nuova'* (Florence: Sansoni, 1961), 44–5, in connection with Canticles and Cavalcanti's sonnet. Dronke cites the sonnet as an example that 'one must reckon . . . with traces of more than one version of the Canticle in a medieval poet's imagination' ('Song' 238).

that the speaker's mind cannot reach the lofty heights of the woman he is discussing and that he can't even manage to know her:

> Non fu si alta gia la mente nostra;
> E non s'è posta in noi tanta salute;
> Che propiamente n'habbiam conoscenza. (di Guinta, *Rime* 64b)

> Our mind never was so lofty
> And never was such beatitude granted us
> That we could really have knowledge of her. (Cavalcanti, trans. Nelson 7)

Cavalcanti thus incorporates a clear sexual message into his description of the lady. Although the knowledge that he laments missing is on one level carnal, on another it is explicitly spiritual and intellectual. The poet has it both ways, of course, for the lady is simultaneously human and angelic. The biblical allusion associates the sensuousness of Canticles with a contemporary woman, but it also suggests that to the extent that the biblical book is an allegory of Christ's love for the Church, the sexual tension between the couple is a metaphor for deeper spirituality.

The sonnet concludes with the impossibility of attaining that which the lady embodies and thus insists upon the gap between her perfection and the poet's struggle to imitate her. The knowledge that he can master is finally textual, like the experience of his poem. The words strain to suggest more than they denote as a means of representing the poet's struggle to do likewise. In this conflict, the angelic lady is mysterious as she seems to hint at a resolution of the dichotomy between spirit and flesh which the lover cannot quite comprehend. Love for Cavalcanti is thus finally indeterminate as his speaker trembles and sighs yet cannot go beyond the intellectual, spiritual and sexual boundaries established by his language. The mysterious lady overwhelms him both as an enigmatic text from Canticles and as a real woman who somehow intimates more about her identity than the poet dares to grasp.

Cavalcanti's opening question as to the identity of the lady challenges the traditional allegorical interpretation of Canticles by implying that she is somehow available as a sexual being. She may be awe inspiring but she is also lovely and desirable. By the conclusion of the poem, however, the speaker is incapable of knowing her. This inability to reach a conclusive synthesis reflects a challenge to the rhetoric of sexual desire in textual form. Cavalcanti explodes the myth of Canticles by using it to break down rhetorical poses for male poets concerned with desire. The combination of beauty and awe connotes fulfilment in the Hebrew text, just as the allegorical readings generally see no difficulty in accommodating both the wonder of beauty and the fear of the numinous. By refusing to go beyond his fear, Cavalcanti underscores the limitations of mind and language when confronted with the transcendental.

Dante's *Commedia* extends the use of Canticles that Cavalcanti's stilnovist lyric employed. Embedded in the text of the *Purgatorio* are biblical echoes

Introduction

from Canticles and the Psalter which simultaneously intensify and destabilize the poem. The relationship between the medieval Italian and the ancient Hebrew as perceived through the Latin Vulgate is rich and complex. The obvious philological and hermeneutic problems of how to construe the biblical texts and their significance for Dante is complicated by the oral residue that surrounds them. That is, the textuality of Dante's long vernacular poem is significantly altered by memories of texts with both written and oral qualities to which his pilgrim refers. The tension between orality and textuality corresponds to the thematic conflicts within the poem between profane and spiritual love. While Dante must progress from passion for Beatrice to love for God he evokes memories from relevant biblical poems likewise charged with conflicting interpretations and alternating oral and written modalities. Whereas Cavalcanti's lyric was primarily concerned with the intense experience of the lady's observer, Dante the pilgrim encounters his own 'donna angelicata' in a context that moves back and forth between the lyric present and an apocalyptic future.

At the beginning of the twenty-first century our electronic media make it abundantly clear that literary texts need not be enjoyed as printed books. We watch televised dramas, listen to poets recite from their verse on records, tape-recordings or compact disks, and some of us even listen to radio dramas. This new kind of orality has even begun to undermine the exclusive hold which the literacy of the printed word has held upon western culture since the late Renaissance. The importance and power of the spoken word are no less relevant to medieval texts even though it is almost impossible for us to document even a partial range of their oral components. Nevertheless, in looking back at the pre-Gutenberg world we ought to consider the place of orality in texts ordinarily read primarily in terms of the printed word.

Paul Zumthor has discussed ways of considering this problem in texts originally designed to be transmitted orally, but many of his ideas are also relevant to Dante's dense textuality. Zumthor suggests considering '*on principle every text . . . as a dance.* By this I mean (admittedly until we find evidence of distinctions of a different nature) that its actual functioning required the same endowment of qualities and brought into play the same powers of expression as did "dance songs" which are in other respects (and in this particular instance) better known: a text, a melody, and (through a rhythmic analysis or an iconographic study) movements.' This, he claims, can help us 'retain the essential "community-like" nature of the medieval poetic text' (89–90). Zumthor's essay points to ways in which we can try to 'see instances of interference, recurrences, repetitions that are probably allusory in nature: exchanges of discourse that create the impression of a whirl of moving textual elements, at every moment linking up with others in provisional compositions' (78). I want to suggest that the allusions of Dante to Canticles and the Psalter should be understood as part of this intertextual whirl. Considered in oral terms, these references unsettle and destabilize the poetic

Introduction

texture in which they appear and in so doing recreate a moving world in which change and uncertainty are dominant qualities.

Near the end of the *Purgatorio*, Beatrice appears before Dante the pilgrim and in so doing causes him to recapitulate his entire experience of love. He describes his sensation in terms of trembling blood:

> Men che dramma
> di sangue m'è rimaso che non tremi:
> conosco i segni de l'antica fiamma.
>
> I am left with less
> than one drop of my blood that does not tremble:
> I recognize the signs of the old flame. (30.46–8, trans. Mandelbaum 280–1)

The echo of trembling from Cavalcanti is provocative, especially since it anticipates a series of older echoes from Canticles. The most obvious of these are annotated in most editions of the poem while less direct allusions have been traced in works by scholars such as Paul Priest and Jean Leclercq. These authorities do not, however, connect the echoes with Dante's sinful state of mind as he stands trembling before Beatrice.

Solomon's Song adds more complexity to Dante's text than has been previously noted. Early in Canto 30, just before the coming of Beatrice, one of the elders sings '*Veni, sponsa, de Libano*' (11). This well-known quotation from Canticles (4.8) could be taken allegorically. A note in Allen Mandelbaum's translation suggests that 'in light of the imminent arrival of Beatrice and of Beatrice's role in the *Comedy* as Dante's guide to the divine mysteries, it seems quite reasonable for Divine Knowledge to be the meaning of *sponsa*, "spouse" here' (396). Attention to orality here suggests other possibilities. The way in which the Italian text yields to Latin could be taken as a measure of greater formality and perhaps a desire to submit to the authority of learning and the Church. These words also call up memories of prayers heard in church, since Canticles was an important source for medieval liturgical readings.

The context of pilgrim Dante's trembling, however, also suggests a carnal understanding of the allusion. Readings like those attacked by Akiba and Origen suit Dante's current condition. Despite his apparent progress up the mountain of purgatory and the gradual disappearance of the *P*s from his forehead, Dante finds himself overcome with sinfulness as he approaches the Garden of Eden at the top of the mount. His movement from carnal love for Beatrice to heavenly love for God is in a sense at the heart of the entire *Commedia* (with the *Vita Nuova* as an introduction). This moment at the end of the *Purgatorio* can thus be seen as pivotal. Dante's pilgrim has internalized much doctrine on his way to his vision of Heaven, but at this point he still feels the passion of his old love for Beatrice with all of its implicitly illicit desire. A carnal reading of the *sponsa* might thus make her into a human bride whom Dante would make his own. The fact that this goes counter to the

Introduction

doctrines of the Church is just another reason for him to tremble. As with Cavalcanti, the consciousness of love is expressed in terms of trembling, but for Dante this experience is terrifying just as it is an echo of his own past. The sounds of Canticles blend into those of Cavalcanti about the lady 'Who makes the air tremble with clarity' all of which remind him of his own trembling: 'when my eyes first lit upon the glorious lady of my mind who was called Beatrice ... At that moment ... the spirit of life which lives in the most secret room of the heart began to vibrate so fiercely that its effect was dreadfully apparent in the least of my pulses; and trembling, it said these words...' (*The New Life* 37–8).[28]

Dante the poet, of course, can use the diverse possibilities of interpreting the biblical text as a means of articulating his hero's state of mind. It goes in various directions simultaneously. Love for Beatrice had led Dante to despair and thence through the inferno and purgatory, on his way to paradise. In this most famous western account of a shift from carnal to holy love, Dante the pilgrim is here suspended between these two extremes. Beatrice appears and asks him how he dared approach:

> Come degnasti d'accedere al monte?
> non sapei tu che qui è l'uom felice?
>
> How were you able to ascend the mountain?
> Did you not know that man is happy here?
> (30.74–5, trans. Mandelbaum 282–3)

Her words are unclear since the connection between Dante's love and happiness needs further explication. Is he to be made happy by fulfilling his love for her or will his happiness be the result of a final sublimation of his love for Beatrice into love for God?

The angels recognize his difficulty and offer him support in the form of the opening verses of Psalm 31 in which David sings of the strength of faith in God. They stop singing at the verse which concludes with the words 'my feet' in the Vulgate: 'ma oltre "*pedes meos*" non passaro' (84). The attention Dante pays to the words sung by the angels brings together voice and text as it suggests a reading of the biblical poem. The psalm begins in a tone of security and certitude: 'In thee, O Lord, do I put my trust' (31.1). This mood continues through the verse that concludes with the reference to feet: 'and hast not shut me up into the hand of the enemy: thou has set my feet in a large room' (31.8). The next section of the psalm registers a very different note. The psalmist complains of his troubles:

---

[28] Dante's original Italian is as follows in Chiappelli's edition: 'quando a li miei occhi apparve prima la gloriosa donna de la mia mente, la quale fu chiamata da molti Beatrice ... In quello punto dico veracemente che lo spirito de la vita, lo quale dimora ne la secretissima camera de lo cuore, cominciò a tremare sì fortemente, che apparia ne li menimi polsi orribilmente; e tremando disse queste parole ...' (*Vita nuova Rime* 19).

Introduction

> For my life is spent with grief, and my years with sighing: my strength faileth because of mine iniquity, and my bones are consumed. (31.10)

Dante has his pilgrim refer to this abrupt shift in tone by ascribing significance to the angelic choice of psalmic text. He interprets the fact that they stop before the shift in tone as an expression of sympathy for him:

> ma poi che 'ntesi ne le dolci tempre
> lor compartire a me, par che se detto
> avesser: 'Donna, perché sì lo stempre?'

> but when I heard the sympathy
> for me within their gentle harmonies,
> as if they'd said: 'Lady, why shame him so?'
> (30.94–6, trans. Mandelbaum 282–3)

Had the angels gone beyond 'pedos meos' in verse 8, the song of the troubles of the psalmist would have reminded the pilgrim of his sinful condition, a task taken up by Beatrice.

Dante's personal translation of the significance of the angelic song need not be understood as exhausting the interpretive possibilities of the choice. The angels may have been hesitating momentarily before continuing or else they may have wanted to save the role of accuser for Beatrice. What is noteworthy here is the way the psalm has been placed in a context that translates it into immediate personal terms for the listener. The biblical text is recalled by Dante and it reverberates in his memory so as to sound 'as if they'd said: "Lady, why shame him so?"' The written text of the psalm has thus been combined with the pilgrim's oral recollection of having heard it sung in various settings. The most obvious of these would have been liturgical, no doubt, but the application of the biblical poem to Dante's personal situation at this point in the *Purgatorio* suggests that the use of the dramatic power of this and similar texts was available as a poetic technique to be deliberately shaped and cultivated.

This passage in the *Purgatorio* is thus an enactment of the tensions it sets out to describe. The central fact to be conveyed is the spiritual condition in which Dante finds himself even after he has supposedly been purged of his sins on the way up the mountain. Dante's text functions by referring to biblical passages that communicate on various levels. Familiarity with shifts of mood and tone in the psalm makes it possible for him to ascribe sympathetic intention to the angelic song and to derive personal comfort from this understanding. That is, the biblical texts, even when silently omitted, continue to resonate in the mind of the pilgrim.

This principle is no less relevant to the earlier quotation from Canticles. There the various possibilities of interpretation conflict with each other to imitate Dante's condition of fear and trembling. As the pilgrim is about to proceed beyond his love for Beatrice as she was on earth, his inner conflicts which that love produced are thematically parallel to the oral and allegorical levels on which Solomon's Song could be understood. Much of his inner psychological state is thus projected by the hermeneutic struggle between the oral and written readings, between his carnal desire for Beatrice as a literal bride who will come with him from Lebanon and his spiritual understanding of her as a means of approaching God. Dante's attitude to his heavenly guide is ambivalent since he is simultaneously in love (not without carnal desire) and in awe of his mistress, who resembles the Bride of Canticles: 'fair as the moon, clear as the sun, and terrible as an army with banners . . . for love is as strong as death' (6.10, 8.6). Thus the fundamental duality of the allusion to Canticles helps to register the emotional intensity of the lover's condition. If this struggle undermines the theological placidity of the *Purgatorio*, it should be recognized that it is part of a larger struggle in which the device of a linear progress from Hell to Purgatory to Heaven is discredited by the inability of Dante the pilgrim to internalize the implications of his external movement towards heaven. The intertextual whirl of allusions and interpretations here helps to authenticate the psychological depth of the presentation of Dante the pilgrim.

Chaucer and Canticles

Chaucerians have long recognized ways in which the Song of Songs echoes through some of the *Canterbury Tales*. In his discussion of the different traditions that operate in the tale of the Merchant (as well as in that of the Miller), James I. Wimsatt connects Chaucer's use of Canticles with the humorous approaches of goliardic poets in *Carmina Burana*. When the Miller or the Merchant allude to Canticles, readers must recognize that, in addition to the spiritual interpretations of these texts which would have satisfied the Church, there must have been more carnal approaches. Wimsatt shows this to have been the case in the *Carmina Burana* and generalizes further in the 'Panel Discussion' that follows his paper in *Chaucer the Love Poet*: 'Bernard is very worried that the monks are going to get some amorous ideas out of the Canticles. Clearly his worry, his concern, was justified: the goliards found plenty of amorous ideas, as would anybody who reads it, I suppose' (97). R. E. Kaske likewise speaks of 'one of the attractive things about Canticles is this tension that exists between the literal reading (which obviously on that level is a very erotic poem indeed) and the spiritual meanings' ('Panel Discussion' 97). That is, despite the fact that very few medieval texts record a carnal reading of Canticles, there are enough of these in existence to support a thesis that posits a carnal text alongside the spiritual commentaries that were officially sanctioned.

In contrast to Dante, whose experiences seem equally open to spiritual and carnal understandings of the echoes of Canticles, Chaucer's pilgrims provide more evidence of the carnal in tales that fit into the genre of fabliaux. The Miller has Absolon, the foolish lover in his tale, serenade under Alison's window on the night she is in bed with her lover Nicholas:

Introduction

> And softe he cougheth with a semy soun:
> 'What do ye, hony-comb, sweete Alisoun,
> My faire bryd, my sweete cynamome?
> Awaketh, lemman myn, and speketh to me!' (I [A] 3697–700)

In the Merchant's Tale, Januarie, the old man married to a young wife, speaks to his wife about making love in his garden:

> Rys up, my wyf, my love, my lady free!
> The turtles voys is herd, my dowve sweete;
> The wynter is goon with alle his reynes weete.
> Com forth now, with thyne eyen columbyn!
> How fairer been thy brestes than is wyn! (IV [E] 2138–42)

Wimsatt's brilliant discussion of these lines and their complex manner of functioning in the tale explores the various ways in which Chaucer manipulates the biblical materials for his artistic purposes in the tale. On another level, however, these passages are oral texts that occur within the context of a more complex rhetorical passage. Absolon is literally singing, while Januarie's words sound almost like a song. Both of these characters seem to be relying on passages from Canticles that they have heard many times in a biblical context which they are adapting here for a carnal purpose. There is, presumably, a difference between the consciousness of the pilgrim–narrator (either the Miller or the Merchant) and his allusive capabilities and that of Chaucer the poet (or, for that matter, Chaucer the pilgrim). Absolon's song to Alison may be akin to that of Adso, the young cleric in Umberto Eco's *Name of the Rose* who responds to his first (and only?) sexual encounter by reciting from Canticles in Latin to his sexually experienced, yet Latinless partner. Of course, Absolon is both more crude and less successful than Adso and remains ridiculous from the outset. The similarity lies in the implicitly carnal reading of Canticles that motivates them both. Perhaps Chaucer the poet was familiar with learned commentaries on Canticles such as that of Hugh of St Clair or the *Glossa ordinaria* (cf. R. E. Kaske [1962] 483) but was his Miller? What about Januarie? I suggest that these biblically inspired texts reflect an oral tradition that was rarely articulated in writing about the Song of Songs as a secular love poem. Absolon and Januarie are Chaucer's contributions to the rare yet significant collection of written texts which testify to the existence of an oral tradition available during his time. Their practice is not unlike that of the goliardic poets cited by Wimsatt and is not necessarily too far from more serious love lyrics in works by Cavalcanti and Dante.

This introduction has been concerned with various aspects of a synchronic pattern whose elements stretch from the Sumerian tradition through the end of the Middle Ages. The principle of balance between the various extremes of the specific traditions is crucial. Even though each specific text can often be situated at some specific point between the polarities of profane and holy, oral and written, carnal and allegorical, domestic and apocalyptic, present and future, the effect of the pattern has been to maintain the archetype in a fully polysemous, indeterminate form. It is this form to which the writers of the English Renaissance seem to have had intuitive access, even as each of them chose a specific mode in which to articulate it.

Chapter 1

WILLIAM BALDWIN'S *THE CANTICLES, OR BALADES OF SALOMON*: THE SHAPING OF HISTORY, SEXUALITY AND SUBSEQUENT ENGLISH POETRY

FIRST COLLECTION OF ENGLISH POETRY

WILLIAM Baldwin's *Canticles, or Balades of Salomon* (1549) modulates a series of related polarities that account for the work's rhetorical and ideational features. These determine the ways in which the work establishes its temporal, conventional and intertextual moorings as it moves back and forth between the poles. As they comprise literature and shape history, the genres of lyric and narrative, poetry and prose, literality and allegory are related to shifts between sexuality and spirituality, as well as between oral and textual modes and sources, and Janus-like oversee the English Renaissance from Chaucer to Marvell. Many of these individual tensions are subtly interrelated so that poetry which is literally plain and lyrical in tone is often sexually suggestive (if not explicit) and produced in a world of oral communication that stresses song, music, sound and performances that do not repeat themselves. These moments are pressed into written texts that provide a narrative explanation linked to a prose allegory. Baldwin's work rewrites the carnal into spirit while it produces literary history which shapes the future both as material events and literary production. The rich texture of Baldwin's work recalls the synchronic pattern first recorded in Sumer as it explores the various facets of the polysemous biblical material and moves back and forth between carnal and allegorical, lyrical and apocalyptic, often recalling rabbinic dialogue between oral and written.

Baldwin was a skilful experimenter in poetic forms whose achievement was appreciated by Elizabethans such as Sir Philip Sidney.[1] His verse translation of

---

[1] In his comments on English poets whom he admired, Sidney included Baldwin after Chaucer: 'I account the *Mirrour of Magistrates* meetely furnished of beautiful parts' (51). Details about Baldwin's life are few. Stephen Gresham cites Lily B. Campbell's summary in her edition of the *Mirror for Magistrates* (21–5), articles by W. F. French ('William Baldwin', *Modern Quarterly of Language and Literature* 2 [1898–99]: 259–67) and Eveline I. Feasey ('William Baldwin', *Modern Language Review* 20 [1925]: 407–18) in addition to other research about Baldwin's

Canticles into seventy-one poems was the earliest collection of English poetry ever published and seems to have had direct influence on the work of later poets such as Spenser, Shakespeare, Donne, Herbert, Milton and Marvell. While Baldwin's *Canticles, or Balades of Salomon* has received little critical attention over the years, many who have noticed it explicitly praise the comparatively high quality of the verse. As part of his survey of Baldwin's status as a major mid-sixteenth-century writer, John N. King points out that 'Baldwin is the only imaginative author of the English Reformation to escape the 1580s censure of earlier Tudor literature and to provide a consciously acknowledged influence on Elizabethan literature' (1982, 360). Anthony à Wood quotes from Baldwin's 23rd poem (corresponding to Song of Solomon 2.17) as an indication 'that Baldwyn's versification is far more smooth and polished than the generality of scriptural translations we have yet met with' (341). The only extended modern study of this work of Baldwin's is Sister Francis Camilla Cavanaugh's doctoral dissertation which provides a critical introduction as well as a series of annotations for each of the poems that Baldwin published. There are, in addition, short descriptions of this work by Baldwin in more general studies by Lily Campbell (*Divine Poetry* 57–9), Stanley Stewart (7, 9) and, more recently, Stephen Gresham (107–9) and Max Engammare (especially 301–4).

PREFACE AND LAYOUT

Baldwin's work juxtaposes different renditions of the biblical text as part of a project to replace popular bawdy verse with a complex poetic tradition that appeals to both extremes of the tensions between flesh and spirit, letter and allegory, lyric and apocalypse, oral and written. It is cryptic at its very core. When, in a preface as well as in the subsequent dedicatory letter to Edward VI, he instructs readers and king to read his work with care, he is presenting a poet's implicit statement about the slippery if not indeterminate nature of language. For Baldwin, the Song of Songs is a dark text which can nevertheless be understood if read intensively and with the guidance of a competent commentator. The 'Wanton wurdes' of the Hebrew text are to be read in various ways which, when combined, will provide necessary aid for the diligent reader. This 'proces of the matter' seems to include a need to confront various textual difficulties and to overcome them through struggle. One obvious level of such problems concerns the way in which the erotic language should be read. The nature of this allegorical method, however, also opens up other levels at which one set of significations supplants another. In Baldwin's text, this happens when the erotic language is read in terms of the conflicts of

---

work as a printer and his death. Gresham's article appeared too late to include the final word on the end of Baldwin's life by David Scott Kasten in 'The Death of William Baldwin', *Notes and Queries* 28 [226] (Dec. 1981): 516–17.

Baldwin's Canticles, or Balades of Salomon

the Reformation. Here the biblical lyrics take on the significance of the Protestant search for the true Church.

Baldwin opens each chapter of his *Canticles, or Balades of Salomon* with a transcription of the translation of the biblical text that appears in the Great Bible.[2] Although that translation is accurate and faithful to the original Hebrew, the language used tends to diminish the level of carnal association. This becomes clear in the context of Baldwin's own translations which follow. John King describes what he calls 'the complex format' of the book as combining 'the prose text from the Great Bible with a commentary, a division of each chapter into individual lyrics in Baldwin's own prose translation, and an amplified verse paraphrase set off from the black-letter text in italic type' (*English* 367). Thus, each of the eight biblical chapters is divided into a series of shorter passages which Baldwin retranslates into prose and then adds a prose 'argument' as well as a poetic version.

Baldwin's 'arguments' can be understood as an indication of the tension between orality and textuality in his work. They provide an allegorical interpretation of the biblical text in ways that are more or less in agreement with the patristic tradition going back to Origen and which thus rely on venerable written authority. In terms of literary genre, the 'arguments' take the timeless moments of the biblical lyrics and rewrite them into a narrative about Christ's love for the Church. As such, the narrative points in the direction of a conclusion that is implicitly apocalyptic, the triumphant union of Christ and Church at the end of time. This kind of closure is then reworked as it interacts with the poems that follow the arguments which reproduce an oral interpretation that adds sound and music on one level and a reinscribed sexuality on another. The poems thus combine what Baldwin calls 'argument' and 'rime' (A.i.v) to form a series of songs that may privilege written over oral as they struggle to maintain the narrative closure imposed on the text by the apocalyptic allegory. Nevertheless, the orally based musical undertone that stresses the sexuality and flexibility resisted by the allegory continues to make itself felt. Baldwin as poet is generally in control of this tension and uses it for striking poetic results.

At the heart of Baldwin's project lies a series of intertwined theological, literary and political issues that make up the major thrust of his view of Canticles. His work connects Protestant doctrine about the superiority of faith to works with his allegorical method of reading which assigns spiritual

---

[2] As John N. King notes (*English* 367), Baldwin provides a translation that is almost an exact version of the Great Bible translation (1540) which had been published by Edwarde Whitchurche, Baldwin's employer. The typeface used in Whitchurche's Great Bible is the same as that in Baldwin's Canticles. In a few instances, Baldwin changed a word or phrase as he reproduced the Great Bible translation chapter by chapter. Thus, for example, in 6.8 the Great Bible refers to 'lx, Quenes. lxxx. wyves, and dameselles without nõbre' (Pt 3, Fol. 41a) while Baldwin corrects 'wyves' to 'Concubines' (h.iii.v), also used by Coverdale (1535) to render the Hebrew פילגשים (Vulgate 'concubinae').

33

significance to the images of the flesh that abound in Canticles. The suggestiveness of these images of sensuous specificity is signified in print by a series of texts that continually rewrite the Bible, as the book moves from one stage of the interpretive process to another. As Baldwin's prose translation replaces the Great Bible text and is then replaced by the argument, the senses are often suppressed, only to re-emerge in the poems which help to restore the oral traditions that have lost prominence in the course of this textualization.[3]

Baldwin's *Balades* can be read as determining in some sense the development of the historical events that transpired subsequent to its publication. Along with the *Book of Common Prayer*, they illustrate Marshall Grossman's claim that literary history precedes and enables the articulation of cultural or material history. Grossman shows that the 'moment in which specifically literary processes mediate our access to "the Real" will be at once literary and historical, because a literary text matters historically precisely when it gives form to exigent experience and thus takes part in the self-constitution of subjects whose choices and actions affect the substance of material history'. In these terms, Baldwin's work functions 'as an active participant in the formation of material experience' (18).

When Henry VIII died in 1547, the future of the Anglican Church was in no sense settled. The heir to the throne, Edward VI, was only ten years old so that his uncle, the Earl of Somerset, had himself appointed Protector and as such took over control of the government. By 1549 Somerset had introduced many changes into the religious practices of the Church. One of the most far-reaching of these, the publication of the *Book of Common Prayer* and its establishment as the standard text for liturgical purposes, preceded the appearance of Baldwin's *Balades* by only a few months. Some of the political turmoil that resulted in popular rebellions seems to have been at least partially motivated by conservative peasant resentment of the religious changes imposed upon them in general and by the publication of the *Book of Common Prayer* in particular. D. M. Palliser points out that the revolt 'in the west country was in the main a protest against the first Edwardian prayer book' (99). At a time when the English government was pursuing an intensive campaign aimed at furthering the reformation of the Church, even a fervent Protestant such as Baldwin had to have been aware of the murmuring and resentment among the conservative forces that wanted to see as little religious change as possible. Baldwin's dedicatory letter to Edward, dated 1 June 1549,

---

[3] In addition to all the apparently conscious play with the different faces of the biblical text, Baldwin's book seems to have undergone a slight printing problem that has resulted in a number of textual variants between the extant copies. Careful comparison between the copy at the British Library and that at the Folger Shakespeare Library suggests that the type was reset for some of the pages, evidently as a result of some minor mishap. Almost all of the variants seem to be insignificant, although in two instances the type may have been reset deliberately to correct errors. My citations are to the Folger copy.

can be understood in the context of the rebellion which would break out later that summer in partial response to the literary activity of Protestants such as Baldwin who were active in court circles. Baldwin's appeal to Edward's Protestant views in the letter are echoed in the text of his *Balades*. His poetic work can be read as an example of firm Protestant support for Somerset's religious innovations and as such seems to have contributed to the motivations of rebels in outlying areas.

The preface to the reader and the dedicatory letter to Edward make it plain that Baldwin wanted his work to be read and considered in more than a cursory fashion. He instructs his readers that

> althoughe I bee not so playne in al thinges as I mought haue ben by meanes of my metres, yet I trust that suche as wyll reade them diligently, shall haue great lyght in understanding the texte. But this I tell the good reader, thou must reade them well, (for it is not once readyng nor twise that can make thee understand them) & in reading note the sentence more than the rime, with the argumentes whiche go before and after the songes. (A.i.v)

This, however, is not yet proof of the 'great lyght in understanding the texte' which Baldwin promises his readers. Some of this is to be found on the level of politics and religion. Baldwin urges the importance of his work to Edward with explicit support for Henry's doctrine that the English king is simultaneously head of the state and of the Church. He explains that his spiritual work is addressed to his temporal king as an indication of Edward's dual political and religious roles and then goes on to connect his poetic work or 'gift' to prophecy 'truly to understand the holy scriptures, that ye may be able through the illuminyng of his holy spirit, to iudge & examin al spirites, & then to besech your maiesty to take in wurth this simple gift' (A.iii.r). That is, Baldwin is suggesting that careful reading of his work could be of spiritual and political value to the young king. On this level, Baldwin is looking forward to his more famous work which he would publish in the following decade, *Mirror For Magistrates*. If he considers the *Balades* potentially valuable for his king's spiritual and judicial education, Baldwin obviously ascribes to them no small degree of political relevance.

At the moment that tensions between English Catholics and Protestants are threatening to escalate into civil war, Baldwin sets up the relations between the Churches in his allegory as simultaneously idyllic and charged with danger. He interprets the verse about 'she that cumeth up by the wyldrenes lyke a spyre of smoke' as an indication that 'whyle the newe conuerted Spouse resteth in the sweete peace of conscience, she waxeth dayly more perfect and perfect: ascendyng from fayth to fayth, from clerenes to clerenes' (e.ii.r). Then he states that the 'perfect Spouse perceyuyng that the other is in the bed of Christe, out of whiche she smoketh up so swetely, prayseth the bed to the Younglynges: syngyng':

> BEholde ye young, behold and see the bed
>   Of Salomon, Christes peace wherin we dwell:
> With thre score men moste strong and myghtie fed
> Beset about, the strong of Israel
>   That faythful are and wyse.
>
> Of whiche eche one doeth hold a cuttyng swurd,
> Expert therwith to stryke and warde in warre:
> Well learnde they be to preache and teache Gods Wurd,
> And with the same to kepe all errors farre
>   From godly men and wyse.
>
> Upon theyr thygh this swurd, Gods Wurd they wear,
> Gyrded therwith for fear of enemies,
> That cum by nyght the feble for to fear
> With priuie trappes of subtyl heresies
>   Whiche fleshly wittes deuise. (e.iii.r–v)

Here Baldwin has integrated the biblical passage about Solomon's bed and his surrounding warriors (3.7–8) into the previous passage about the two churches. While the 'perfect Spouse' is presumably pleased to see the newly converted spouse in Christ's bed, her words are of strength and might, of swords and cutting. Despite the pastoral idyll in which the wives of Solomon regard each other amicably, those who refuse to convert and who subject believers by night with 'priuie trappes of subtyl heresies / Whiche fleshly wittes deuise' will have to face the warriors of the king.

There is a more explicitly political way of reading Baldwin's use of the pastoral convention. In Chapter 7 there is a well-known passage in which the lovers speak of going out to fields and villages. Baldwin renders the verses as follows: 'Cum my Beloued, let us goe furth into the field, and let us lodge together in the villages. In the mornyng we wyl ryse, and goe se yf the uines be flowred, and whether the Pomegranades be shot furth. Ther wyl I poure out all my loue upon thee' (k.iv.v). As in the previous passage, for Baldwin the language here is fraught with meaning. He explains 'that abrode in the worlde, whiche here is called a fyelde and countrey, there are many that know not Christe' (l.i.r) and has the Church suggest that she and Christ go out and convert them. The poem ('The Spouse to her Beloued. lviii') extends the agricultural imagery suggested in the biblical passage (fields, vines, 'Pomegranades', flowering) with phrases such as 'bedewed with grace', 'pleasaunt shower', 'get fruite,' 'fruitful fayth', 'wedes' and 'foxes'. The general technique is quite similar. He provides the erotic imagery from the Bible with a spiritual level of meaning that shifts the significance of love to a metaphor for the relation between Christ and the Church. In so doing, however, he also imposes a Protestant ideology onto the pastoral convention so that the fields become a source for good 'dedes and doctrine' where 'fayth' is fruitful. In the context of peasants in rebellion against the enclosure of fields as well as in protest against the English *Book of Common Prayer*, Baldwin is making a bold statement about Protestant truth and the ultimate significance of the Bible. The allegorical methodology of interpretation allows language to slip into a series of significations that co-opt the entire religio-political world into the pastoral imagery of the poem. If Edward did, in fact, read this book with care, it was an invitation for him to continue the process of the Protestant protectorate despite the uprisings. In a curious way, the process of interpreting this pastoral reverses the apparent valorization that favours the fields over the city. In the end, the contemporary conflict between the rural peasants and the Tudor regime concluded, for Baldwin, by the strengthening of the monarch and, by extension, the acts of his protector(s) in the struggle to reimpose order and obedience upon the rebels 'abrode in the world'. The triumph of the city over the country is thus another of the strange reversals that make Baldwin's allegory rich and complex.

The theological focus with which the collection begins is traditionally allegorical. Sensuous objects and experiences in the biblical text are identified with the theological problem of how to understand the physical world of the Bible. At this level, the physical experiences of Canticles appear as metaphors for spiritual search and discovery. A 'swete smelling ointment' (Song of Songs 1.3) becomes 'the oyntments of gyftes spirituall that runne out of his fragraunt smellyng brestes' ('Argument' to poem ii, 'The Younglynges to Christ', a.ii.r). In the poem, the biblical 'We wyll runne after thee' gets interpreted as movement from 'grosnes of the flesh' to 'the trueth' as the younglings run after Christ. Then, in the following poem, 'The Spouse to the Younglynges, [iii]' the spouse explains the significance of the biblical verse in which she declares 'the King hath broughte me into his priuie Chaumber' (Song of Songs 1.3):

> Kyng Christe (ye young) whose loue (ye sawe) I sought,
>   Hath kyssed me with his swete peace and grace.
> He hath by fayth my troubled conscience brought
> To peace and rest: his pleasaunt Chaumber place. (a.ii.v)

The desire which seems clearly erotic in the biblical text has become a spiritual search for grace and rest.

Baldwin's use of erotic language to refer to his spiritual quest is made poetically complex by the tension between oral and written. As we read the poem, the sounds of the rhymes along with the regular iambic rhythms reintegrate the oral world into the written text. Although it is by now quite clear that his having 'kyssed' her 'with his swete peace and grace' is not to be understood in a simple, carnal fashion, neither has the sensuousness of 'kiss' or the orality of 'sweet' been entirely lost. These are complex metaphors of spiritual experience which are based upon the contrast between orality and textuality. Another aspect of this is the sense of colloquial discourse and implicit drama in the stage directions that the 'Argument' provides here. The poem is meant to be understood as the words of the 'Spouse to the younglinges' that is, the statement about the 'privie Chaumber' is contextualized as the preaching of the Church. The interpretive language in which she encourages and preaches juxtaposes oral and written modes. First the directions of the 'Argument' establish an imaginative setting which is itself a balance between the orality of ordinary speech and the textuality of written expression: 'Christe seyng the readinesse of the Younglinges . . . he sendeth furth his spouse . . . Who prechyng to theym the mercies of God . . . syngeth very pleasauntly' (a.ii.v). Then Baldwin introduces parenthetical comments to the younglinges in the poem of the spouse: 'Kyng Christe (ye young) whose loue (ye sawe) I sought'. The poem thus combines formal diction with oral address. This technique recurs throughout Baldwin's *Canticles*.

The thematic movement from flesh to truth and from works to grace and faith is formally presented in a regular iambic pentameter quatrain with a rhyme scheme that is normally *abab*. This is the pattern that opens and closes Baldwin's *Canticles* and it serves as a formal arrangement that frames the dozens of other patterns with which the collection experiments. Although some of the other stanzaic patterns are repeated as the work proceeds, none appear as often as this one. Twenty of the poems[4] more or less conform to it, each having between two and eleven stanzas with occasional variation on the rhyme scheme. The constant return to this fairly simple formal arrangement of iambic pentameter quatrains establishes an important way in which Baldwin integrated form and content in his collection. The verse patterns that are more striking and elaborate do not repeat as much as this one so that they provide a formal mode of variation in contrast to the almost regular recurrence of the iambic pentameter quatrain. Baldwin's return to this form is similar to Shakespeare's use of rhymed couplets to conclude scenes in his plays. All but three of the eight chapters of Baldwin's *Canticles* begin and/or end with poems made up of iambic pentameter quatrains.[5]

This formal aspect of the poems is clearly related to their orality. The appearance of the lines on the page is a representation of how they sound when read aloud. They are not, of course, the equivalent of recordings but rather representations of the conflict between the textual and the oral. In this case, the regular return and the sense of frame that the iambic pentameter quatrain provides is important in connecting us to the world of mid-Tudor speech. The way in which normal English speech rhythms tend to be iambic is, of course, a major explanation for the success of iambic pentameter as the most common English verse form. In this first collection of English verse, the

---

[4] Those numbered 1, 3, 5, 6, 9, 11, 14, 17, 20, 23, 25, 29, 31, 33, 39, 43, 60, 61, 65 and 71.
[5] The first chapter begins and ends with this form (poems 1 and 11), the second concludes with it (23), four and five begin with it (29 and 35), and like the first chapter, the eighth begins and ends with this same stanzaic pattern (60 and 71).

poet was anticipating this development as he intuitively recognized the regularity of the iambic sound patterns.

Although Baldwin's poems apparently avoid sexuality as they allegorize physical detail into Christian doctrine, they generally return to the flesh to help articulate the nature and intensity of the spiritual world. In the opening 'ballad', the reader must explore poetic sources which are rooted in sexually charged carnal imagery, as well as in the textual silence of the printed page. A significant difference between Baldwin and the rendition of Canticles in the Great Bible appears in the second verse of chapter one. The Great Bible version renders: 'O that he wolde kysse me with the kysses of his mouthe: for thy loue is more pleasaunt then wyne' (A.iv.r). On the next page, Baldwin translated 'for thy teates are better than wyne' (a.i.r). He then elaborated in the opening song of 'The Churche unto Christ':

> The Kisse o Christe, whiche I of thee requyre
> Thy grace, thy peace, thy loue (my Loue) it is:
> Whiche whyle I lacke, thy Fathers wrath and iyer
> Condemneth me for my fyrste fathers misse.
>
> The lawe (alas) the dutie of our hyer,
> Skarce kept in ought, doeth styll agaynste me hisse:
> Wherfore o Christe who quenched hast his fyer,
> Through loue and grace, delyuer me from this.
>
>   Whiche styl to crave the more I me encline
> Bycause thy Teates, thy consolacion swete
> Muche better be than any kynde of wine: (a.i.r–v)

Marvin H. Pope summarizes the textual tradition with regard to the reading of 'teates' for 'loues' here: 'The reading "your breasts" by LXX (*mastoi sou*) and Vulgate (*ubera tua*) appears mistaken, although there are grounds for the choice, since the words dôdîm, "love(s)" and *daddayim*, "breasts," "teats," appeared the same in the ancient consonantal orthography, *ddm*' (298). Thus Baldwin could be understood as merely providing his readers with an alternative reading for the unusual Hebrew word דודיך. Nonetheless, the poetic effect of his choice of words here is to focus directly upon the more sensuous significance of the word and to explain it in terms that are allegorical. That is, Baldwin clearly wants the 'breasts' of Christ to be understood metaphorically as sources of spiritual nourishment. He provides a general view of chapter one, using words of the Great Bible (the literal 'loves'), but in his own translation of the passage and in the poem, he makes use of the more striking metaphor of 'teats'. He attempts to avoid any carnal understanding of the words by making the connection with Christ explicit and somehow asexual.

Baldwin's approach to language here is considerably more complicated than it appears. The biblical text takes on a theological tone in the poem and thus fits into a Protestant world view that is simultaneously religious, political and social. The most striking aspect of this view concerns the way in which Baldwin exaggerates the extent to which the original Hebrew makes use of 'wanton wordes' (A.i.v). The Great Bible version is made more sensuous just at the moment that the poetic treatment allegorizes the breasts into a metaphor about Christ's concern for mankind as a nursing mother. Instead of arguing that there is no sexual significance to the passage, Baldwin recognizes one at the outset. It is not, however, part of a world of 'fleshly pleasures and delytes' but one explicitly positioned in contrast to a society with the sexual values supposedly rife in Henry's court. In his preface to Edward, Baldwin writes of his hope that verse such as his 'myght once driue out of office the baudy balades of lecherous loue that commonly are indited and song of idle courtyers in princes and noble mens houses' (A.iii.v). Baldwin's point then is that the presence of sexual language in the biblical text is part of Christ's world of charity.

The length of the opening poem of the book is a clear reflection of the textual pleasures that Baldwin can be read as singing. From a passage which is two-and-a-half verses in the Hebrew, Baldwin produces six lines of prose translation (42 words), ten lines of prose argument (in smaller type, 92 words), and forty-eight lines of poetry (412 words). The rhyme scheme of the poem is fairly simple. Most of the lines are organized into four-line stanzas with alternating rhymes. The rhymes, however are often interrelated so that the first three stanzas use the same two kinds of rhyme (*ababababab*) as do the final two. This sort of intricate attention to formal detail is part of the processing of orality into the textuality of the printed work that Baldwin's text fashions.

The issue here concerns the way in which Baldwin engages the various polarities: oral and textual, literal and allegorical, sexual and spiritual. The carnal suggestiveness of the biblical text gets spiritualized as it is interpreted by Baldwin in a textual process of transformation that leads from the literal prose of the Great Bible to the carefully shaped verse of the *Canticles or Balades*. As he makes his way from one voice of the original text to another, Baldwin is working out a delicate balance between his various polarities. When he tries to spiritualize 'the baudy balades of lecherous loue', he is likewise balancing oral and written, literal and allegorical. The result he achieves locates the excitement of the sensual in the tension between oral and written.

One might argue (with a cue from Roland Barthes) that the central pleasure for Baldwin is that of constant refashioning of texts. As his book moves more and more firmly away from a carnal understanding of the biblical material, it seems to take more and more pleasure in its elaboration of new texts that sing the praises of spiritual desire in many different ways. Literal prose translation makes way for prose interpretation which finally yields carefully rhymed poems. The innovative attention Baldwin paid to the formal shape of his translated verses was clearly a source of considerable literary pleasure for him. The external look of the poems is generally connected to the poet's concern with thematic content. These two aspects of the poems work together in ways that must be sought out and synthesized by the reader, albeit with major emphasis on 'sentence' as Baldwin recommends in his preface: 'in reading note the sentence more than the rime' (A.i.v).

In his opening poem, Baldwin thematizes his interest in transforming erotic motifs into spiritual doctrine. He does this by acknowledging the carnal level of the biblical material which he goes on to treat as a spiritual metaphor. This is very different from standard Protestant practice. Martin Luther's commentary on Canticles provides a useful foil. After complaining bitterly of medieval use of allegory, Luther's account of the opening of Solomon's Song gingerly sidesteps the carnal level of the language. In general, it states, Solomon's Song 'deals with the greatest of all human works, namely, government'. Luther accounts for kisses in terms of 'the custom of the people of that day. Among us kisses are held in less esteem. However, kisses are signs of love and favor'. He then goes on to explain the passage that Baldwin would render 'for thy teates are better than wyne'. 'Breasts', Luther claims, 'refer to doctrine, by which souls are fed so that "the man of God may be perfect for every good work" (2 Tim. 3:17)' (196–7). Luther considers erotic aspects of the biblical text but denies their carnal significance. Baldwin, on the other hand, begins his poem with a movement 'fro[m] vayne to perfect blisse / To perfect fayth, from wurkes of worldly myer' (a.i.r). The carnal level of the biblical text is thus understood as an appeal to recognize 'wurkes of worldly myer' as something to be replaced with faith.[6] The sexually charged breast imagery of Solomon is transformed into a rejection of carnality by the traditional view of the speaker as Christ.

The attention to breast imagery is continued in the fourth poem, 'The Younglynges to Christe'. There is a similar movement from generalized 'love' in the Great Bible translation (pt 3, fol. 40r) of Canticles 1.4 to Baldwin's prose version: 'we wyl thynke more of thy teates than vpon wyne'. The poem rehearses the theme, familiar by now, of faith as the means of overcoming the condition 'Where wurkes are allto lyght' (a.iii.r). Once again, however, it is significant that the emphasis on theological grace is accompanied by the imagery of 'teates':

---

[6] Cf. poem 3 'The Spouse to the Younglynges' based on 'The Kyng hath brought me in to his priuie Chaumber' (Canticles 1.4). Baldwin interprets the private chamber as Christ's 'pleasaunt Chaumber place' where mankind can be saved. Here the reader's tendency to interpret the biblical text in sexual terms is broadened to include the struggle between the flesh and the spirit:
    For whan the Lawe, that no man can fulfyl,
    Had made me dead and coulde me not reuiue.
    Because the fleshe full sore agaynst my wyl
    Mayntaynd with sin, dyd styl agaynst me stryue. (a.ii.v)
The poem thus expands the interpretive stance of the reader into a general comment on the nature of human flesh and the concomitant need for a generalized spiritual solution.

> Thy fruitful teates that are so fyne,
>   Thy consolacions sweete,
> We wyll remember more than wyne:
>   Whiche are for vs most meete. (a.iii.r)

Baldwin's opening poem is also marked off by a number (18) of marginal references to other biblical passages evoked by the verse. These provide additional scriptural voices that add to the tensions developed in the text. Central here are the passages that seem to gloss 'kiss'. On the surface it appears as if the poet were merely trying to clarify to the reader that the apparent carnal reference in the biblical text is really spiritual. Nevertheless, the contexts in the proof texts increase the complexity of the texture. First, the margin invokes Genesis 29 where Jacob first met Rachel and then Laban her father (his uncle). Although the biblical passage makes it clear that his kiss was one of greeting, it was hardly devoid of emotional (including sexual) significance: 'And Jacob kyssed Rahel, and lyfte vp hys voyce & wepte' (Great Bible, pt. 1, fol. 12r [b iiiir]. Jacob's kiss marks a moment of intense feeling as he recognizes that he is living out the terms of the quest his father had set for him: 'se thou take not a wyfe of the daughters of Chanaa[n] but aryse & gett the to Mesopotamia to the house of Bethuel thy mothers father: and there take the a wyfe of the daughters of Laban thy mothers brother' (Gen. 28.1–2, Great Bible pt 1, fol. 11v, [b iiiv]). Indeed, soon after Jacob's kiss we find that 'Rahel was bewtyfull & well fauored. And Jacob loued Rahel' (fol. 12r). So Baldwin's reference to 'Gene. xxix' intensifies the significance of 'kiss' by bringing to it the various levels of anticipation and desire that characterize the narrative about Jacob.

The other biblical voices are no less charged with emotion. In 'ii. Kin. xiiii' (generally referred to as 2 Samuel 14.[33]), David's kiss of Absalom carries with it all the intensity of a parent – child relationship cursed by the desire for vengeance and power. Like Jacob's kiss, David's occurs in the midst of a narrative charged with an intrigue of passionate and tragic proportions. Baldwin brings the voices of that story as well into the margin of his text. This is likewise the case in Luke 7.[36–50] in which the sinful woman kisses the feet of Jesus and in Luke 22.47–8 where Judas betrays his master. In all these cases, the marginal voices cry out to complicate the 'Kisse' demanded by the speaker. Sexuality and passion are in the margin to intensify the 'grace' and 'peace' of the poetic text.

Baldwin's approach is furthermore complicated by the language of descriptive landscape which it adapts as part of the poetic processing of the Bible. The celebration of spring is connected in the Hebrew with romantic longing in a landscape. Baldwin's prose renders the scene with delicacy:

> Nowe the wynter is past, the rayne shower is goen, and departed. The flowers haue appeared in our land. The singing tyme is cum. The Turtles voyce was heard in oure lande: The fygge tree hath brought furth her buddes, and the

flowred vines haue yelded theyr smell. Up therfore my Loue, make haste my darlyng: and cum O my doue in to the holes of the rocke, into the hyd ladder degrees, and shewe me thy face and let me heare thy voyce: for thy voyce is swete, and thy face beautiful'. (d.i.v – d.ii.r)

The word rendered 'singing' here is problematic. Coverdale (fol. 580) and Matthew (pt 1, fol. 245v) suggest 'twystinge,' while the Geneva (fol. 281r) and the King James translators kept 'singing'. Another, possibly preferable meaning of the Hebrew word is that rendered by Robert Etienne (Stephanus) whose Latin 'putationis' or 'pruning' (fol. 213b) is ordinarily accepted by scholars of the Hebrew Bible.[7] The fact that Baldwin ignored this reading emphasizes his desire to connect the biblical text with his ideological concern with preaching and song. His 'argument' for the passage focuses on this orality: 'Christe seyng hys Spouse ready to ryse, encourageth her to make great haste: and exhortyng her to preache, declareth howe bothe the tyme and place is nowe fit therefore, openly syngyng' (d.ii.r).

The oral connection between song and preaching is significant here. At the very moment that Baldwin was shifting from allegorical narrative back to the lyric mode with its attention to the world of sound as reflected in the shape of the poem on the page, he was also at pains to connect the informal world of orality with the official, textual world of the church and preaching. The poem that he produced maintains the balance:

> OF vnbelefe now is coulde wynter past,
>   The stormes lykewyse of blyndnes, and of trust
> In mannes deuice, the whiche dyd ouercast
> The truth, are goen: are knowen to be but rust.
>
>   And loe the flowers of faythful men and iust
> In the erth, our lande, in beautie bud and bloom:
> So that the tyme for which thou long didst lust,
> The syngyng tyme, the tyme to preache is cum.
>
>   The turtles voyce, the voyce of the holy gost,
> The wurd of God sincerely as it ought
> Was heard abrode in our landes litle coast,
> And as it shoulde, effectually hath wrought.
>
>   The fyg tree loe, her blossomes furth hath brought,
> The budded vines haue yelded out theyr smel:
> The faythfull folke to whom my truth was tought,
> In fayth and wurkes, excedyngly excell.

---

[7] Marvin Pope translates 2.12b 'Pruning time has come' (365) but comments: 'It is difficult to decide here between the two meanings of *zamir*, "pruning" or "singing." The ancient versions and authorities, LXX, Aquila, Symmachus, Vulgate, Targum, Rashbam opted for "pruning"; Rashi, Qimhi, Ibn Ezra, and most moderns favor "singing"' (395).

> Aryse therfore my spouse, my special Loue,
> Make haste, make spede, purely my wurde to preache:
> And cum to me, cum, cum to me my doue,
> To whome I geue myne holy goste to teache.
>
> Cum to the Rocke, to me thy stedy leache,
> Cum to the hoales, the merites of my death:
> Cum to the hyd degrees of fayth, that reache
> To perfectnes, assisted by my breath.
>
> Then turne to me thy face, and let me hear
> Thy voyce aloude, lyke thunder in the ayer.
> Thy preachyng voyce is pleasaunt to myne ear,
> And in myne iye thy face is very fayer. (d.ii.r–v)

The poem celebrates spring and rebirth in song but it does so by transforming the biblical attention to love in a natural landscape into Christian truth in an allegorical scene where each natural element has a higher, spiritual meaning that clarifies and elaborates upon mere nature. Thus the movement from winter to spring becomes identified as one from unbelief, blindness and rust to truth. The second stanza conflates the natural world's 'beautie, bud and bloome' into its biblical equivalent (in Baldwin's translation), 'the syngyng tyme', which, in turn gets interpreted as 'the tyme to preache'. The poem presents the tension between oral and written as it represents each side of the polarity in different ways. Nature is included in imagery that focuses upon the world and its experience. The 'wynter' is 'cowlde', 'stormes . . . ouercast', 'flowers . . . bud and bloome', 'the fygtree . . . blossomes', 'budded vines' yield 'out theyr smel', 'Rocke' and 'thunder in the ayer' are associated with the 'very fayer' beloved. At the same time, all of the images are explicitly interpreted in Christian terms in accord with the allegorical mode of reading textually practised by the Church. That is, the orality of the biblical original is adapted by a textual practice so that it conforms to the written way of understanding. As this kind of formality is being achieved, however, the poet also processes his text into the stanzaic pattern of rhymed iambic pentameter that provides the vocal or musical norm for the entire collection. All this is part of the tension behind the primary allegorical image of song as preaching.

A more extraordinary instance of the allegorization of nature occurs in chapter three where the biblical text speaks of a woman's search for her lover. Baldwin's prose translation renders the first four verses as follows:

> BY nyghte, in my bed sought I for hym whome my soule loueth. I sought him but I found hym not. I wyl ryse nowe and goe about the citie, by the lanes & stretes wyll I seke him whome my soule loueth. I sought hym, but I founde hym not.
>
> The kepers whiche goe aboute the citie, founde me. Haue ye not seen hym, whome my soule loueth? Whan I was a little passed furth from them, I founde him whome my soule loueth.

I got holde upon hym, and wyll not let hym go agayn, untyll I haue brought hym into my mothers house, and in to the Chamber of her that bore me. (d.iv.v)

The standard allegorical understanding of the identity of the woman in search here is that she represents the Church. Some commentators discern a comparison between the Synagogue and the Church. Thus, according to Richard F. Littledale, the sixth-century commentary attributed to Cassiodorus distinguishes between 'the earlier reference . . . to the Primitive Church of the Jews, but here to the Gentile Church, bound far more closely to Him in love' (123). Baldwin enlarges upon this and attributes these verses to 'the newly converted' Protestant Church. His 'Argument' describes the conversion process:

> AT the desyer of his Spouse, Christe cummeth upon the mountaines of Bather, the harde harted foxes that destroyed his vineyardes, mekenyng through his grace, theyr loftie stomakes: so humbling them that they acknowlegyng theyr wyckednes, do repent and recant the false doctrine that they taught. And nowe receyued through fayth and humilitie into the felowshyp of Christes holy Churche, they confesse and openly publish the vaynenes of theyr former lyfe and of the tradicions and glorious wyl wurkes, which they so stifly mayntayned, singyng. (e.i.r)

In the passages that follow, Baldwin continues his interpretation of the biblical text as presenting two churches, one perfect and one newly converted. These two share the attentions of Christ with love and respect.

The poetic language that deals with the two churches takes up the pastoral motif from the biblical text but extends this to include an urban pole that implicitly threatens the idyllic atmosphere. The false, fleshly, urban pole is contrasted with the purity and truth to be found in the fields. In the context of this contrast between city and country lurk the darker fears of war and violence that threaten to destroy the idyllic world which the *Balades* present. In the course of engaging with these difficulties, the reader is expected to choose between the forces of love and those of error.

The first song of 'The new converted Spouse to the Younglynges. xxiiii.' develops most of these themes in seven stanzas each of which has a short chorus of one line. The poem makes use of imagery which contrasts light with darkness, and flesh with spirit and concludes with what is implicitly presented as spiritual enlightenment. The explicit theological references make the Protestant message unmistakably clear. The first stanza presents the initial condition of the speaker's fleshly and spiritual darkness:

> IN wysedome of the flesh, my bed,
> > Fonde trust in wurkes of mannes deuise,
> > By nyght, in darkenes of the dead,
> > I sought for Christe, as one vnwyse,
> > Whome my soule loueth.

Kisses of their Mouths

She alludes to the Roman Catholic Church in terms such as 'flesh', 'wurkes of mannes deuise' and 'darkenes of the dead'. The next stanza contrasts the imagery of 'nyght' and death with faith:

> I sought hym long, but founde hym not,
> Because I sought hym not aryght:
> I sought in wurkes, but now I wot
> He is found by fayth, not in the nyght,
> > Whome my soule loueth.

The urban context of the Roman Catholic darkness is inscribed with images of blindness and falsity:

> I wyll vp (thought I) and get me out
> In lanes and stretes my Loue to fynde:
> And wandre others wurkes about,
> To seke hym in that citie blynde,
> > Whome my soule loueth.

> I sought hym there but coulde not spede,
> The watche that of that citie been,
> False preachers there founde me in dede:
> Of whom I askt yf they had seen
> > Whome my soule loueth.

Literal experience in London 'lanes and stretes' (as opposed to the Great Bible translation 'in the wayes, in all the streets') for the Hebrew 'in the market stalls and the streets' (בשוקים וברחובות) begins with a sense of narrowness which is then metaphorically extended towards darkness by making 'that citie blynde'. The 'watchmen' of the Great Bible become 'False preachers' who neither watch nor see. Soon thereafter we find that indeed,

> They saw hym not, nor greatly past
> My soule that sought hym to confounde:
> But whan I was a lytle past
> Fro them and theyrs, than hym I founde
> > Whome my soule loueth.

> I caught hym quycke, by fayth and grace,
> And wyll not suffre hym depart,
> Tyl I haue brought hym to the place
> Where I hym sought with blynded hart,
> > Whome my soule loueth.

> Tyl I hym bryng into the place
> Of vnbelief, my mothers house
> And Chaumber: that she may embrace
> His wurde, and be with me his spouse,
> > Whome my soule loueth. (e.i.r–v)

After extending the blindness of the city to the former state of the speaker ('blynded hart'), the poem concludes with reference to the conversion of the speaker's mother who is presumably the Roman Catholic Church. The imagery of darkness leads directly to 'the place / Of vnbelief' which is then to be converted by Christ. The final image ('embrace / His wurde') returns to the metaphor of sexuality which has been explicated through the poem in Protestant terms that stress belief and faith over works. The language of the poem avoids explicit figures of light and sight except in reference to Christ. The imagery that attracts our attention is fully negative so that the poem moves from flesh to spirit in metaphorical terms as well. The conclusion of spiritual oneness between the churches is the final point and it is achieved by means of doctrine rather than imagery.

Others among the poems establish formal play with sound patterns as a substitute for the sexuality of the biblical text. Their rejection of carnality functions as a means of focusing attention on spirituality. In the second chapter, the biblical text describes the lover's embracing of his beloved. Baldwin's prose translation is almost identical to that of the Great Bible: 'His left hand is vnder my head, & his right hande shall embrace me'. The 'Argument' distinguishes between the significance of the actions of the two hands,[8] for this verse reads 'left hand' as an expression of adversity: 'So feruent is the Churches zeale to bring all creatures to the loue of her Beloued, that it causeth the wycked, and suche as hate the truthe, to persecute her: whiche also for a whyle Christ suffereth, to trye whether she be constant in the truthe or no' (c.iii.v). The poem develops this theme of adversity as trial in five-line stanzas which consist of a tetrameter quatrain followed by the single-word refrain: 'Continually'.[9] The theme here is fairly simple. 'His left hande of adversitie' is juxtaposed against 'his ryght hande [which] wyll embrace / His Churche with all prosperitie, / Continually'. The continuity of the '*b*' rhymes here parallels the thematic notion of 'Continually' that establishes eternal warfare between good and evil, suffering and prosperity, perversity and truth. The formal inscription of theme in stanza form sets up a mode that later poets like George Herbert would pick up and develop.

The ninth poem 'The Spouse to the Younglynges' complicates the pattern somewhat. It reverts to the original technique of disassociating the biblical text from the imagery which is oriented to the body and then refashioning the allegory in ways that recuperate the sexual suggestiveness in a context that clearly stresses the spiritual allegory articulated through the senses. The Great Bible version reads: 'Whan the kyng sitteth at the table, he shal smell my Nardus: a bundle of Myrre is my loue vnto me: he wyll lye betwixte my

---

[8] This kind of reading is likewise true for poem 32 'MY mynde thou hast whole rauyshed' where Baldwin's poem distinguishes between the eye which has ravished and that which is detestable because of its 'iudgement of the flesh' (f.iii.r). Here, as with the hands in poem 16, there is no biblical suggestion of the moral distinction between the eyes.

[9] Cavanaugh refers to this poem in her discussion of Baldwin's use of the refrain (66).

breastes. A cluster of Camphore in the vineyardes of Engaddi, is my loue unto me' (A.iv.v). Baldwin's prose tones this down somewhat: 'WHyle the kyng was in his restyng place, my Narde yelded furthe the sauoure. My Beloued is to me a bundle of Myrrhe, he wyl tary betwene my brestes: a cluster of Cypres is my loue vnto me in the vinyardes of Engaddi' (b.ii.v). The nard in this version is not directly connected to the action of the lover as in the earlier text where the lover's smelling of the nardus of the beloved could connote sexual activity. Baldwin's prose here is a more literal rendition of the Hebrew original which would have been readily accessible to him through the Latin of Robert Etienne: 'nardus mea dedit odorem suum' (fol. 213v). In a similar manner, having the lover 'tary' rather than 'lye' reduces some of the sexual tension in the passage. Baldwin's allegory further disconnects many of the sensuous nouns from their bodily associations:

> Than dyd my Narde, myne oyntment of belief
> Yelde furth the smell, the fruteful wurkes of faythe.
> Among the which my charitie for chief
> God doeth accept, and most of value wayeth. (b.iii.r)

The Kyng's 'couche' is 'my quiet conscience', 'narde' becomes 'oyntment of belief', its smell 'the fruteful wurkes of faythe', and so on. At the same time, there is a metaphorical tension that develops in the poem which is not altogether different from the sexuality in the prose of the Great Bible.

> Betwene my brestes, suche cumfort as I show
> To all that nede, delyteth for to dwel.
> Ye Christe my Loue from whom all fayth doeth flow,
> In me his Churche so pleasauntly doeth smell,
>
> That to my taste he is the goodly grayne
> Of Cypresse swete, whiche commonly doeth spryng
> Among the vines, the elect that do remayne
> In Engaddi, Gods truth, the true kyddes spryng. (b.iii.r–v)

Some of this is, of course, the result of the breast imagery which is similar to some of the other poems. Here, the breasts of the Church remain a dwelling place for Christ and Baldwin makes no attempt to avoid the image. At the same time, other sensory experiences are brought together to extend and define the sexual language. Taste, smell and sight combine with the breast imagery to move the reader from the world of the senses to the truth of the spirit which is conveyed in a series of phrases which Baldwin must interpret. This takes place in the final quatrains of the poem which move from the breast imagery to references to the olfactory and the gustatory but conclude with God's truth in a poetic technique that anticipates the metaphysical mode of a poet like George Herbert. The final rhyming words of the last quatrain are the homonyms 'spryng'. The first of these is the verb meaning 'grow' (cf.

Oxford English Dictionary v1 sense 8) while the second is a noun denoting a flow of water (cf. *OED* sb1 sense 2.a). These two different senses of the word move readers past the biblical imagery of wood (Cyprese) and place (Engaddi) and then spring or catapult us through the homonyms to an insight into the divine connections between the world of the senses and God's truth.

The 'true kyddes spryng' is the deepest sense of the natural wonder of Engaddi, literally the fountain of the goat or kid. Baldwin included 'Engaddi' meaning 'iye or fountayne of a kyd' in his list of 'Hebrue wurdes' with their literal 'interpretation' at the end of his book (n.iii.r). This information is conveniently available at the conclusion of the Etienne Bible.[10] About Engaddi, Etienne had commented 'Fons siue oculus hœdi vel fœlicitatis: aut ex Hebræo & Syro, fons siue oculus incisionis, vel scissuræ. Nomen urbs, ubi fuit mare mortuum. 1. reg. 24 a. ezech 47. b. cantic. 1d' ([Pt 3] fol. 10r [bb2r]).

This biblical site on the western shore of the Dead Sea is well known today as a rocky oasis where fresh water abounds despite the stark and arid surrounding mountains. Even in ancient times this site was renowned for both power and fertility. David and his supporters chose this spot as a fortress when Saul was pursuing them (1 Samuel 24). Josephus referred to it (*Antiquities* 9.1.2) as a 'city situated on Lake Asphaltis [i.e. the Dead Sea] ... [where] are grown the finest palm trees and opobalsamum' (6.5–7). Ezekiel prophesied that a river would one day flow from the Temple mount to the Dead Sea and that it would reclaim the entire region from its present condition as a wasteland:

> Nowe when I came there, there stode many trees vpon ether syde of the ryuer bancke. Then sayde he vnto me: Thys water that floweth oute towarde the east, and runneth downe into the playne felde, commeth into the see: and from the see runneth out: & maketh the waters whole. Yee, all that lyue & moue, wherunto thys ryuer commeth, shall recouer. And where thys water commeth, ther shalbe moch fysh. For all that cõmteh [sic! should be 'commeth'?] to this water, shalbe lusty and whole. By this ryuer shall the fysshers stāde from Engaddy vnto En Eglaim, & there spread out their nettes: for there shalbe great heapes of fysh, lyke as in the mayne see. As for his claye and pyttes, they shall not be whole, for why? it shalbe occupyed for salt.
>
> By this ryver vpon both the sides of the shore, there shall growe all maner of frutefull trees, whose leaues shall not fall of, nether shall their frute perysh; but euer be rype at theyr monethes: for theyr water runneth out of theyr sanctuarye. (Ezekiel 47. Great Bible, Pt 3, Fol. 107b–108a. [DD iiiv–DD iiiir])

Baldwin undoubtedly knew the biblical reputation of En-Gaddi and could have been aware of the Josephus passage since various editions of the ancient

---

[10] This section of Etienne's work has a separate title page (*Hebraica, Chaldaea, Græcâque & Latina nomina virorum, mulierum, populorum, idolorum, vrbium, fluuiorum, montium, cæterorumque locorum quae in Bibliis vtriusque testamenti sparsa sunt, restituta, cum interpretatione latina.* Lugduni, 1537) with separate folio pagination and signatures.

historian had been published in Latin, Greek and French by the 1540s. It is noteworthy that the passages from 1 Samuel (described as 1 Kings in many early Bibles as well as in the Roman Catholic tradition) and Ezekiel appear in the passage cited above from the Etienne Bible. In any case, the 'true Kiddes spring' suggests connections with Christ as the lamb or 'kid' of God in addition to the Christian associations of the fish imagery from Ezekiel.

Baldwin's poetic use of this material depends upon a mindset that assumes a correspondence between biblical language and spiritual truth that includes the deeper significance of place names. The meaning of the names he inserted into his poems is poetically relevant to the form and content of the verse. As the final quatrain jumps from spring to spring, the connections between Christ and God's truth spring out at the younglynges and presumably at the reader as well. Baldwin's imaginative use of language thus connects the various levels of meaning at which his poem functions. The conjunction of rhyme with a biblical place attaches a whole range of oral associations to the poem and conclude its exploration of sensuous images with an insistence on the inevitable connection between physical detail and metaphysical significance.

In some of his poems, Baldwin treats the conflict between flesh and spirit so as to establish an apparent reading on a literal, even sexual level only to reinterpret these patterns in a manner that reinscribes the sexual as an aspect of the spiritual. In 'The Spouse to the Younglynges. xl.' this pattern gets especially intense as Baldwin's translation of the language of the Bible seems to get more and more explicitly erotic:

> MI Beloued put in his hande at the Hole, and my bowels swelled within me. I arose that I myght open to my Beloued, and my hādes dropped myrrhe, and my fingers wer full of tryed mirrhe. I opened the bolte of my dore to my Beloued: but he was goen & past. (g.iv.r)

Baldwin's 'Argument' twists and even adds to the eroticism which it views as a metaphor for spirituality:

> THe Churche beholdeth Christ, and would gladly receyue hym, for her soule deliteth in his dewy head, but her flesh can not away with the nyghtdroppyng heares, which caused her as though she had ben perfect, to reason with Christ, and to thynke that he woulde haue her put on her coate agayne, whan as in dede he woulde haue her cum naked to put on the coat whiche he wyll geue her. Thus is the poore churche deceyued through fraylie of the flesh: whiche he consyderyng and seyng the dore shut, that is the spirite so hyndred in carnal iudgement, that she can not receyue hym, thrusteth in his hande, that is his power, grace, and helpe, through the hole of the dore, that is the eleccion whyche remayneth in olde Adam the dore of the flesshe, whiche through his grace he openeth. Whiche the Spouse felyng, confesseth: syngyng. (g.iv.r–v)

This allegorical reading complicates the biblical scene considerably. It explores the tension between flesh and spirit in terms of clothing as opposed to nakedness, works in contrast to grace, reasoning with Christ in contrast with faithful acceptance through election. At the same time, it is an example of that which it would have the Church relinquish. As an example of reasoned wit, the reading itself implies that its own methods are ultimately to be rejected in favour of Christ's 'power, grace, and helpe, through the hole of the dore'. It also extends the sexual tension and desire in the biblical text so that the woman's hesitation to 'cum naked' to her lover becomes an image of her 'frayltie of the flesh'.

The poem Baldwin produced from these materials explores the metaphor of spiritual eroticism as it carefully constructs a poetic technique that requires the reader to imagine a 'fleshly' scene and then reject it. The suggestive opening of the biblical text becomes an almost explicit reference to sexual activity:

> MY Loue dyd put his hande of myght,
>   In to my hole of fleshly sence:
> Whereby myne inwarde partes outryght
> Dyd swel and ryse, through influence
>   Of grace.

The 'fleshly sence' of the Spouse is apparently nourished and supported by 'grace' but the specific details as to how the move from one to the other is possible remains unclear. By the end of the next stanza, this gap is widened:

> Than vp I rose with diligence
> To open that he mought cum in
> Whome I doe loue, by whome my sence
> Of fleshly wit was made so thin.
>   By grace.

At this point the grace that the speaker needs is apparently in conflict with the 'sence / Of fleshly wit'. The thinness of the wit is perhaps a suggestion of its quality as a sheer piece of negligée which, despite its own attractiveness, must be relinquished in sexual activity which is itself only a metaphor for that which is opposed to the flesh. This becomes clear later in the poem when the Spouse gives up the carnal, only to find that Christ has gone:

> The doar bar eke that made me slacke
> To let hym in that knocked fast
> My carnal sence I thrust abacke:
> But Christe before was goen and past,
>   Helas. (g.iv.v)

The rest of the poem focuses on her subsequent search for Christ and her suffering at the hands of 'The tryauntes that the citie watche' (h.i.r). As the poem proceeds, it makes clear that the fleshly images which it began by invoking can, in fact, be detrimental to spiritual understanding. In the end, the Spouse tells the Younglings:

> I charge you yf ye chaunce to fynde
> Christe my Beloued that dwelles aboue,
> Ye shew hym how sore I in mynde
> Am sycke, and languish whole for loue
>   Of grace. (h.i.r)

That is, the poem that begins with apparent sexual imagery soon forces the reader to abandon such 'fleshly' thought. In the end, however, the experience of the poem is one of alienation and lack of closure. The search for the Beloued goes on but the searcher is 'sycke' and languishes. The entire poem is a kind of 'fleshly wit' which must be reinterpreted and emptied of its carnal readings. This activity is not, however, one that the text can finally achieve. The project of providing 'suche songes [that] myght once driue out of office the baudy balades of lecherous loue' (A.iii.v) is fundamentally threatened. There is a gap between the fairly clear plan that called for songs that would be fully suitable for spiritual purposes, and the darker moments of some of the canticles. Perhaps this is part of the significance of Baldwin's use (A.ii.r) of Miles Coverdale's term 'Cantica canticorum' or 'Songs of Songs'.[11] There are many songs in this collection and they do not necessarily make up a spiritually unified narrative.

The most striking illustration of Baldwin's use of sexuality as an important rhetorical device in his work occurs in the seventh chapter of the Song of Songs. Baldwin's five poems that comprise this section work together as a unit which develops different kinds of sexual tension. The general pattern is similar to what has appeared earlier. The allegory replaces especially provocative biblical imagery with spiritual equivalents but just when the sexuality seems to have almost disappeared, the poems bring it back, even when the biblical original makes no such demand. As this process refashions the chapter, the underlying message about spirituality becomes more and more apparent.

The first of these poems is drawn from five biblical verses which purport to describe the beloved with a series of comparisons, many of which have

---

[11] 'Salomons' Balettes, called Cantica Canticorum.' fol. dlxxix. Stanley Stewart claims that the 'lyric conceptualization of the Canticles represents a continuation of the reaction traced by Miss Campbell to its source in the Great Bible (1539), where the translator altered the title of the Song of Songs in such a way as to suggest a lyric or musical piece. Thus, "Canticum Canticorum Salomanis" became "Ballet of Balettes of Salomon"' (6–7). While it is true that Campbell does quote the title in the Great Bible as 'The Ballet of Balettes of Salomon: called in Latin Canticum Canticorum' (57), she does not claim that this was the first use of the term 'balette' (or ballad). In fact, Coverdale had used it in his 1535 reading. Max Engammare traces parallel uses of singular and plural titles back to 'les premiers commentateurs et traducteurs du Ct' (110).

appeared before in the biblical text. Most obvious in its technique is the stanza parallel to Song of Songs 7.2 which Baldwin renders as follows in prose: 'The cumpas of thy thighes are lyke a goodly iewel whiche is wrought by the handes of a cunning wurkman' (k.ii.v). The poetic version reads:

> The cumpas of thy thyghes, thy power for to beget
> And to engendre suche as to my truth must stycke,
> Because it styl bringthe furth, withouten stop or let,
> Is lyke an endles lynked chayne, Of Gods own hand made tricke
>   Alwayes to remayne. (k.iij.r)

The allegorical shift from literal thighs to God's truth is perhaps predictable here, but it is significant to note that the shape of the woman's body as presented in the biblical text contains no reference to sexual fruition.[12] Nonetheless, Baldwin's poem reads the thighs in terms of 'power for to beget'. The biblical imagery of jewelry and 'wurkman' disappears in favour of 'an endles lynked chayne, Of Gods own hand made'. The poem is more explicitly carnal in this stanza than the text which inspired it. Of course, this is in contrast to the way in which Baldwin allegorized many additional details of the bride's anatomy such as her navel (7.3) and breasts (7.4): 'Thy Nauyl rounde, that is the holy Byble boke' or 'Thy brestes, thy ready help to comfort them that nede' (k.iij.r).

The next poem, 'Christe to his Spouse. lvi.' is remarkable for the way in which it apparently supports a carnal understanding of the biblical text. Baldwin's translation sets out the biblical text quite clearly:

> O how fayer & louely art thou my Darling in plesures? Thy stature is lyke a Palme tree. I sayd: I wil clyme the palmtre, and take hold of the hye branches. Thy brestes also shal be lyke the vineclusters, the smel of thy nostrels lyke the smel of apuls. Thy throte shalbe lyke the best wyne, mete for my beloued to drinke, with his lyppes, and to chewe with his teeth. [Canticles 7.7–10] (k.iij.v)

The 'Argument' makes no attempt to allegorize here. Instead, it focuses on the poetics of description that characterize the passage: 'Christe hauyng praysed his Spouse particulerly, begynnyng at her feete and goyng upward to her head, where as he was wunt to begyn at the head, and thence to go dounwarde: procedeth as he was wunt, with moste ernest affeccion syngyng' (k.iij.v).

This passage is one of the few for which medieval literary tradition seems to

---

[12] The passage is translated 'Thy thighes are lyke a fayer iewel' in Baldwin's version of the Great Bible text (k.ii.r). Coverdale had first rendered 'Thy thees are like a fayre iewell' while Thomas Matthew translated 'Thy thiges are lyke a fayre iewel / which is wrought by a cōnyng worke master' (pt 1, fol. 247r [Gh.vii.r]). The Geneva version comments on the entire first section of chapter seven that 'He describeth the comelie beautie of the Church in euerie parte w^c is to be vnderstand spiritually' and then renders 'the iointes of thy thighs are like iewels' [282r]. The Authorized Version used the Geneva rendition.

53

have provided a carnal reading which Baldwin could certainly have known. While exegetes and theologians compared the tree to the cross, as well as to Mary,[13] at least one of Chaucer's pilgrims had another view. In the 'Merchant's Tale', Januarie's garden serves as a *locus amoenus* where his young wife May has sexual relations with both husband and Damyan, her lover. She has Damyan 'clymbe upon a tree / That charged was with fruyt' (Merchant's Tale, 2210–11) where she soon joins him for another sort of climb that James I. Wimsatt has associated with the mounting of the palm in Canticles. He points out that 'the sexual implications of these images could not escape the medieval reader; all are humorously relevant to the Merchant's Tale' ('Chaucer' 86). Wimsatt, however, balks at viewing Chaucer's 'attitude toward the Canticles' as 'daring if not outrageous'. He sees an 'ironic disparity between the lovers . . . and Christ and Mary . . . Every echo of Canticles emphasizes the contrast between the carnal reality portrayed in the tales and the spiritual ideal that was found to be expressed in the Bible.' It is thus fairly easy for him to characterize the erotic moment in the tale as an 'amusing, disgusting spectacle . . . their version of the sponsus' words: "I will go up into the palm tree . . ."' (88–9). Whether or not Chaucer's 'ideal' view of the biblical text required traditional Christian allegory, his use of imagery from Canticles in the Merchant's (and the Miller's) Tale can be understood as evidence of the availability of a carnal reading during the Middle Ages. This would certainly have been more oral than written but it must have been a significant aspect of any reader's initial perception of the words from Solomon's Song.

Baldwin's text exploits the carnal potential of these lines for a different purpose. Although his poem begins in a mood that seems to suggest the approach of Chaucer's Merchant to the biblical text, the final two stanzas of his lyric clarify the ambiguities of the earlier verses. The poem has six stanzas, each of which concludes with the same refrain. At the outset, the reader is struck by the carnal suggestiveness of the language:

> OH howe fayer, howe fayer art thou my ioye?
>   How louely my Loue, how louely art thou alse:
> Oh my spouse how wanton and how coy
> Thou art in delites whan I doe thee enhalse.
>   O my Darlyng.
>
> Lyke thou art in stature to the tree,
> Of Palmes, for no wayght can let thee for to grow:
> And thy brestes are lyke as semeth me,
> To clusters of grapes, that rype hang doune below,
>   O my Darlyng.

---

[13] See Wimsatt, 'Chaucer' 89.

Words such as 'wanton', 'coy' and 'delites' tend to encourage the reader to take the 'Darlyng' in the refrain as a fleshly woman whose body is being compared to a tree. In the middle of the third stanza, however, just as the language becomes most suggestive, the poet shifts ground by referring to 'my church' and 'younglinges':

> Clyme wyll I the Palme tree then I sayde,
> And wyl by the frutes and braunches hye take holde:
> I myself (my church) wyll be thyne ayde,
> And sit thee vpon, to make thy younglinges bolde,
>   O my Darlyng.

Suddenly the carnal reading is in doubt. The significance of 'Darlyng' is not as obvious as it seemed in the first two stanzas. There remains some question as to the status of the addressee at this point. The parentheses around 'my church' back us away from a straightforward carnal reading but also from an unequivocally allegorical approach. Stanza four reverts entirely to the earlier carnal mode where it seems clear that the addressee of the poem is a woman with breasts and body odour reminiscent of fruit:

> There wyll I thy dugges so fruitful make,
> That they shall be lyke the clusters of the vine:
> And the smell that thou shalt of me take,
> Shall reike fro the nose lyke sent of appuls fyne,
>   O my Darlyng.

Here Baldwin is, perhaps, closest to the French tradition of 'blason' which had been developed by Clément Marot and his circle just a few years before the publication of the *Balades of Salomon*. The French poets, however, addressed their blazons to specific parts of the female anatomy with no interest whatever in spirituality.[14] If these poems by Baldwin are to be understood in terms of this tradition, it should be clear that they are part of his concern for 'songes [that] myght once driue out of office the baudy balades of lecherous loue' (A.iii.v). That is, as opposed to the exclusively carnal interest of this French tradition, Baldwin's attention is both biblical in inspiration and balanced midway between carnal and spiritual.

It is in the final two stanzas that the allegorical nature of the poem becomes obvious. The imagery of the body is glossed to point in the spiritual direction

---

[14] Most famous of Marot's blasons is his epigram LXXI 'Du beau tetin' (99–102). On the tradition, see Alison Saunders, *The Sixteenth-Century Blason Poétique* (Bern: Peter Lang, 1981); Cathy Yandell, 'A La Recherche du Corps Perdu: A Capstone of the Renaissance Blasons Anatomiques', *Romance Notes* 26 (1986): 135–42; Nancy Vickers, '"The blazon of sweet beauty's best": Shakespeare's *Lucrece*', Geoffrey Hartman and Patricia Parker, eds, *Shakespeare and the Question of Theory* (New York and London: Methuen, 1985), 95–115.

so that 'throte' becomes 'voyce', wine becomes 'truth', and 'frende' is 'byshop':

> Make wyll I thy throte, that is thy voyce
> So moyst with the muste of truth my chefest wyne,
> That my frende, my byshop shall haue choyce
> Of doctrine to preache out of those truthes of thyne,
>   O my Darlyng.

This makes it possible to conclude the poem with a series of images that retain much of their sensuous and physical associations without obscuring the ultimately spiritual significance of this sort of language. The mystery of the spirit which both is and is not of the body finally begins to make itself felt:

> There shal he haue meate and drinke at wyll,
> To chew with his teeth and lyps: there shal he haue
> Misteries, wheron to vse hym styll.
> Of the shall he learne hymself and moe to saue,
>   O my Darlyng. (k.iv.r)

The manner in which poems 55 and 56 both move back and forth between carnal and spiritual metaphors is an important aspect of the tension they exhibit between orality and textuality. The traces of an oral tradition in Chaucer's 'Merchant's Tale', which would have taken the language of Canticles about climbing a palm tree as a sexual reference, remain (even for a twentieth-century scholar of medieval literature) qualified by the claims of the official written tradition which read Canticles as an exclusively spiritual allegory. Wimsatt explains this cogently in part of the 'Panel Discussion' that follows his essay in *Chaucer the Love Poet*:

> you don't find very important, serious uses of it [i.e. Canticles] in vernacular poetry. The Latin goliards were willing to use it despite their knowledge, their familiarity with the tradition; but the secular, vernacular poets just wouldn't presume to use it, as far as I can see. This indicates to me a very strong consciousness of the spiritualization of Canticles, the denial of the carnal sense, which Bernard emphasizes time and again in his sermons to the monks. (96–7)

My point here is that the written tradition should not be taken as an exclusive perspective from which to read all presentations of Canticles. Baldwin moves back and forth freely from the carnal to the spiritual and this reflects a similar movement between the oral and written traditions. Despite the views of figures such as Origen or Bernard, there is another tradition at work here but it was primarily conveyed orally. The poets of the English Renaissance can be read as balancing the tensions between erudite written tradition and popular oral culture. Some of these tensions get transferred to the actual pages of the early books in the terms of the formal arrangement of the words on the page.

This can be understood as an attempt to bring back the world of oral sound to the silent printed page. Baldwin's combination of formal experimentation with verse patterns and deliberate confusion between carnal and spiritual is part of his very significant contribution to the development of English lyric poetry.

Although Baldwin's text is clearly relevant to mid-Tudor modes of perceiving the past and perhaps in making these speak to political events as they would soon unfold, it is no less important to us as it looks forward to the poetic practice of later and more famous poets.[15] The poems in this first collection of verse to be published in England often bear a striking resemblance to the poetic practices of Spenser, Shakespeare, Donne, Herbert, Milton and Marvell. In the absence of clear-cut historical evidence that these later poets read Baldwin's *Canticles*, I shall limit the discussion to ways in which some aspect of one or more of Baldwin's poems suggests a parallel in the work of a later writer.

Parallels between Baldwin and Edmund Spenser are striking, especially in the *Amoretti*. Since these instances are at the heart of Spenser's own treatment of Canticles, however, I shall defer this discussion until the relevant section of the subsequent chapter. Suffice it to say that a major English poet who is reported to have done his own translation of Canticles can be expected to have known of Baldwin's work, especially when it is curiously parallel to poetic choices made by this classical Elizabethan.

One of Baldwin's poems provides a context for reading a famous line from Shakespeare's Sonnet 130. The octave of the sonnet concludes:

> And in some perfumes is there more delight
> Than in the breath that from my mistress reeks.

There seems to be general agreement among modern editors and commentators that today's pejorative associations with the word 'reek' cannot be documented before the eighteenth century.[16] Hallett Smith annotates 'is

---

[15] Cavanaugh discusses Baldwin's connections to earlier and contemporary poets. Her treatment of the influence of Wyatt and, to a lesser extent, Surrey is especially perceptive (45–9, 52–3).

[16] Although there is a natural tendency for a twentieth-century reader to respond negatively to this word, it is generally true that in early texts the word is either neutral or positive. For example, Adam's account to Raphael in *Paradise Lost* about his earliest memories is quite positive. The 'balmy sweat' and 'reeking moisture' are part of what Fowler calls 'a magnificent piece of microcosmic grandiloquence' (Carey and Fowler 828):
> As new waked from soundest sleep
> Soft on the flowery herb I found me laid
> In balmy sweat, which with his beams the sun
> Soon dried, and on the reeking moisture fed.

Likewise in *Of Reformation*, Milton uses 'reake out' as part of a metaphor of a seething pot, which, when 'set to coole, sensibly exhale and reake out the greatest part of that zeale, and those Gifts which were formerly in them, settling in a skinny congealment of ease and sloth at

exhaled (without pejorative connotation)' (*Riverside Shakespeare* 1773) while John Kerrigan claims that 'reek was more neutral than offensive for early readers, close to "emanates" or "exhales" . . . [The] *Oxford English Dictionary* confirms that, in the sense "To emit an unwholesome or disagreeable vapour," the verb is unrecorded before Swift' (360). Stephen Booth cautions the modern reader

> against hearing this word as the simple insult it would be if a modern writer had written the line; the primary energy of 'to reek' and 'a reek' was still in communicating the ideas of emitting vapor and of vapor emitted; the narrow modern senses, 'to stink' and 'a stench,' which focus attention on the quality of vapor emitted, do not emerge until the late seventeenth century. However, commentators often over-caution modern readers: both the verb and the noun were already well on their way toward their modern meanings in Shakespeare's time; although 'to reek' and 'a reek' could be used neutrally . . . (454)

Booth's 'neutral' reading is very much in accord with the *Oxford English Dictionary* which quotes Shakespeare's sonnet as an illustration of the fourth meaning in its first instance of the verb: 'Of smoke, vapour, perfume, etc.: To be emitted or exhaled; to rise, emanate. Obs.' Nicholas Udall's translation of Erasmus's *Apophthegmes* is also cited. Its potentially positive association with perfume, is, however, qualified by the cynicism of the source, Diogenes:

> Diogenes hauing gotten perfume, rubbed and enointed his feete therewith, contrarie to the common vsage of all other folkes. And to soche persones as made a great wondring therat, he saide: Thus I doe because that perfume being powred vpon the head, reketh out into the aire: but from the feete it ascendeth vp to the nasetrelles. (107).

The parallel between 'reketh' and 'ascendeth' is of major import here, but the association of perfume and feet affects its otherwise positive associations. This also contributes to the spirit of Shakespeare's sonnet which can be read as less than complimentary to the mistress.

Baldwin, however, provides an unequivocally positive context for 'reek.' In 'Christe to his Spouse. lvi.' nature is a source of richly positive imagery with which Christ associates his bride.[17] She is likened to trees and grapes in totally positive terms before the following passage:

> And the smell that thou shalt of me take,
> Shall reike fro the nose lyke sent of appuls fyne. (k.iv.r)

the top' (*Complete Prose* 1.536). That is, Episcopacy forces the best of ministers to allow their learning and zealousness to steam off or evaporate (i.e. reake out) leaving a skinny congealment. Contemporary readings notwithstanding, 'reek' remains a positive term, 'an exhalation; a fume emanating form some body or substance'. It is only 'in mod. use, a strong and disagreeable fume or smell' *OED* sb. 3.

[17] See the discussion of this poem at pp. 54–6 above.

Baldwin's poem makes it unquestionably clear that 'reek' could have had positive associations in the mid-sixteenth century and thus establishes a context for an understanding of Shakespeare's line that is not ambiguous. Although none of this is new with regard to the non-pejorative associations editors have posited, it locates such a use of the word in mid-Tudor literary practice and suggests a possible contact between Shakespeare and Baldwin.

Baldwin's treatment of one early passage from Canticles has a number of elements that are parallel to one of John Donne's 'Holy Sonnets'. In 'The Spouse to her beloued' [6], Baldwin develops a poem from the text of Canticles 1.7: 'O Thou whom my soul loueth, tel me wher thou fedest, & where thou restest at none tyde: least I begin to wander after thy felawes flockes' (a.iv.v). The poem applies the predicament of the shepherdess in search of her shepherd to the situation of the Church in search of Christ. The Spouse sings of her difficulties:

>   O Christe my Loue, beloued of my soule,
>   I know that thou delyting in the lyght,
>   In midday tyme, when men in fayth be hole,
>   Doest feede and rest, through pleasure and delyght.
>
>   But in what place thou doest thee feede and rest,
>   I am not sure: wherefore I thee desyer
>   To teache me that, least I with all the rest
>   By wandryng wyde, defyle vs in the myer.
>
>   The Churche malignant with her many mockes,
>   To be thy felow boldly doeth her boast,
>   And in thy name hath gathered myghty flockes:
>   Whiche straye abrode welnygh in euery caost.
>
>   Newe foldes, new faythes, she dayly doeth diuice
>   Her flockes to feede, wherein alas they stray:
>   And as for thyne she counteth of no price,
>   Fraying by force, all shepe from them away.
>
>   Yet in thy name her office she doeth holde,
>   Makyng her vaunt that she the true Church is:
>   Enforcyng all that would be of thy folde,
>   Suche weedes to eat, as she hath sowen amis.
>
>   That I therfore lead not thy yong awrye,
>   Nor fall among thy fayned felowes flocke,
>   Enfourme me where thou doest thee feede and lye,
>   O Christ my lyght, my shepherd, and my rocke. (a.iv.v–b.i.r)

The thematic similarity between this poem and John Donne's Holy Sonnet, 'Show me dear Christ' is fairly clear. Both poems address Christ and ask that he identify the 'true Church', both refer to and dismiss Roman

Catholic claims, and both are in some sense readings of Canticles. Of course, Donne need not have turned to Baldwin for the doctrine that the Church is the Bride of Christ. It is, however, significant that Baldwin frames the issue of the nature of the true church in terms of feminine sexual appeal. The biblical text is shaped into a woman's appeal for her lover to make himself known lest she 'fall among thy fayned felowes flocke'. Donne's version of this motif reworks and ironically disrupts male concern about the woman's behavior with other men as the bride becomes sexually available to as many believers as possible: 'Who is most trew, and pleasing to thee, then/ When she'is embrac'd and open to most men' (350). With Baldwin's poem as an intertext for Donne's sonnet, this final couplet can be read as an updated re-enactment of the allegorization and subsequent restoration of sexuality to the text of Canticles.

Baldwin's careful attention to problems of printing and the arrangement of verse on the page looks forward to the work of George Herbert. While the superiority of Herbert's achievement is clear, it is significant to note that both were working in a poetic tradition that was explicitly concerned with countering the appeal of the erotic tradition. Isaak Walton quotes from a letter that Herbert wrote to his 'dear Mother for a New-years gift' in 1609/10 that he would 'reprove the vanity of those many Love-poems, that are daily writ and consecrated to *Venus* . . . For my own part, my meaning (*dear Mother*) is in these Sonnets, to declare my resolution to be, that my poor Abilities in *Poetry*, shall be all, and ever consecrated to Gods glory' (Herbert 363). In addition, Baldwin's play with unusual verse forms suggests a similar development in Herbert. Both poets experimented with verses that combine a more or less standard stanza with a refrain of only a few syllables. Baldwin's poem 'Christe to his Spouse. viii.' has six stanzas with four lines of hexameter concluded with a single line of dimeter. A number of the other poems (8, 10, 12, 15, 30, 36) juxtapose trimeter stanzas with two- or four-syllable refrains. Alternatively, Baldwin uses tetrameters and pentameters but concludes each stanza with dimeter or even monometer lines (cf. numbers 16, 19, 21, 37, 40, 45, 49, 56, 70). This fairly unusual poetic practice looks forward to Herbert who employs similar techniques in such poems as 'Employment (1)', 'Grace', 'The Starre', 'Vertue', 'The Pearl. Matth. 13.45', 'The British Church', 'Gratefulnesse', 'Peace' and 'Longing'.

Baldwin and Herbert also share ways of interconnecting form and meaning in terms of the shape of the stanza. One of Herbert's best-known poems, 'Easter Wings', establishes at least some of its meaning by varying the length of the lines to achieve visual form. Herbert's poem takes on the visual shape of a pair of wings just as its sound patterns contract and expand and its thematic development discusses spiritual flight. One of Baldwin's simplest lyrics anticipates the way 'Easter Wings' makes use of short lines to achieve a delicate poetic effect:

Baldwin's Canticles, or Balades of Salomon

Christe to his Spouse. x.

LOe thou my Loue, art fayer:
   Myselfe haue made thee so,
Yea thou art fayer in dede,
Wherefore thou shalt not nede
In beautie to dispayer:
For I accept thee so
   For fayer.
For fayer, because thyne iyes
Are lyke the Culuers, whyte:
Whose simplenes in dede
All others doe excede:
Thy iudgement wholly lyes
In true sence of spryte,
   Moste wyse. (b.iii.v)

The opening line is very close to Baldwin's rendering of the biblical text (Song of Songs 1.15): 'Loe thou art fayer my Loue, Loe thou arte fayer: Thou hast doues iyes' (b.iii.v). The word 'fayer' is repeated through the first stanza (1, 3, 7) and echoes in the rhyme 'dispayer' that concludes line 5. In a similar manner, the focus of the second stanza, the eyes of the Spouse, sets the rhyme pattern which recurs in the fifth and seventh lines of the stanza and finds echoes in the long 'y' sound of 'whyte' and 'spryte' (lines 2 and 6). The simplicity of the message that the spouse is fair because Christ accepts her as such and because of her eyes which are like culvers (doves) is finally reduced to the disyllabic concluding line 'Moste wyse'. The effect of the short lines at the end of each stanza is to emphasize the simple theme that fair appearance leads to wisdom. The apparent effortlessness of the verse matches its form.

As Baldwin's lyric progresses from the external appearance of the 'fayer' Spouse to her inner qualities of judgment and wisdom, it also hints at a poetic tension between the complexity of formal shape and the simplicity of stated theme that gets greater attention in some of the later poems. In 'Christe to his Spouse. x.' there is only the slightest conflict between the formal attention to rhymes, length of lines and stanzaic structure and the desirability of 'simplenes in dede'. The textual manipulation of line length matches the demands of oral sound so that the two become different ways of perceiving the same poetic object. The implicit pressure of the allegory to eradicate the poetic process that creates it (as the biblical text about the 'fayer' beloved is shifted into praise for her wisdom) is counterbalanced by the continued attention to an image such as 'the Culuers, whyte' in the second stanza. That is, oral and written aspects of the interpretive process balance similar tensions on the level of formal poetic organization and produce a poem that is simple yet complex, oriented to the flesh, yet spiritual, unusual to look at on the page, yet rhythmically smooth to the ear. Herbert's carefully crafted pattern poem is much more textually sophisticated than Baldwin's work as it replaces the movement from trimeter to monometer with a gradual reduction from pentameter to monometer and back to pentameter in each of two stanzas. Despite these obvious differences, however, it is significant that both poems develop within the context of a two-stanza structure and that Herbert makes use of short lines such as 'Most poore' or 'Most thinne' which resemble Baldwin's concluding line 'Moste wyse'. Herbert can be understood to have been extending a mode that Baldwin introduced into English verse.

These parallels between Baldwin's work and passages in major Elizabethan and Jacobean verse make it clear that the *Canticles, or Balades of Salomon* should be read as a significant precursor to some of the best poetry of the later Renaissance in England. Whatever the other links in the intertextual chain that connect this book with these poets, their successors are likewise related to it. Famous cruxes from Milton and Marvell illustrate ways in which Baldwin can be heard in these later works. Near the beginning of his visit to Adam and Eve in *Paradise Lost*, Raphael explains that earthly food is not 'unsavourie . . . / To spiritual Natures' (5.401–2). He points out that:

>   food alike those pure
> Intelligential subsances require
> As doth your Rational; and both contain
> Within them every lower facultie
> Of sense, whereby they hear, see, smell, touch, taste,
> Tasting concoct, digest, assimilate,
> And corporeal to incorporeal turn. (5.407–13)

The importance of the continuity between sense and spirit is paramount for Milton's vision here and elsewhere in the epic. It is part of a larger integration of flesh and spirit that depends upon a reading of Canticles that is apparently in conflict with that of Baldwin. Nevertheless, Baldwin too, reserves a place for the larger signification of digestion in his allegorical grasp of the biblical poetry. In 'Christe to his Spouse. xxxvi.' Baldwin has Christ sing the praises of 'food diuine':

> EAt my frendes and drynke,
>   My Spouses mylke and wine:
> My wurde whiche to the brynke
> Is full of food divine,
>   Both meat and drynke.
>
> My Frendes whome I loue moste
> Drynke, drinke tyll ye be drounk:
> Drynke tyll my holly goste
> In you be throughly sunke,
>   Drinke and be drunke. (g.ii.v)

Baldwin's interest here is fairly clear. Where the biblical text denotes only the eating, drinking and possible intoxication of the beloued, Baldwin points to the spiritual significance of this process. The attention to heavy drinking is certainly justified by the Hebrew text and Baldwin's 'be drunke my best beloued' reflects the reading Etienne provided ('& bibite, & inebriamini charissimi' 213v). As the drinking gets more intense, the sense of inebriation is equated with the internalizing of God's spirit: 'tyll my holly goste / In you be throughly sunke'. For Baldwin this presumably recalls the miracle of the wine in John 2. For Milton, however, this can be understood as a celebration of the baroque openness of carnal experience to spiritual realms. Raphael literally eats and extracts the spirit that is 'thoroughly sunke' and insists upon literal participation in the meal in prelapsarian Eden.

Andrew Marvell's poetry is well known for its unusual refashioning of earlier poems into texts that are strangely evocative. 'The Garden' has provided scholars with a text that recalls a variety of other poems.[18] This dense and ironically crafted poem begins with a celebration of a garden which develops a biblical focus so that Eden is unavoidable as a relevant analogue. On the level of surface 'plot', Marvell's narrator praises the garden as superior because its flowers and trees can provide 'Garlands of repose' as opposed to the wreaths from individual trees that served as crowns for victors in ancient contests of athletic, literary and civic excellence. He continues: 'Fair quiet, have I found thee here, / And Innocence thy Sister dear!' (9–10). The argument to Baldwin's fourteenth poem, 'The Churche to the Younglinges' explains that 'the Churche hauing compared Christe to an apple tree, declareth to the Younglynges the cause why she so dyd, swetely syngyng as foloweth' (c.ii.v). The poem expands upon the image of the shadow of the apple tree which provides 'help and refuge', 'quiet rest'. Marvell's 'Garden' likewise sees 'Fair quiet' as the product of a retreat into nature. From the quiet rest of the tree's shade, Baldwin's poem moves on to the fruit of the tree which is like manna to taste, thence to a 'fall at Christes fete', and concludes with reference to wine and love:

---

[18] In the course of his well-known essay on Marvell's argument, Frank Kermode treats 'The Garden' as 'a poem of the anti-genre of the naturalist paradise' (336) and refers to a number of sixteenth- and seventeenth-century French and English poets whose works are relevant to Marvell. Kermode also connects the poem to the Song of Songs: 'Nothing is more characteristic of Renaissance poetry than the synthesis of spiritual and erotic in poetic genre and image. It was encouraged by centuries of comment on the *Canticum Canticorum*' (336–7). Stanley Stewart concurs: 'important aspects of poems like . . . Marvell's "Garden" are not fully understood until seen in the context of the allegorical tradition of the Song of Songs' (10). The final chapter of his *Enclosed Garden* ('Marvell and "The Garden Enclosed"' 150–83) is devoted to just such an analysis. More recently, Robert Wilcher has referred to a number of mid-seventeenth-century poets whose work Marvell might have known including James Shirley, Joseph Beaumont, Thomas Stanley, Abraham Cowley, Thomas Randolphe, Katherine Philips, Mildmay Fane and Edward Benlowes (130–41).

> I Whiche dyd long my Loue to know,
>   Who is the apple tree of lyfe:
> Haue sit doune in his Shade below,
> Whiche is his help and refuge ryfe.
>
>   In this trees shade is quiet rest
> For all that truly therin trust:
> In whiche to sit for them is best,
> Who to fynde rest in soule, doe lust.
>
>   For whyles I rested me in the shade
> Of Christes helpe, there dyd I eate
> The frute therof, Gods sprite, whiche made
> Me feele the taste of Manna meat.
>
>   Wherof the relice is so swete
> Vnto my Throte, whyle I it chew:
> That doune I fall at Christes fete,
> For this his foœd, high thankes to shew.
>
>   For whyle I sat vnder his wyng,
> And trusted whole in power diuine:
> Than dyd he lead me lyke a Kyng,
> Into his wurd, his house of wyne.
>
>   In whiche whan I holp from aboue,
> Was well refresht, my Kyng set vp
> His standard strong, whiche is his loue,
> For me, and all that taste his cup. (c.ii.v–c.iii.r)

Marvell's poem can be read as an ironic reconsideration of the tradition developed by Baldwin. Baldwin's notion of Christian 'rest' is presented in language that is simultaneously sensuous and spiritual. The images of eating, 'Manna meat', the 'relice . . . so swete' and 'doune I fall' all have their analogues in Marvell's account of physical pleasure in 'The Garden':

> What wond'rous Life in this I lead!
> Ripe Apples drop about my head;
> The Luscious Clusters of the Vine
> Upon my Mouth do crush their Wine;
> The Nectaren, and curious Peach,
> Into my hands themselves do reach;
> Stumbling on Melons, as I pass,
> Insnar'd with Flow'rs, I fall on Grass. (33–40)

Baldwin's rich world of metaphor is simultaneously sensuous and spiritual, while Marvell's imitates such a world of internal peace with ironic mockery. Baldwin provides an illustration of what Frank Kermode refers to as the anti-genre of 'the libertine garden of the Platonic *solitaire*' (337). The perfection of the fall in Baldwin ('at Christes fete') is ironically gentle in Marvell ('I fall on

Grass'), intimating the fallenness of the sensuous pleasures celebrated in the stanza. Read from the perspective of Baldwin's poem, then, Marvell's 'Garden' ironically problematizes the simplicity of Baldwin's allegorical world. Although Baldwin succeeded in holding onto spiritual peace by means of juxtaposing flesh and spirit in the allegory, Marvell's poem implicitly mocks this.

Such a reading of Baldwin's mid-sixteenth-century *Balades* is essentially a call to reread subsequent English literature in terms of the intertextual pressures that Canticles imposes on later Renaissance writers in England. The ways in which Baldwin portrays the various polarities that his work spans look forward to similar interests and concerns in the work of Spenser, Shakespeare, Donne, Aylett, Milton and Marvell, as well as marginal figures such as the Ranters. The instability of Baldwin's allegories that first drain their biblical texts of sexuality and then reinscribe the poems with something similar establishes an uneasy sense of apocalyptic closure on *The Canticles, or Balades of Salomon*, but contrive to allow the individual lyrical moments to reassert themselves as they escape into the timelessness that can also be read as the future, material and literary. In one sense, then, Baldwin's project can be read as framing the poetry of love to be produced by the yet unborn poets of Tudor and Stuart England in the language and sensibility of Canticles. Baldwin's work reasserts the ancient synchrony found in Sumerian poetry, in the allegorized biblical lyrics, in Cavalcanti and in Dante. Likewise, it intertextually charges later poems such as the *Amoretti*, *Venus and Adonis* and *Paradise Lost* with similar baroque patterns that conflate the holy and the sexual.

Chapter 2

CANTICLES, BALDWIN AND SPENSER'S *AMORETTI*

BALDWIN's *Balades* provide insights into Spenser's *Amoretti* that support and extend recent readings of the sonnet sequence. The complex ways in which late medieval poets used the language of Canticles to articulate perceptions about love and femininity are integrated into Baldwin's text and look forward to the less obvious pressures of the Song of Songs on later poems. Spenser's *Amoretti* recall the biblical language of Canticles so as to lend a mysterious numinous quality to Elizabeth Boyle. The lady is both human and divine, a person in her own right and a symbol for the divine presence. As Spenser's persona suffers through the sequence he may appear to progress from desire for his 'fayrest proud' (2.9) to 'pure affections bred in spotlesse brest' (84.5). This, however, is not quite in accord with the sense of the sequence since from the very beginning he is aware of her 'Angels blessed looke' (1.11) and at the end he is 'alone now left disconsolate' (89.5). The sequence is thus more lyrical than narrative as it resists closure. The lady's simultaneously divine and human nature problematizes the poems as she regularly avoids the persona's pursuit without ever rejecting him. This pattern is parallel to the way in which the lovers in Canticles rarely seem to unite. They avoid each other more often than they enact their desires for union and in so doing maintain a highly charged atmosphere of desire.

The nature of the intertextual pressures from Canticles on English poets after Baldwin is complicated. Traditional studies of 'influence' are important as they isolate specific passages and explore their relation to a poet's work, but they often ignore playful manipulation of the source if the connection is not obvious. Spenser's relation to the Song of Songs was treated in some detail by Israel Baroway in an article that set out 'to demonstrate that in an ultimate sense, Spenser's "*Canticum canticorum* translated" is not completely lost, even though its original form seems irrevocably gone. It still lives, though without its name, in a few passages of the *Epithalamion*, the *Amoretti*, the *Faerie Queene*, and *Colin Clouts Come Home Again*' (24). Baroway's urbane, clearly argued essay identifies the biblical sources of much of Spenser's imagery and explores ways in which an 'Oriental reader' would have understood the ancient Hebrew poem. It does not, however, address Spenser's use of these materials, either in the ways the biblical text had shifted diachronically from ancient times through the Renaissance or in the effects of these changes on Spenser's perspective. Baroway's account of the influence of Canticles on Spenser assumes that an early twentieth-century reading of the Bible (Moulton 1448–50) approximates Elizabethan reading and interpretive practices. That is, Baroway's methodology may establish that Spenser was influenced by the Song of Songs, but its explanation of the significance of the parallels merits further consideration. My interest here will be limited almost entirely to the *Amoretti*.

Baroway's work has prompted numerous other scholars to consider Spenser's use of Canticles. A. Leigh DeNeef refers to the Song in a number of contexts and suggests that 'a reexamination of the sequence in terms of its biblical – rather than liturgical – imagery is long overdue' (184). William C. Johnson claims that 'Spenser's heavy reliance on the lush imagery of the Canticles affirms that he does not reject physical love for a purely spiritual love' (34). He goes on to speak of 'fairly obvious echoes of the Song of Songs' (62, in relation to *Amoretti* 4). John N. King points to the tradition in which 'the Bride of the Song of Solomon was commonly interpreted as an allegorical figure' so that 'the Church of England inherited a network of epithalamic imagery based upon the scriptures and mediated through the Roman-rite liturgy' (*Spenser's Poetry* 157). He cites George Scheper's seminal article in *PMLA* to help establish that 'Spenser's vantage point is akin to the allegorization of the Song of Solomon in many Protestant sermons' (173). Carol Kaske sees in the Anacreontic poems that appear at the end of *Amoretti* 'the same flickering sexual suggestiveness as in the *Song of Songs*' (278). As these and other scholars show, many of Spenser's sonnets in the *Amoretti* are closely connected to a series of images that had been associated with the Song of Songs by earlier poets.

Most of the scholarship that deals with Spenser and the Song of Songs is part of a more general interest in the balance between spiritual and physical in the *Amoretti*. Charlotte Thompson claims

> that Spenser has arranged his love story into a design that repeats in expanding and ascending strata through the so-called three worlds – sublunary, celestial, and supercelestial – of conventional Elizabethan thought. A system of analogies binds these strata together and ultimately unites the speaker's small, temporal *amoretti* to the supernal *Amor* of God. (277)

Anne Lake Prescott, near the end of her discussion of the relevance of Marguerite de Navarre to Spenser's sonnets, suggests that

> Marguerite's chansons make it even easier to hear the religious overtones of *Am.* 67–70 and to consider Spenser's unusual treatment of the old belief, so often forgotten in all Christian centuries, including our own, but never quite dead, that sexual love can participate in and body forth divine love, that the love that moves the sun and the other stars can move us into each other's arms. (61)

William C. Johnson shows that

> the progress of the courtship is also depicted analogously. While the drama of human passion is played out between lover and lady, and between the lover as lover and the lover as poet, a simultaneous progression of Divine Passion, as recorded primarily in the liturgy of Lent-Easter, is portrayed. Furthermore, liturgy itself is another form of analogue in which, and through which, mundane ritual time and mundane formal rite suggest the timelessness of the always-already, not-yet reality of God's interactions with mankind. (19–20)

Although he only treats him in passing, Anthony Low claims that Spenser 'represents what I would call the "official" position – that is, society's and Christianity's position – on love and marriage' (8). He regards '*Epithalamion* (with *Amoretti* as its preface and *Prothalamion* as a kind of variant or pendant) as the only finished instance of the arduous journey to the altar' (31–2).

A related aspect of the discussion of the connections between the spiritual and the physical in Spenser's sonnets addresses the issue of structure. Carol Kaske sees the *Amoretti* in terms of the poems published with them: 'By drawing out a single love story through three successive stages – courtship, betrothal, and marriage – and through three successive genres – sonnet-sequence, Anacreontic, and epithalamion – Spenser has incorporated the virtues of each and even made psychologically realistic tensions out of their limitations' (295). In his 'Introduction' to the *Amoretti and Epithalamion* in *The Yale Edition of the Shorter Poems of Edmund Spenser,* Alexander Dunlop points out that while the narrative of these two works treats a 'hopelessly enamored' poet whose lady

> eventually accepts him . . . Yet the wholeness of this simple story is brought into question by the uncertainty of narrative progression from sonnet to sonnet and even from work to work, or more precisely by our inability to say with certainty whether or not the segments of *Amoretti and Epithalamion* are in fact parts of a larger work. (592–3)

He points out that 'the most absolute disruption of the narrative sequence is the placement between *Amoretti* and *Epithalamion* of four playful poems of trivialized mythology about Venus and Cupid in the manner of the Greek poet Anacreon . . . which violate the narrative continuity of the book' (593). M. Thomas Hester focuses directly on these Anacreontic poems and points to their conventional and 'epigrammatic emblem genre' (185). Cupid and Venus intimate conventional aspects of love since for Spenser

> all views, all motifs, all poses, therefore, are 'types' of love which shadow the Christian antitype: 'Love is the lesson the Lord us taught' – we should love '*lyke* as we ought' . . . It is through a typological examination of different 'kinds' of love that the lyricist learns both 'naturally' and 'supernaturally' what love is (an image of and participation in divine love). (187)

Canticles, Baldwin and Spenser's Amoretti

It is significant that Hester sees the 'mode of presentation in the sonnets' (187) in terms of intertextuality. That is, the *Amoretti* as a series of 'little loves' cite a great many different approaches to love and then understand even the pagan sources in terms of Christianity. Thus, when the conventional themes are translations from Marot (Hester 183), they are nonetheless part of a continuum between physical and spiritual explored by the work as a whole. Whether Marot is present in the *Anacreontics* or in the blazon-like tradition of Sonnets 15 and 64,[1] these materials become a way of presenting love in terms of ultimate spirituality.

Attention to some of these intertextual connections provides a broader context for reading the *Amoretti*. My point here will be to show how Baldwin's work and its relevance to Spenser's project and performance help to present the intertextual tradition about Canticles that Spenser might have known in terms of references to specific texts from *The Canticles, or Balades of Salomon*. I am not aware of any previous attempt to make a connection between Baldwin and Spenser. The intertextual pressures of Baldwin and Canticles on the *Amoretti* help to focus on the ways in which language echoes traditions with experiences that shift and change the subtle meanings beneath the surface of the poetic text. The tensions traced and elaborated in previous chapters between poetic elements that are sexual, sensuous and oral but also religious, symbolic, and written, achieve a delicate balance in Spenser's *Amoretti*, not unlike Baldwin's *Canticles* and the ancient and medieval tradition.

Spenser's third sonnet makes use of light imagery to admire the lady's 'sovereyne beauty'. Baroway read it as an 'impassioned expression of the neoplatonic "idea" of beauty' in distinct contrast to the poems influenced by Canticles which feature 'the rhapsodic praise of physical perfection' (29). Some accounts of Spenser's Italian sources[2] connect this sonnet with one by Tasso, which also includes images of light ('le gran fiamme ond'arsi'), amazement ('maraviglia'), silence ('Tace la lingua') and sighs ('E son muti i sospiri accesi e sparsi').[3] Most of Tasso's sonnet, however, explores other figures while Spenser treats more fully the ways in which the lady's light amazes and silences his speaker.

The octave of Spenser's sonnet begins by establishing the poet's inability to deal with the lady's light:

---

[1] See pp. 76–8 below.
[2] See Scott 194. Veselin Kostić goes so far as to assume that Spenser's sonnet is a poor imitation of Tasso: 'Tasso shows a more sensible judgment of the inner harmony of the poem. Both poets describe a situation which was very common in the sonnet literature of the time: the poet is so enchanted by the sight of his mistress that he is unable to say anything. Yet, Spenser introduces in the first quotrain [sic] the idea of the purifying effect of love which is not relevant to the central theme of the poem. The fourth line, in particular, looks like a patch, like something that has been interpolated, but not fused, into the poem' (54).
[3] The Tasso sonnet appears as XXII in a recent edition of *Rime d'amore* (Gavazzeni, et al.), 26. I am indebted to Ms Camille Seerattan at the Folger Shakespeare Library for her translation of this sonnet.

> THe soverayne beauty which I doo admyre,
>   witnesse the world how worthy to be prayzed:
> the light wherof hath kindled heavenly fyre,
>   in my fraile spirit by her from basenesse raysed.
> That being now with her huge brightnesse dazed,
>   base thing I can no more endure to view:
> but looking still on her I stand amazed,
>   at wondrous sight of so celestiall hew.

The 'heavenly fyre' that she kindles to raise him from baseness causes admiration that amazes and inspires wonder. The poetic mode here is closer to Guido Cavalcanti than to Tasso. Anthologies of Tuscan verse by Bernardo di Giunta made Cavalcanti's work available to sixteenth-century readers.[4] As indicated in the discussion of Cavalcanti's sonnet in the Introduction,[5] this poem treats a speaker's wonder and awe about a woman who inspires him with such intensity that he cannot express his predicament even as he manages to do so in verse. Ezra Pound's final version of this sonnet[6] has a suggestive, almost Spenserian, quality:

> Who is she that comes, makyng turn every man's eye
> And makyng the air to tremble with a bright clearenesse
> That leadeth with her Love, in such nearness
> No man may proffer of speech more than a sigh?
>
> Ah God, what she is like when her owne eye turneth, is
> Fit for Amor to speake, for I can not at all;
> Such is her modesty, I would call
> Every woman else but an useless uneasiness.
>
> No one could ever tell all of her pleasauntness
> In that every high noble vertu leaneth to herward,
> So Beauty sheweth forth as her Godhede;
>
> Never before was our mind so high led,
> Nor have we so much of heal as will afford
> That our thought may take her immediate in its embrace.
>   (*Pound's Cavalcanti* 46)

---

[4] Di Giunta's first collection appeared as *Sonetti e canzoni di diversi antichi autori toscani* and was published by the di Giunta family press in Florence in 1527. Di Giunta included an introduction in which he praised the work of the Tuscan poets he had included. In 1532, the same collection was reissued by the Sabio brothers in Venice under the title *Rime di Diversi Antichi Autori Toscani in Dieci Libri Raccolte*.

[5] See Introduction 21–3.

[6] Pound published four versions of this sonnet, all of which appear in David Anderson's edition *Pound's Cavalcanti*. The translation cited first appeared in Pound's *Guido Cavalcanti rime: editione rappezzata fra le rovine* (Genoa: Edizioni Marsano, 1932). Anderson cites a review of this edition by A. Hyatt Mayor in which the reviewer suggests that the 'quaint language is not a pastiche of pre-Shakespearean sonnets . . . Pound is matching Cavalcanti's early freshness with a color lifted from the early freshness of English poetry' (xxiii).

Canticles, Baldwin and Spenser's Amoretti

In an important article on the *Amoretti* and the stilnovist tradition, O. B. Hardison distinguishes between 'two apparently clashing motifs... the *donna angelicata* and the "cruel fair"' (210). He sees Spenser as avoiding the Dantesque and Petrarchan traditions which require the deaths of Beatrice and Laura:

> Spenser's concept of 'Eros sanctified' enabled him to use the *stil novo* motifs while avoiding the drastic either/or attitude that made the death of the lady the price of love's fulfillment. Instead of placing the 'cruel fair' and *donna angelicata* sonnets in separate sections of his cycle, Spenser begins with a section in which both are included. (215)

It is significant that Cavalcanti's verse provided a stilnovist poetic practice that likewise combined the elements of angel and trembling, without the death of a lady.

Spenser and Cavalcanti share a biblical awareness of the disturbing aspect of a lady whose attractions inspire love and awe at the same time. Both poets treat the effects of love on the lover – speaker and his world and extend the significance of attraction beyond the limits of sexual encounter. Cavalcanti and Spenser both echo the biblical perception of a love relationship that locates the joys and pains of lovers in a landscape that contrasts previous desolation and wilderness with present fertility and beauty that is nonetheless threatening. The biblical topos locates itself at the point in the lover's feelings for his beloved that sexual desire is mixed with numinous awe. More relevant to Cavalcanti's stilnovist practice in general and thus to the context of Spenser's third sonnet in particular is the poet's consciousness of the unresolved duality of the lady who is both angel and woman, fair and terrible.

Spenser's sonnet concludes, not unlike Cavalcanti's, with a treatment of the poet's view of his own inability to express what he has experienced:

> So when my toung would speak her praises dew,
>   it stopped is with thoughts astonishment:
> and when my pen would write her titles true,
>   it ravisht is with fancies wonderment:
> Yet in my hart I then both speake and write
>   the wonder that my wit cannot endite. (*Amoretti* 3)[7]

It is significant that Spenser's version of Cavalcanti's predicament includes the poet's ability to capture both speech and writing in his 'hart' if not with his pen. That is, Spenser's poem is part of the initial concern of the *Amoretti* with literature and poetic inspiration. The poem rephrases the despair of Cavalcanti at articulating his wonder with a determination to have 'hart' direct 'wit' which has been amazed at the lady and her light.

---

[7] All citations to Spenser's *Amoretti and Epithalamion* are to the *Yale Edition of the Shorter Poems of Edmund Spenser*.

It is relevant that the experience of wonder in both Cavalcanti and Spenser is parallel to a similar experience in the Song of Songs, where the speaker testifies simultaneously to the beauty of the lady and to the terror she inspires. That is, the biblical text introduces the various themes of the sonnets by Cavalcanti and Spenser. Cavalcanti's language reinscribes the biblical scene in terms of a transcendent experience with a woman who intimates a mysterious otherness. In Dante she becomes Beatrice whose dual carnal and spiritual significance is so troubling for the poet. For Spenser, Cavalcanti's despair at not being able to describe the woman or apprehend her with knowledge ('conoscenza'; cf. Pound's 'thought') becomes an almost aggressive insistence upon trying to overcome the daze she has inspired. Somewhere in the background lurks the fear of the terrible, the wonder that 'wit cannot endite' yet the speaker resolves to try and confront her.

Allegorical explanation for this passage is described by Baldwin in the argument to his 'Christe to his Spouse. xlix.' 'Whan Christe hath magnified his Spouse with no lyttle cōmendacion, yet is he not satisfied: but that the yonglynges maye lyke her the better, procedeth farther, comparyng her to the mornyng, to the sunne, to the moone, and to a banner: and as it were wundryng at her excellencie' (I.iii.r). Spenser's poem recognizes that the woman is a source of ravishment whom 'he can no more endure to view', yet in his 'hart' (and in the rest of the *Amoretti*) he will try to 'speake and write / the wonder' that extends beyond his 'wit'. Baldwin had established a poetic precedent for reading wonder as simultaneously spiritual and carnal even though his poems generally resolved the tension spiritually. Spenser's sonnet echoes both Cavalcanti and Baldwin as he makes the object of his wonder include both flesh and spirit.

These dual elements of the lady parallel the allegorical division between flesh and spirit that Baldwin articulated so fully in his *Balades*. The intertextual pressures of the mid-Tudor poems help to clarify ways in which Spenser's sonnets are responsive to both carnal and spiritual modes of interpretation. Sonnet 4 illustrates this duality quite clearly. On the surface, the poem seems to be a celebration of the new year and spring, replete with the sexual suggestion of images such as 'wanton wings and darts of deadly power', 'lusty spring' and 'new love to entertaine'. Baldwin's *Balades* provide a poetic context that accommodates nature and sexual desire to a rhetorical scheme which allegorizes carnal language as spiritual longing. At the centre of Spenser's enterprise is a presentation of love that simultaneously addresses a real woman as object of desire and figure of God. This is most explicitly thematized in Sonnet 68 which is addressed to Christ but which concludes with an appeal to the lady: 'So let us love, deare love, lyke as we ought, / love is the lesson which the Lord us taught.' In Sonnet 4 the poet begins with an account of the coming of a new year (both January and March seem to be suggested) and then refers to the role of love in the coming of spring:

>   and soone about him dight
>   his wanton wings and darts of deadly power.
> For lusty spring now in his timely howre,
>   is ready to come forth him to receive:

The final couplet is addressed to the lady as 'faire flowre' telling her to 'prepare your selfe new love to entertaine'. This fairly straightforward sonnet about courtship in terms of spring and love is, however, closely linked to Baldwin's *Balades* which reads love and nature in spiritual terms. In particular, 'Christe to his Spouse. xx.' allegorizes the landscape of spring into a series of Christian values.[8] For Spenser's sonnet, this suggests that 'lusty spring now in his timely howre' may be more closely connected to prayer and Easter than appears likely in the sequence before Sonnet 68. At the very least, Baldwin's treatment of the passage from Canticles provides a different perspective available to Spenser's persona, even if he himself fails to comprehend at this point. The entertainment that the persona promises the lady may be more spiritual than he recognizes. The motif of spring as a metaphor for preaching as song is part of Spenser's sonnet as it moves from the new year to lusty spring. The lady as 'faire flowre' is asked to prepare for 'new love' which in Sonnet 68 becomes Christ's lesson. At this point in the sequence the intertextual pressures of Baldwin and Canticles prepare the ground for a motif that will get explicit development in later sonnets.

Baldwin's pressures on the *Amoretti* requires a slight adjustment of earlier views of the relation between Spenser and Canticles. Israel Baroway singled out *Amoretti* 15 as an illustration of how the poet was 'moved by his desire to direct the reader's attention to the standards of value rather than to the members of the body, to the interfusing connotations of the high symbols rather than to the eyes, the teeth, the locks, the forehead, and the hands themselves' (35). He was connecting Canticles 5.11, 14–15 with Spenser's sonnet that compares various parts of his lady's body to precious treasures (gems, ivory, gold, silver). For Baroway, the relevance of the biblical verses was to 'suggest beauty . . . in symbols of transcendent value' (35). Baldwin, however, clarifies the use of biblical imagery here with a striking image that Spenser chose to repeat. The relevant phrase comes from an earlier passage in Canticles where Solomon's 'tabernacle' is described: 'The pyllers made he of siluer, the coueryng of golde, the stayres of purple: in the middes therof is made a pauement of loue for the Daughters of Ierusalem' (e.iii.r). In his poem based on this passage, Baldwin describes the pillars of the Tabernacle as composed of 'syluer shene'. This is the exact comparison that Spenser uses to describe his lady's hands: 'if siluer, her faire hands are siluer sheene' (15.12).

Baldwin's poem is, however, more than a 'source' for Spenser's image. It points to the way in which 'carnal' imagery is read as Christian and spiritual

---

[8] See pp. 43–4 above for discussion of this poem.

and thus indicates how Canticles establishes an important interpretive mode for both poets. Baldwin's practice is quite clear. The opening stanza connects 'Salomon' with Christ and the carnal imagery ultimately points to the passion:

> KIng Salomon, kyng Christe the prince of peace,
>   Made for hymself a tabernacle clere,
> Of trees that swete in Libanus increace,
> A carnal corps, wherof the pyllers were
> Of syluer shene, the sylynges fyne of golde:
> Swete for to smell, and goodly to beholde. (e.iii.r)[9]

The 'carnal corps' is thus a mode for transmuting the biblical imagery into a type of the passion. As the poem continues, other elements of the tabernacle (e.g. stairs and pavement) likewise take on aspects of the passion so that the poem can conclude in general about Christ's flesh that clearly connotes Christianity:

> Cum see his flesh, beleue that for your sake
> He dyed therin, and rose agayne to lyfe:
> That by his blood he myght them ryghteous make
> That trust in hym, and cleaue vnto his wyfe.
> Cum furth to see this Salomon your kyng,
> Who may alone your soules to glory bring. (e.iii.v)

Spenser's use of Baldwin's image 'siluer shene' to describe his lady's hands is part of a similar interpretive strategy. Like Baldwin's poem, his sonnet rests on a polarity between the flesh and that which transcends it. In Spenser, the position of transcendence is attached to the lady's mind in the final couplet:

> But that which fairest is, but few behold,
>   her mind adornd with vertues manifold. (15)

The polarity between Christ's 'flesh' and his resurrected 'lyfe' is parallel to that between 'this worlds riches' in the sonnet (Saphyres, Rubies, Pearles, Yvorie, Gold and silver) and the mind of Elizabeth Boyle. She is once again the 'donna angelicata' who is simultaneously woman and angel, flesh and spirit.

One of the most striking sets of echoes of the Song of Songs has been recorded by various scholars [10] in response to Sonnet 64. Here too, however, it is the example of Baldwin that helps to control and determine the ways in which the biblical materials are most relevant to Spenser's work. Without reference to Baldwin, Baroway could do little more than note the general parallel with Canticles:

---

[9] The signature e.iii mistakenly appears on the preceding page.
[10] E.g. Baroway 39–40, DeNeef 39–40, 70–1, Gibbs 120–1, Johnson 180–1.

> The beauty of this passage [*Amoretti* 64] derives, like that of the garden passage of *Canticles*, not from the singling out of details, but from the sensuous and sedative suggestiveness of the whole group; and though there are no exact parallels in olfactory imagery between the two poems, the technique and the general flavor of the descriptions are singular enough to cast the strongest of suspicions upon the source of Spenser's inspiration. (40)

DeNeef is concerned with the motif of captivity which he finds 'behind Spenser's use of the Song of Songs at this dramatic point in the sequence' (71). Baldwin's allegorical approach to the Song of Songs is, however, the most obvious interpretive mode to apply here. At the very point that the erotic imagery becomes most striking in Spenser, the biblical imagery is equally powerful and serves to sacralize the lady.

As Baroway has shown, the most relevant passage from Canticles here is from 4.10–16. Baldwin renders some of the biblical text as follows:

> O howe fayer are thy brestes my syster my spouse? they are more pleasaunt then wine, and the smell of thyne oyntmentes passeth al the spices. Thy lippes o my loue are a dropping hony combe, milke and hony is vnder thy tongue . . . The fruites that growe in thee, are lyke a Paradise of Pomegranades, with fruite trees, Camphor, Nardus, and Saffron, Fistula, and Synamom, with al trees of Libanus. Mirrhe, Aloes, and all the best spices. (f.iii.r – v)

The interpretive problems are clear. What is the significance of the imagery of milk, honey, fruit and spices? How are these connected with the speaker's erotic fascination with the lady's breasts? Baldwin's poem ('Christe to his Spouse. xxxiii.') solves these problems in traditional Christian terms. The breasts are charity and the lips scripture:

> HOwe fayre thy Dugges, thy charitie is my Spouse,
>   My syster swete, more fayre they are than wyne:
> Thy sauour eke of my gyftes glorious,
> Do passe all odours, be they neuer so fine.
>
>   Thy lippes my Loue the hunney combe are lyke,
> From whiche my prayse doeth drop al men among:
> My scriptures eke that are not muche unlyke
> Hunney and mylke, doe vnder lye thy toung.
>
>   Thy garmentes gay, my merites whiche thou hast,
> Do sauour swete, lyke the mount Libanus.
> My Spouse, thou art an orchard locked fast
> Of pleasaunt trees, my elect most bounteous.
>   . . .
>   The planted trees and frutes whiche grow in thee,
> Of Pomegranates are lyke a paradise,
> Beset about with fruites that pleasaunt bee,
> Of cumly heygth that spryng in goodly wyse.

> In thee doeth grow spykenarde and Calamus
> With saffron, Camphor and the swete cypres,
> And all the trees that grow in Libanus:
> Sweete Cynamome, strong Myrrhe and Aloes. (f.iii.v – f.iv.r)

Baldwin's combination of the imagery of Canticles with the Church, scripture, truth and faith helps to clarify the significance of Spenser's sonnet as well. The allegory stresses the sexuality of the woman and derives much of its power from the sensuousness of the imagery. The experience of the body, be it olfactory, gustatory or even sexual, is made to be relevant to Christ and his message.

Spenser's sonnet sequence in general and his famous catalogue of flowers from 64 in particular are concerned with the interrelations between various levels of language and meaning. At issue in this sonnet is the connection between the oral sexuality of a kiss and imagery that addresses woman as flower. Spenser frames the latter as a means of describing his experience of the former:

> COmming to kisse her lyps, (such grace I found)
>   Me seemd I smelt a gardin of sweet flowres:
>   that dainty odours from them threw around
>   for damzels fit to decke their lovers bowres.

As the imagery shifts from 'lyps' to 'flowres' the poet is apparently recounting a narrative experience of a particular kiss that carried with it olfactory recollections. The lady is associated with the odors of flowers which leads to a long catalogue of her parts in terms of flowers:

> Her lips did smell lyke unto Gillyflowers,
>   her ruddy cheekes lyke unto Roses red:
>   her snowy browes lyke budded Bellamoures,
>   her lovely eyes lyke Pincks but newly spred,
> Her goodly bosome lyke a Strawberry bed,
>   her neck lyke to a bounch of Cullambynes:
>   her brest lyke lillyes, ere theyr leaves be shed,
>   her nipples lyke yong blossomd Jessemynes:

The anomaly here is the strange way in which the apparently sensuous flower imagery carries with it distinguished levels of meaning. The sensuous level of the poem is concerned with connecting the grace of her kiss with a 'gardin of flowres' that provides a pictorial means of presenting a strikingly erotic analogue to the kiss: the lady's head and breasts. At the same time, however, the rhetorical arrangement of these details alludes to the biblical mode of describing a woman from head down as in the passage from Canticles cited by Baroway. Like the connection between the grace of the lady's kiss and the theological significance of the word, the rhetorical associations from Canticles

Canticles, Baldwin and Spenser's Amoretti

help to facilitate the convergence between the levels of sense and spirit. Spenser has deliberately chosen to confuse the two kinds of grace. He has likewise stressed the biblical 'sound' of the Hebraic dative of comparison ('lyke unto') in the description in order to help conflate holy and sexual here. In thematic terms, he is sacralizing sexuality as his courtship moves toward the conclusion of Sonnet 68: 'love is the lesson which the Lord us taught'.

Spenser, however, adapts the topos with the addition of the catalogue of flowers which is transcended almost before it is completed. That is, the final couplet undermines the point of the catalogue which appears to have been an attempt at describing aspects of the fragrance and beauty of the lady. As the catalogue moves below the woman's head, the sexual tension rises. The description of the similarities between her breasts and flowers marks a high point in the daring of the poem which began with a kiss and proceeds to the sexually suggestive partial nudity at the end of the catalogue. The final couplet, of course, reverses this moment by rejecting the implicit sexuality along with the comparisons. If the lady has been assumed to be like the fragrances of all the plants, in the final couplet she turns out to be superior to them all:

> Such fragrant flowres doe give most odorous smell,
>   but her sweet odour did them all excell. (64)

Unlike Sonnet 15 which defines the lady's ultimate superiority in terms of her mind, this final couplet invokes her odour which simultaneously maintains the poetic fiction that compares her body to flowers and yet values her above these. Not unlike Baldwin's 'Christ to his Spouse. lvi.' this is Spenser's extension of Marot's blazons. Baldwin was spiritualizing the body and its mysteries in terms of female anatomy:

> There wyll I thy dugges so fruitful make,
> That they shall be lyke the clusters of the vine:
> And the smell that thou shalt of me take,
> Shall reike fro the nose lyke sent of appuls fyne,
>   O my Darlyng.[11] (k.iv.r)

Like Baldwin, Spenser has revised the French blazon tradition into another indication of the spiritual potential of the physical. The olfactory sense represents the lady and yet does not. It is 'her sweet odour' which puts her above and beyond the 'gardin of sweet flowres' to which she is compared. The language of sensuous appeal and of allegorical spirituality are here combined so that neither can provide a final statement about their complex, almost inexpressible, partnership. More than any of Spenser's other sonnets, this one juxtaposes the various matrices of meaning found in Canticles and in

---

[11] For an extended discussion of this poem, see pp. 54–6 in Chapter 1.

Baldwin's arrangement of them: oral and written, sensuous and spiritual, literal and allegorical. The binary opposites line up neatly here as they are linked into the transcendence of the couplet in the nasal poetics of the olfactory.

The association of Christian and sexual love which informs many of the *Amoretti* reaches its highest pinnacle in the celebration of Easter in Sonnet 68. The speaker begins by addressing Christ as he prays that 'we . . . with loue may one another entertayne', and then shifts his attention to his lady as he concludes:

> So let us love, deare love, lyke as we ought,
>   love is the lesson which the Lord us taught.

This movement is at the core of Spenser's sequence as poem after poem seems to redirect the reader's attention from carnal desire to spiritual longing. This sonnet recalls the way in which Baldwin explicated Canticles so as to reveal the allegorical text beneath the apparently erotic verses. Here, however, Spenser has reversed the ordinary order of the interpretive process. Instead of Baldwin's movement from sensuous detail to its spiritual significance, this sonnet begins with the spiritual high of Easter and concludes with an insistence upon the connections between Christ's love for mankind and the mutual feelings of the loving couple.

Baldwin's work helps to support some accounts of the influence of Canticles on Spenser's sonnets. For example, Baroway points to 'the possible influence' of Canticles 2.10–13 on Amoretti 70: 'The adjurations, "goe to my loue," "bid her . . . soone ready make," "make hast . . . sweet loue," are epithalamic in tone, much like "Arise, my loue, my faire one, and come thy way." The references to the passing of winter and to the advent of spring with its flowers are similar too' (43, note 28). Johnson is evidently convinced and sees the poem as 'moderated by the unmistakable reference to the Song of Songs and its associations with marriage'. He cites the same passage from Canticles: 'My welbeloued spake & said vnto me, Arise, my loue, my faire one, & come thy way. For beholde, winter is past: the raine is changed, and is gone away. The flowers apper in ye earth: the time of the singing of birdes is come, & the voice of the turtle is heard in our land (Song of Songs 2.10–13)' (206). In both the Bible and the sonnet, winter is past and flowers appear but, on the surface, there is not much more of a connection. It is easier to justify Baroway's 'possible influence' than Johnson's 'unmistakable reference'. Baldwin's poetic version of the biblical passage establishes at least one more parallel. In the fifth stanza of 'Christe to his Spouse. xx.' Christ calls to his spouse 'Aryse therfore my spouse, my special Loue, / Make haste, make spede, purely my wurde to preache' (d.ii.v).[12] In Spenser's sonnet, the

---

[12] See pp. 43–4 above for further discussion of this poem.

penultimate line establishes the parallel: 'Make hast therefore sweet loue, whilest it is prime.'

Baldwin's poem provides more than mere verbal parallels, however. The shift from winter to spring is interpreted as a movement from 'vnbelefe' to faith and 'the syngyng tyme' is explicitly 'the tyme to preache'. This allegorical view of spring is not irrelevant to Spenser's sequence since love for his lady has just been explicitly connected to agape. Baldwin's version of Canticles allows us to read the *carpe diem* motif as a call to spiritual regeneration. The address to spring becomes much more than an opportunity for pagan lust; it associates winter with 'blyndnes', 'stormes' and 'ouercast' skies and springtime with song, 'the voyce of the holy gost', truth, 'fayth and wurkes'. Such a reading is, of course, fully in accord with recent accounts of the integration of profane and holy in the *Amoretti*.

The lover in Spenser's *Amoretti* reaches a high point of religio-sexual tension as he focuses his attention on his lady's breasts. Although he has already described them in some sense (Sonnet 64), in Sonnets 76 and 77 he is more direct. The first of these poems presents the lover's passionate desire and thoughts:

> FAyre bosome fraught with vertues richest tresure,
>   The neast of love, the lodging of delight:
> the bowre of blisse, the paradice of pleasure,
> the sacred harbour of that hevenly spright:
> How was I ravisht with your lovely sight,
>   and my frayle thoughts too rashly led astray?
> Whiles diving deepe through amorous insight,
> on the sweet spoyle of beautie they did pray.
> And twixt her paps like early fruit in May,
>   whose harvest seemd to hasten now apace:
> they loosely did theyr wanton winges display,
> and there to rest themselves did boldly place.
> Sweet thoughts I envy your so happy rest,
>   which oft I wisht, yet never was so blest. (76)

The sonnet that follows continues to focus on the lady's breasts, but does so in what Baroway calls 'symbolic, not realistic images' (41):

> Was it a dreame, or did I see it playne,
>   a goodly table of pure yvory:
> all spred with juncats, fit to entertayne
> the greatest Prince with pompous roialty.
> Mongst which there in a silver dish did ly
>   twoo golden apples of unvalewd price:
> far passing those which Hercules came by,
> or those which Atalanta did entice:
> Exceeding sweet, yet voyd of sinfull vice,

> That many sought yet none could ever taste,
> sweet fruit of pleasure brought from paradice
> By love himselfe and in his garden plaste.
> Her brest that table was, so richly spredd,
> my thoughts the guests, which would thereon have fedd. (77)

The parallel attention paid to the lady's breasts in Canticles has led to general scholarly recognition of the biblical debt here, even though most agree that while Spenser may have been inspired by the Song of Songs, he does not seem to be referring to any specific passage. Baroway indicates that: 'the imagery of the *Song of Songs* has not always precipitated clearly and purely. Many of the strains are faint. Few of the pictures conform closely to those in the scriptural song' (45). This, however, does not prevent him from theoretical speculation about Spenser's 'symbolic' mode in describing the lady's breasts as: 'twoo golden apples of unvalewd price'. Baroway suggests that 'here is the intimate description of the body through symbols which deprive the image of erogenic qualities' (42). Johnson adds that in Sonnet 77 'the references to the table, the dish, the guests, and the desire to be fed have their analogue in the Communion service as well' (223).

On a stylistic level these two sonnets provide an intense illustration of Spenser's flesh–spirit continuum throughout the sequence. The 'FAyre bosome' that 'ravisht' him in Sonnet 76 becomes 'sweet fruit of pleasure brought from paradice / by Love himselfe' in 77. The two poems explore both sides of the tension, and in this way work out between them many of the conflicts that Spenser's sonnets engage. Just as the 'bosome' of 76 becomes the communion 'table' in 77, the literal appears allegorical and orality shifts into textuality. As this is happening, Spenser's version of biblical naturalism (e.g. 'twixt her paps like early fruit in May') is balanced against the transformation of classical myth into Christianity: 'far passing those which Hercules came by, / or those which Atalanta did entice'. Together the two sonnets provide a fairly explicit model for the process by which the various tensions of the Baldwinian project become enmeshed in Spenser's sequence. Baldwin's various versions of his biblical source (i.e. prose translation, argument and poem) take on sensuous and even explicitly sexual levels of meaning as they proceed to spiritualize Canticles. This process is reflected by the many tensions delineated in the previous chapter. Spenser's focus upon his lady's breasts in Sonnets 76 and 77 recapitulates Baldwin's stance which often appears to endorse a straightforward carnal reading of Canticles, but soon after clarifies that these images connote more than they first seem to signify. The classical golden apples need to be reconsidered as part of Eden, not unrelated, perhaps, to Dante's account of the top of Purgatory. The 'sweet fruit of pleasure brought from paradice / By love himselfe and in his garden plaste' needs to be processed in the mind of the reader very much like the classical world had to be Christianized before it could signify for Spenser. The hermeneutic in this case is fairly straightforward. The carnal passion and interest in Sonnet 76 drives the poet's thoughts to a literal desire for the lady's breasts, but these thoughts then lead the lover (and his readers) to the allegorical significance of the breasts and desire for them which infuse the image with spiritual meaning. This kind of transcendental meaning does not, however, undercut the carnal level of the previous poem. Instead it reveals another aspect of fleshly experience which is balanced against the world of religious love.

Near the end of the *Amoretti* are sonnets that examine what it is that makes the lady 'fayre'. William C. Johnson has pointed to connections between sonnets 79 and 81 and parallel passages in Canticles that treat the pulchritude of either the lady or the man (225, 229). Once again, however, it is Baldwin's allegorical developments of the relevant biblical passages which make the references striking. In 79, Spenser's speaker addresses his lady and explains that 'the trew fayre, that is the gentle wit, / and vertuous mind, is much more praysd of me' . Her true beauty is 'deriv'd from the fayre Spirit, from whom al true / and perfect beauty did at first proceed' (79). In 81, the speaker distinguishes between the physical 'fayre' described in the octave and based on 'works of natures wonderment' and her wisdom which is 'the worke of harts astonishment'. The parallel passage in Canticles records a male speaker's catalogue of feminine beauty. Baldwin's version begins: 'LOe thou art fayer my Loue, thou arte fayer, thou hast doues iyes, besyde the tyer thervpon. Thy heares are flockes of Goates, whiche are shoren from of mount Gileal. Thy lyppes are lyke the red scarlet threde, and thy spech is swete' (f.i.r). His poetic rendition of this passage elaborates upon the allegorical significance of each of the lady's bodily parts. Her 'iyes' signify 'iudgement simplenes', 'heares are 'truthes moste principal', her 'teath' are 'argumentes most strong,' and

> Thy lyppes, thy speche is lyke the skarlet red,
> Whiche for the elect, thy sauiour Christ doest preache,
> Afflicte in fleshe, with bloud his crosse bebled,
> To faythfull folke a swete and pleasaunt speache. [f.i.v]

The interpretive method here is allegorical. Each bodily detail is associated with a value which is explicitly spiritual. This does not negate the world of sensuous experience, but associates it with something larger. This is precisely Spenser's approach to his lady's physical attributes. The octave of Sonnet 81 contains the biblical list of bodily parts: 'fayre golden heares', 'fayre when the rose in her red cheekes appeares, / or in her eyes the fyre of love doe sparke', 'Fayre ... her brest', 'fayre ... with smiles'. All these are then compared to her speech which is fairest and which, as with Baldwin, is based upon the allegorical association of mouth with language:

> But fayrest she, when so she doth display
>   the gate with pearles and rubyes richly dight:
>   throgh which her words so wise do make their way
> to beare the message of her gentle spright. (81)

Spenser does not use the specific biblical image of the scarlet thread but his 'gate with pearles and rubyes' has a spiritual equivalent that is clearly linked. The fair lady is thus connected to Christ's bride, the church, which is an important aspect of Baldwin's view of the lady in Canticles.

When the final sonnets of the *Amoretti* treat the separation between lover and his beloved, some readers have been disconcerted. The sequence is supposed to lead to the marriage celebrated in *Epithalamion* with which it was first published, yet it concludes with poems that lament the absence of the lady. Alexander B. Grosart suggested that Sonnets 86 and following do not belong in the sequence: 'Pity that ever the Poet gathered together the others that follow. They seem to me to bear on surface and in substance their own evidence of having been inspired by a different object and under wholly different circumstances' (Spenser, *Variorum* 7.2.452). Twentieth-century scholars are not ordinarily so completely dismissive. Louis Martz sees no difficulty: 'I do not feel the abruptness and uncertainty that some have found in the conclusion of the *Amoretti*' (150). A. Leigh DeNeef imports a metaphor from the *Faerie Queene* to account for the conclusion:

> the Blatant Beast, having already escaped from Calidore's iron chains and threatened the poet himself, enters the sonnet sequence and forces the lovers apart by interpreting their reformed love as a lie. In the face of that public slander, the lover fails to be consoled even by contemplating 'the Idaea playne,' and he ends the sequence mourning his absent beloved. (74–5)

John N. King ascribes the problem to suspense: 'The transitory disturbance over the lady's absence during the three final sonnets may be designed to create some sense of suspense prior to the final union in *Epithalamion* (*Spenser's Poetry* 171)'. Carol Kaske treats the final sonnets and other 'blocks of incongruous material . . . by subdividing the story told by the volume into an emotional progression of not two but three stages . . . courtship . . . betrothal . . . and marriage' (272–3). Donna Gibbs is not disturbed by the apparent difficulty:

> Although, in sonnet LXXXVI, the lover records a breach in their peace, it is caused by some outside force, and presumably is not permanent, since in the very next sonnet the lover waits for the return of his 'love' with confidence that her presence will restore the contentment he has lost. Her absence in this and in the next two sonnets is not explained, but it does not seem due to punishment or withdrawal of favour on the mistress's part. (163)

William C. Johnson is no less sanguine:

> The violence of emotion expressed in 86 apparently subsided, some reconciliation has occurred and, for an unexplained reason, the lady and lover are parted for a period of time . . . in the *Amoretti* the lovers, although apart, remain betrothed; the poet, 'lyke as the Culuer on the bared bough,' waits expectantly for the reunion. (244–5)

The Song of Songs as interpreted by Baldwin provides another kind of explanation of the separation which can be connected to the structure of the sequence and to its ultimate connections to the apocalypse. In the biblical text there are a number of instances in which the female speaker complains of her inability to find her lover. Although she is successful in locating him in one instance (3.1–4), in another she is not so lucky. The city watchmen find and beat her. Baldwin translates:

> I opened the bolte of my dore to my Beloued: but he was goen & past. As sone as my Beloued spake, my soul cam out. I sought hym, but I founde hym not: I called, but he gaue no answer. The watchmen y^t went about the citie, found me, smote me, and wounded me: They that kept the wall, toke away my gaberdin. I charge you o ye daughters of Ierusalem, that yf ye fynde my Beloued, ye shew him how that I am louesycke. (g.iiii.r)

Baldwin's allegorical explanation here views the failure of the woman to open her door immediately as an indication that 'the poore churche [is] deceyued through frayltie of the flesh' (g.iiii.r). This is the underlying reason for her inability to find him when she finally decides to open the door. Her condition is captured in some of the stanzas of 'The Spouse to the Younglynges. xl.':

> I sought him long but coulde not fynde,
> I called hym, he answered not:
> Awhyle he left me to my mynde,
> Because at fyrst I opened not.
>   Helas.
>
> . . .
>
> I charge you yf ye chaunce to fynde
> Christe my Beloued that dwelles aboue,
> Ye shew hym how sore I in mynde
> Am sycke, and languish whole for loue
>   Of grace. (h.i.r)

Spenser's speaker in the final sonnets of the *Amoretti* is in a condition similar to that of the Spouse in Baldwin. The mood of 'long weary dayes' and 'sorrow' (87.2, 13) as well as the 'darknesse of the night' and the 'shadowes vayne' which can only be dispelled by the absent lady's 'heavenly ray' (88.3, 6, 7) come at the end of the sequence. There is a promise of final closure but only on a level that imposes a narrative connection between the *Amoretti* and the *Epithalamion*. Spenser's sonnet sequence concludes with a poem that leaves the speaker disconsolate, joyless and dark. This final poem is linked to

Canticles by the Culver or dove in its opening line which refers back to the 'dove's eyes' of the Bible (Song of Songs 1.15). Baldwin's tenth poem is based on this verse:

> LOe thou my Loue, art fayer:
>   Myselfe haue made thee so,
> Yea thou art fayer in dede,
> Wherefore thou shalt not nede
> In beautie to dispayer:
> For I accept thee so
>   For fayer.
>
> For fayer, because thyne iyes
> Are lyke the Culuers, whyte:
> Whose simplenes in dede
> All others doe excede:
> Thy iudgement wholly lyes
> In true sence of spryte,
>   Moste wyse. (b.iii.v)

This poem provides a link between Sonnets 79 and 81 on the concept of 'fayre' and 89. Baldwin and Spenser each explore the spectrum that leads from physical to spiritual. Baldwin suggests that one connection between 'fair' and doves is the colour white which he associates with 'simplenes' and 'iudgement'. There is also a connection between classical associations between Venus and doves which make this poem part of Baldwin's project to produce poetry to rival 'the baudy balades of lecherous loue' (A.iii.v). That is, his poem intimates that doves are essential to love because of their associations with simplicity and judgment rather than because they were supposedly sacred to Venus.

Spenser's concluding sonnet continues the mood of grief and darkness from the two preceding poems, and in so doing adds another aspect to the biblical analogy. The speaker begins by comparing his condition to that of a female dove which longs for the return of her mate:

> LYke as the Culuer on the bared bough,
>   Sits mourning for the absence of her mate:
>   and in her songs sends many a wishfull vow,
>   for his returne that seemes to linger late.

The associations with the Song of Songs here are subtle, but noticeable. The *Oxford English Dictionary* lists a figurative meaning for 'culver' which it illustrates with quotations from medieval texts obviously quoting Canticles: 'An appellation of tender affection'. The illustrations come from the *Ancren Riwle* ('Cum to me, mi leofmon, mi kulure'), Wyclif's translation of the Song of Songs 6.8 ('Oon is my culuer, my parfit') and Caxton's *Vitas Patrum* ('She herde oure lorde whiche callyd her sayenge:

Come to me my spowse, my culuer or douue'). There is, therefore, an excellent chance that the word had biblical associations for Spenser. In addition, the gender of the culver makes it analogous to the spouse in search of her Beloued or Christ in Baldwin's *Balades*. By comparing himself to the female dove who longs for her male mate, Spenser was associating the bird with the biblical dove from the Song of Songs.[13] This lends support to the other parallels between Spenser's speaker in the *Amoretti* and the allegories developed by Baldwin.

The parallels between Baldwin and Spenser suggest ways in which Canticles provided a metaphor for Spenser's speaker to explore his love and its spiritual implications. There is, however, a significant difference between the spirit of the 1549 poems and that of Spenser almost half a century later. It is at this point that the relevance of Canticles to the *Epithalamion* is crucial. As readers move from the *Amoretti* to its companion piece, they must contemplate the pagan or natural aspects of flight and love before returning to the dove of Canticles in its guise as 'truest turtle dove'. The poetic apparatus for effecting this is the Anacreontic poems which deal with the flight of Cupid, doves and bees. The description of the bride in stanza 10 of the *Epithalamion* then returns to the imagery of Canticles from *Amoretti* 64 as it directs the reader's attention down the lady's body from 'goodly eyes' to 'brest' and 'paps', concluding with 'all her body like a pallace fayre'. That is, Spenser has the 'merchants daughters' gaze at the bride whose appearance makes them 'forget your former lay to sing':

>   Her goodly eyes lyke Saphyres shining bright,
>   Her forehead yvory white,
>   Her cheekes lyke apples which the sun hath rudded,
>   Her lips lyke cherryes charming men to byte,
>   Her brest like to a bowle of creame uncrudded,
>   Her paps lyke lyllies budded,
>   Her snowie necke lyke to a marble towre,
>   And all her body like a pallace fayre,
>   Ascending vppe with many a stately stayre,
>   To honors seat and chastities sweet bowre.

---

[13] As Carol Kaske, M. Thomas Hester and others have pointed out in various ways, the conclusion of the *Amoretti* is far from the end of the work Spenser published in 1595. The *Anacreontics* and the *Epithalamion* continue the love motif and, in a sense, the latter suggests a kind of closure in terms of marriage. One aspect of this development concerns the Song of Songs. The *Anacreontics* function as what Hester calls a 'centerfold' in which the emblematic conventionality of the imagery contrasts with the movement from the Culver of *Amoretti* 89 to the 'truest turtle dove' in the *Epithalamion* (24). That is, the wings of the dove are replaced in the *Anacreontics* by those of Cupid:

>   But when he saw me stung and cry,
>   He tooke his wings and away did fly (*Anacreontics* 5–6)

and by the 'gentle Bee' which 'with his loud trumpet murm'ring, / about him flew by hap' (*Anacreontics* 25–6).

> Why stand ye still ye virgins in amaze,
> Upon her so to gaze,
> Whiles ye forget your former lay to sing,
> To which the woods did answer and your eccho ring.
> *(Epithalamion* 171–84)

Although much of the language here is very close to that of the *Amoretti* (especially 15 and 64), the intensity is slightly different. The catalogue concludes with the lady's 'snowie necke' so that the reader's attention which moved consistently down in *Amoretti* 64 here concludes by 'Ascending uppe . . . / To honors seat and chastities sweet bowre'. The rhetoric from Canticles is somehow less sexually charged here, more public and formal. The style is, perhaps, even a little less biblical than that of the *Amoretti*. The imitation of the Hebrew dative ('lyke unto') is simplified here into a plain simile ('lyke'), while the lover's gaze has become that of the 'merchants daughters'. The balance between holy and carnal has likewise been resolved into honour, chastity and the amazement of the virgins. Courtship has yielded to the formalities of the wedding day. This mood continues into the following stanza which treats the lady's 'inward beauty'. The emphasis is on 'constant chastity . . . and mild modestie'. Here Spenser moves away from the balances of Baldwin and the daring of courtship.

Baldwin's approach to Canticles is then, more relevant to Spenser's *Amoretti* than to its sequel. The rhetorical modes of the *Epithalamion* are somewhat different from those of the sonnets. The conventions of classical pastoral in which woods answer and echoes ring are dominant here. As the poem approaches the altar, the biblical doves which were replaced by those of Venus in the *Anacreontics*, are in turn replaced by 'th' Angels which continually, / About the sacred Altare doe remaine' (229–30). The biblical sexuality that was simultaneously carnal and holy is a part of the background here perhaps, but it is superseded by the language of Christian humanism.

The delicacy of Spenser's work would be ruined by a heavy-handed application of Baldwin's allegorical approach to Canticles. The kind of reading that I want to propose is designed as an alternative to others rather than one that demands exclusive authority. Baldwin's allegory need not operate at all times in this sequence to make its suggestiveness extend the possibilities of meaning. On one level these sonnets seem to have a connection to Spenser's personal life. Nonetheless, a reading that insists too stridently on an exclusive identity between the lady and Elizabeth Boyle unnecessarily reduces the scope of the sequence. At the point that she is analogous to the Spouse in Baldwin and thus to the Church, it would be absurd to deny the intertextual hints in order to maintain a reading that can only accommodate psychological realism. On the other hand, none of the hints and analogies should be pushed so far as to ignore other possibilities. The model of analogy that functions best here assigns different positions for different sonnets along axes that connect a series of abstract dichotomies. The most obvious of these is the tension between the allegorical and the carnal, but similar distinctions can be accommodated between the textual and the oral, and between apocalypse and domesticity. In each of these cases, the initial terms are more or less parallel and can be understood as articulating aspects of a related reading. This is likewise the case with the opposite terms. Allegorical, textual apocalypse establishes a pattern of meaning in the sequence that moves toward a sense of narrative closure which is finally resisted by the unexpected conclusion of the sequence. Spenser's sonnets engage the dichotomies of Baldwin's *Balades* so as to maintain both poles of the various axes in a delicate balance.

Chapter 3

CANTICLES AS ERASED CONVENTION IN *VENUS AND ADONIS*

UNLIKE the Canticles tradition which moves from Baldwin and Spenser in the sixteenth century to Aylett, the Ranters and Milton in the seventeenth, Shakespeare's *Venus and Adonis* is unremittingly secular. His narrative poem focuses on the absence of the numinous as the verse establishes its style by ignoring the underlying traditions which had become irrelevant to the poet's purpose. Like Ovid's poems and Canticles, Shakespeare's narrative is somehow an erasure of earlier mythic texts that celebrated the numinous in terms of balance between conflicting dichotomies. Shakespeare deals with the secular text of Ovid which was itself a rewriting of a religious myth. Beneath the surface of *Venus and Adonis* we can trace elements of the erased text of numinous sexuality which included the biblical text as well as its more well established classical 'source', but the poem itself generally ignores these materials. Shakespeare's erotic narrative thus provides a useful foil against which to view the other texts considered in this study.

Shakespeare's *Venus and Adonis* is a secularized version of a mytho-erotic text rooted in Semitic traditions adopted and refashioned by the Greco-Roman world and as such is roughly parallel to the Song of Songs, which can likewise be read as a humanized version of an older pagan fertility myth. Ovid's *Metamorphoses*, the generally acknowledged 'source' for Shakespeare's poem, is itself far removed from what must have been the original spirit of the myths it interprets. Suave, witty, urbane, and ironic, Ovid's poem has little of the spirit of the Olympian religion that one senses in Homer or Hesiod. The concerns of Ovid's Venus are much more those of a mortal woman afraid of her lover's interest in hunting than those of a goddess. Ovid's story, however, is rooted in an ancient middle-eastern fertility myth in which a god descends into the underworld and is later resurrected. The hero's marriage with the goddess of love was celebrated in terms of sexual abandon that knew neither shame nor hesitation. Ovid's secularization of this myth ironically emphasizes the eroticism by ignoring most of the sexual encounter between Venus and Adonis.

The mythic roots of Ovid's tale were certainly known during the Renaissance. George Sandys summarized the details of the ancient solar and vegetation myth in his 1632 commentary on Ovid which collects most of the information about the *Metamorphoses* which Shakespeare could have known:

> Now *Adonis* was no other then the Sun, adored under that name by the *Phaenicians*; as *Venus* by the name of *Astarten*: for the Naturalists call the upper Hemisphere of the Earth, in which we inhabit, *Venus*; as the lower *Proserpina*: Therefore they made the Goddesse to weepe, when the Sun retired from her to the six winter signes of the Zodiacke; shortning the daies, and depriving the earth of her delight and beauty: which againe he restores by his approach into *Aries*. *Adonis* is said to be slaine by a Bore, because that beast is the Image of the Winter; salvage, horrid, delighting in mire, and feeding on ackornes, a fruit which is proper to that season. So the Winter wounds, as it were, the Sunne to death, by deminishing his heate and lustre: whose losse is lamented by *Venus*, or the widdowed Earth, then covered with a vaile of clowds; Springs gushing frõ thence, the teares of her eies, in greater abundance; the fields presenting a sad aspect, as being deprived of their ornament. But when the Sun returnes to the Aequator, *Venus* recovers her alacrity; the trees invested with leaves, and the earth with her flowrie mantle: wherefore the ancient did dedicate the month of Aprill unto *Venus*. And not only the *Phaenicians*, but the house of *Judah* did worship the Sun under the name of *Tamuz*, the same with *Adonis*: for *Adon* in Hebrew signifies Lord, and he the Lord and Prince of the Planets, they calling his entrance into the signe of *Cancer*, the revolution of *Tamuz*. (493)

Sandys pointed to the parallels between the middle-eastern material and the Greek story and intimated that they were different ways of referring to the same natural truths, or 'the same in the allegorie' (493). His stress on the natural significance of the myth allowed him to pass over the more explicitly sexual aspects of the material. Nevertheless, his account of 'the feasts of Adonis' does include reference to temple prostitution that evidently characterized middle-eastern idol worship: 'The women that would not cut their heare, were enjoyned to prostitute themselves unto strangers, and to offer the hire of their bodies unto Venus. This lamentation for the death of Adonis is mentioned by the Prophet Ezechiel: for so Thamuz is interpreted in the vulgar translation' (492–3). An ancient account of these matters can be found in *The Syrian Goddess* (De Dea Syria) attributed to Lucianus Samosatensis. The narrator in this work describes different holy places in Syria which he visited. He tells of:

> a great sanctuary of Aphrodite of Byblos in which they perform the rites of Adonis, and I learned about the rites. They say, at any rate, that what the boar did to Adonis occurred in their territory. As a memorial of his suffering each year they beat their breasts, mourn, and celebrate the rites. Throughout the land they perform solemn lamentations. When they cease their breast-beating and weeping, they first sacrifice to Adonis as if to a dead person, but then, on the next day, they proclaim that he lives and send him into the air. They also shave their heads, as do the Egyptians when Apis dies. The women who refuse to shave pay this penalty: For a single day they stand offering their beauty for

sale. The market, however, is open to foreigners only and the payment becomes an offering to Aphrodite. (13–15)

The mythic roots of the tale of Venus and Adonis were no less clear to medieval readers. The anonymous French *Ovide Moralisé* (fourteenth century) combines its reading of Adonis as Jesus with a view of the latter as the spirit of natural rebirth in accord with vegetation myths. The long French poem retells Ovid's *Metamorphoses* quite expansively and then adds a series of poetic commentaries on the allegorical significance of the individual stories. The first explanation of the meaning of the tale of Adonis sees him as a figure of carnal pleasure ('luxure' [10.3708]). The following 'sentence' moves in a very different direction. Here the physical beauty that characterizes Adonis renders him the lord of the world, the saviour and the guarantor, who will deliver all mankind from reproach and sin:

> En qui toute biautez habonde,
> Adonin, li sires dou monde,
> Li sauvierres et li garans
> Qui tout delivra ses parans
> Et de reprouche et de pechiez. (10.3796–800)

This fairly obvious Christianization becomes even more specific as the enraged boar issuing from his hiding place is likened to 'crazy Jews' who put him to death, but the grace of God turns the death devised by the Jews into resurrection, germination and flowering:

> C'est cil que li pors enragiez,
> Issans d'espesses repostailles,
> C'est de tenebreuses entrailles
> Des folz juïs, fist metre à mort,
> Mes la grace Dieu fist le mort
> Que li juïf firent morir
> Resordre et grener et florir: (10.3801–7)

This important French text documents one way in which the medieval mind treated Ovid and his mythic roots.[1] On the one hand there is a moral reaction against Ovid's apparent delight in carnal pleasure which gets recorded as a rejection of 'luxure'. At the same time, however, the medieval poet accepts Adonis as a Christ figure intimately bound up with traditions that get written off as 'folz' but which are simultaneously expressions of rampant anti-Semitism as well as a vague awareness of the middle-eastern roots of the Adonis story.

---

[1] The medieval French poet is not unlike Sir James Frazer who claimed that 'the ceremony of the death and resurrection of Adonis must also have been a dramatic representation of the decay and revival of plant life' (227).

Erased Convention in Venus and Adonis

There is a rich variety of significance in the myth Shakespeare treats here. According to J. W. Lever's survey of the scholarship as of 1962, *Venus and Adonis* has been read as comic, tragic, sensual, moral and didactic and romantic (20–2). A. C. Hamilton treats the 'philosophical level of the poem' (8) while Heather Asals calls attention to 'the Neoplatonic details present in the poem' (33). More recently, William Keach has stressed its deep, even confusing ambivalence (53) while Heather Dubrow develops a complex analysis of 'psychological acuteness we normally associate with Shakespeare' (24). My interest here is to examine the process whereby Shakespeare's text humanizes the myth by encompassing all of the conflicting readings outlined above and many more. I will proceed primarily by focusing on the Song of Songs, a text generally ignored in Shakespearean scholarship, and show how attention to parallels between the biblical poem and Shakespeare point in very different directions. The biblical parallels appear relevant to underlying traditions (such as those presented in the above selections from Ovid, Lucianus and the *Ovide Moralisé*) that are not immediately connected to Shakespeare's poem. These silences point to the ways in which the narrative shifts the reader's attention away from the balances between holy and sexual, oral and written, lyric and apocalypse which form the essence of the Canticles tradition.

The humanization of myth relies upon a process in which principles of orality and textuality interrelate to fashion a complex synthesis in our reading of Shakespeare's text. The poem is a written account of a narrative which purports to recount the oral communication between Venus and Adonis as fashioned and shaped by a narrator. Formal aspects of the poem such as rhyme and rhythm help to determine the sound of the oral material that is recorded in written form in this work of the early 1590s. The interplay between an oral tale and the technology which produces it as a printed text is part of a tension that gets expressed in parts of the poem as instances of self-reflexive pondering by the narrator as to the interactions between art and reality. It is parallel to a similar ambivalence in the Canticles tradition which reads a humanized poem about carnal love as an allegorized account of the relations between God and men. In contrast to the other texts treated in this book, *Venus and Adonis* adjusts the techniques of balance to avert the religious glance focused in each of the other works. The themes of the narrative such as sexual desire and tragic grief humanize the underlying myths as they shape a secular world which attempts to divert attention from the religious otherness implicit in the mythic sources.

The balance between the oral and the textual in *Venus and Adonis* serves to attract the attention of the reader away from the issues of transcendence and otherness that this tension promotes in the other works which deal more directly with the Canticles tradition. Whereas in both Shakespeare and the Bible there is an oral text that has been silenced by the written word, the textuality of *Venus and Adonis* calls attention to a secular avoidance of mythic or cosmic issues in order to focus on the earthly humanity of the couple. While a synchronic reading of the Canticles tradition calls attention to oral traditions that complicate the apparent absence of the divine from the biblical text, Shakespeare's orality gives precedence to artistic rhetoric which seems to have deliberately silenced much of the underlying myth. The darker religious traditions that Elizabethan culture recognized in the story are conspicuously avoided in the narrative. The mythic details highlighted by someone like Sandys are almost suppressed by the actions and language of the protagonists of the poem.

On the level of theme, Shakespeare has left many of the parallels to Canticles undeveloped. There is, for example, a pattern of structural development in the love of Venus which recalls a similar development in Canticles. In both Shakespeare and the Bible the movement is from love and desire to death, with a major role for nature as background enabler as well as source of atmosphere. The similarities and parallels need not have been consciously fashioned. Shakespeare's poem can be read as a response to the conventions of the Elizabethan love lyric and the traditions established by the various sixteenth-century Bibles (e.g. Great Bible 1540, Geneva Bible 1560, Bishops' Bible 1568) as well as by Baldwin's *Balades* (discussed extensively in Chapter 1). All of these were well enough known to have made their mark upon the expectations of readers in the 1590s. Nevertheless, the awe-inspiring seriousness of the biblical parallels is ignored or forgotten as Venus moves from the comedy of her desire to the tragic suffering of her grief. Her emotions (like ours as we hear her) stress the limitations of human existence and ignore her role as transcendent goddess.

There is a general parallel between the development of Shakespeare's poem and that of Canticles. *Venus and Adonis* proceeds from an erotic seduction scene to the death of Adonis and the mourning of Venus. This pattern is similar to one in Canticles as the biblical poetry treats erotic longing, darkens this with various references to war and violence and then, near the conclusion, extends its account of love to include jealousy and death. This similarity in thematic structure makes it possible to read specific parallels between the two texts as related to the movement of plot. Conventions of biblical love poetry which can be taken as governing the lyrical expression of erotic emotion and desire lie behind those biblical passages that are echoed in the first section of *Venus and Adonis*. Although the elements of jealousy and death, a motif which occurs at the conclusion of Canticles, connect both works through the language they use, the theme itself is conspicuously absent in the section of Shakespeare's poem that treats the mourning of Venus. In *Venus and Adonis* we focus almost exclusively on the characters as individual people without an option to reflect their mythic otherness.

The poem begins with the first of many attempts by 'Sick-thoughted Venus' to woo Adonis. She wants him to postpone his hunting and promises

Erased Convention in Venus and Adonis

> for thy meed
> A thousand honey secrets shalt thou know.
> Here come and sit, where never serpent hisses,
> And being set, I'll smother thee with kisses.
> (*Poems, Venus and Adonis* 15–18)

This declaration of feminine desire is similar to the opening of the Song of Songs, where the woman longs for her beloved's kisses: 'Let him kiss me with the kisses of his mouth: for thy love is better than wine' (1.2). The parallel between the two passages is not mere coincidence. While Venus is reversing the traditional Petrarchan situation in which the male 'woos' a less than passionate woman, the conventions to which the Elizabethan reader was attuned included more than just the world of Petrarch and the biblical expression of feminine desire could be significant for gauging the effect of her words. Venus is actively and even aggressively seeking the love of a very unenthusiastic Adonis, and in doing so she is abandoning the traditional role of the coy lady. The reader may be amused at the reversal of the Petrarchan situation, and realize that the literary expression of Venus's desire for Adonis is without support from the most obvious codes of social and literary behaviour. In expressing herself in this unconventional way, she cuts herself off from the standard models of response. At the same time, the biblical text about feminine longing for kisses provides an alternative kind of traditional support for her mood. If so, however, the associations between the goddess and the biblical passage tend to disregard the allegorical mode in which Renaissance readers traditionally had been urged to read Canticles. Venus's desire in Shakespeare is this-worldly and sexual. To search out allegories about Christ's love for the Church is not relevant in *Venus and Adonis*. If these are part of the cultural context of the Canticles tradition, Shakespeare's poem ignores them, and in so doing provides another signal of its secular spirit.

The love and desire that Venus expresses is echoed in the natural landscape in which the poem takes place. Near the outset, she addresses Adonis as 'field's chief flower . . . / More white and red than doves or roses are' (8, 10). This is part of a rhetorical ploy that sees him as greater than nature:

> Nature that made thee with herself at strife
> Saith that the world hath ending with thy life. (11–12)

As the goddess claims mythic superiority for her lover, she departs further and further from the real world that he inhabits until she manages to dislodge him from his horse. Even so, her attention is in vain as he rejects her favours. The lover she would like to encounter in Adonis would presumably have regarded her with a passion as intense as her own. After all, Mars, the god of war had

>   learn'd to sport and dance,
> To toy, to wanton, dally, smile and jest,
>   Scorning his churlish drum and ensign red,
>   Making my arms his field, his tent my bed. (105–8)

The kinds of passionate love found in the Sumerian poems,[2] or in the longing of both lover (cf. 4.9–11, 7.1–9) and beloved (2.1–7, 5.10–16, 7.10) in Canticles seem to be what Venus has in mind as she urges him to kiss her:

> Touch but my lips with those fair lips of thine –
> Though mine be not so fair, yet are they red –
> The kiss shall be thine own as well as mine.
> What seest thou in the ground? hold up thy head,
>   Look in mine eye-balls, there thy beauty lies:
>   Then why not lips on lips, since eyes in eyes? (115–20)

Here it is most obvious that Shakespeare has reversed standard Petrarchan love language in order to make Venus look ridiculous. She uses love conceits similar to those Donne would develop in a poem such as 'The Good-Morrow' ('My face in thine eye, thine in mine appears' [89]). Nonetheless, the lover she attempts to inflame with her mythic language stands in obvious contrast to the embarrassed Adonis who 'burns with bashful shame' (49) in response to her excesses. Although the inversion of the conventions of love here is based primarily on the reversal of traditional sex roles, part of the irony flows from the absence of the biblical passion. The mutual desire of lover and beloved in Canticles is the norm against which Venus's entreaties should be gauged.

The biblical context is ironically parallel. Like Venus, the woman in the Song of Songs refers to her beloved as 'white and ruddy, the chiefest among ten thousand' (5.10) and then goes on to compare his appearance to aspects of nature such as ravens (11), doves (12), spices and sweet flowers (13). Unlike the Shakespearean poem, however, Canticles follows the idyllic description of the lover with an account of the mutuality of their love in a paradisal garden:

> Whither is thy beloved gone, O thou fairest among women? Whither is thy beloved turned aside? that we may seek him with thee. My beloved is gone down into his garden, to the beds of spices, to feed in the gardens, and to gather lilies. I am my beloved's and my beloved is mine: he feedeth among the lilies.
>   (6.1–3)

The difference between the behaviour of the biblical lovers and that of Shakespeare's couple is important. The biblical text helps to support and extend the expectation of Venus that Adonis will conform to the mythic

---

[2] See Introduction, 12–16.

Erased Convention *in* Venus and Adonis

conventions she calls up. As he refuses to do this, his action insists upon the ironic distance between the biblical analogues of her language and her sullen, fretful beloved.

The ironic tension between Shakespeare's Adonis and the erotic myth that underlies Canticles is likewise supported by the description of the young man's horse. Here the biblical parallel is part of a larger rhetorical device in the Hebrew text which integrates horse imagery into a description of the beloved: 'I have compared thee, O my love, to a company of horses in Pharaoh's chariots. Thy cheeks are comely with rows of jewels, thy neck with chains of gold. We will make thee borders of gold with studs of silver' (1.9–11). Although the immediate relevance of 'a company of horses in Pharaoh's chariots' to love or beauty may not have been clear to an Elizabethan reader, the passage is striking and memorable. Its tone implies that there was a connection and that this is somehow related to the jewels that embellish the beloved. These lines could be understood to provide a conventional context for a love lyric that the narrator of *Venus and Adonis* mimics. The detailed attention to the horse of Adonis can be read as an adaptation of the biblical convention in order to register a richly comic rejection of its mythic seriousness. Instead of the horse introducing a context for passionate or at least sincere presentation of a love scene, it serves to portray a comic fall: Venus pushes Adonis from his horse:

> The studded bridle on a ragged bough
> Nimbly she fastens – O how quick is love! –
> The steed is stalled up, and even now
> To tie the rider she begins to prove:
>   Backward she push'd him, as she would be thrust,
>   And govern'd him in strength, though not in lust. (37–42)

In addition, the 'studded bridle' may echo the 'studs of silver' of Pharaoh's horses, but their context calls for laughter. The mythic power of the goddess of love is replaced here with strength to push her love object but not in the sexual mode that she desires. The Ovidian mimicry of love is supported by the reversal of the biblical horse motif.

Further on in the poem, the narrator has occasion to return to this horse motif in a similar manner. The biblical text furnishes a pattern that compares the beloved to Pharaoh's horses and then dwells upon her rich trappings that could refer back to the horses or else to the woman. Shakespeare's narrator represents this pattern by describing Adonis's horse in terms that make him into a thinly disguised sexual metaphor. He then concludes the description by juxtaposing the motif of animal as metaphor for the conventional human emotions of lovers with the specific narrative situation in which Adonis finds himself. That is, after a long passage that describes the horse and its 'romance' with a female, the poem suddenly focuses again on Adonis who has been abandoned by a horse more inclined to love than its master. Even this passage, however, is not quite in accord with the spirit of convention that the biblical poem suggests. The jewelry that bedecks the beloved, like that which adorns Pharaoh's horses, is meant to convey a smooth, poetic connection between the material things described, the love object and the general condition of love. One leads almost unavoidably to the other. In *Venus and Adonis*, there is a rejection of this world of convention in favour of a more natural realistic poetic. Thus, when Adonis's horse rejects his trappings in favour of love, he is also rejecting the convention which connects those 'rich caparisons' directly with love:

> What cares he now for curb or pricking spur,
> For rich caparisons or trappings gay?
>   He sees his love, and nothing else he sees,
>   For nothing else with his proud sight agrees. (285–8)

Whether the narrator is presenting conventional passionate love (as with the horse) or rejection of male desire as in the case of Adonis, the language is anti-mythic as it alludes to the conventions of love in order to reverse or reject them. There is even a possibility of colloquial punning throughout the poem on 'horse' as a sexual term. Gordon Williams points out that the word is often 'equated with woman' (163). He actually cites *Venus and Adonis* where, he states, 'the stallion is developed into a traditional figure of overmastering passion, invertedly representing Venus's powerful desire' (164). As a verb 'horse' could, according to Eric Partridge, mean 'to possess a woman' (*Dictionary of Slang* 571) or 'to mount a woman – as though she were a horse' (*Shakespeare's Bawdy* 123). Although Adonis remains unaware of such punning, Shakespeare and his readers surely relished the irony of this and related colloquialisms associating sexual experience with horses. In our case, the horse imagery can be seen as establishing the material from Canticles as a convention of love to be referred to in order to reject or reverse it.

Although the initial section of *Venus and Adonis* continues on considerably before shifting into the second part, the goddess anticipates the darker conclusion of the poem in a passage in which she reminds Adonis of the identity of another of her lovers: Mars, the god of war. She apparently means this as a part of her rhetorical plea for the serious attention of Adonis, yet her language underlines the parallels between love and war:

> I have been woo'd as I entreat thee now,
> Even by the stern and direful god of war,
> Whose sinewy neck in battle ne'er did bow . . .
> Over my altars hath he hung his lance,
> His batter'd shield, his uncontrolled crest . . . (97–9, 103–4)

Although Venus is primarily concerned here with convincing Adonis to value her as the beloved of Mars, she is also implying that her idyllic colloquy with her mortal beloved could be ended abruptly by the interference of the war-god. Her statement, however, likewise recalls various biblical passages which stress the warlike aspect of the beloved. In a well known descriptive section of Canticles that addresses the woman and directs attention to her body, moving from head to breasts, her neck is presented as follows: 'Thy neck is like the tower of David builded for an armoury, whereon there hang a thousand bucklers, all shields of mighty men' (4.4). This passage thus provides a conventional connection between lyrical sexuality and a celebration of war. For Shakespeare, however, the woman's body is the source of war as well as delight. As the poem continues, the gender identification is reversed so that neck and shields resist the biblical convention and revert to Mars. This adds an ominous quality to the rhetoric of Venus and associates war and violence with her former lover rather than follow the biblical convention which makes war an aspect of the woman. As Venus retreats into the classical myth which assigned clearly gendered roles to love and war, she ignores the biblical perspective readers may recall in which love is both delightful and warlike. Her failure to recognize the parallel is part of the ironic significance of the biblical echo.

As Shakespeare's poem moves toward its final section, in which Venus mourns the death of Adonis, a key passage from Canticles weaves in and out of the poetic texture of the narrative. In the final chapter of the biblical poem, the woman exclaims:

> Set me as a seal upon thine heart, as a seal upon thine arm: for love is strong as death; jealousy is cruel as the grave: the coals thereof are coals of fire, which hath a most vehement flame. Many waters cannot quench love, neither can the floods drown it: if a man would give all the substance of his house for love, it would utterly be contemned. (8.6–7)

Echoes of this passage may be heard in the Shakespearean poem as early as the narrator's description of Adonis as a 'dying coal' soon after his horse has deserted him to follow the jennet:

> He sees her coming, and begins to glow,
> Even as a dying coal revives with wind. (337–8)

If the coal here is relevant to the 'coals of fire, which hath a most vehement flame' from Canticles, it functions, like the other biblical conventions in this poem, to call attention to a parallel with significant mythic force. At the same time, the tone of the poem either rejects the irrelevance of the similarity or else uses it to call ironic attention to the absence of the numinous. Adonis's identity as a 'dying coal' has all too little to do with love, as opposed to the biblical coals which are explicitly those of love which cannot be extinguished. When Venus attempts to interpret the significance of the horse's actions, she too makes use of the coal image:

Kisses of their Mouths

> Affection is a coal that must be cool'd;
> Else, suffer'd, it will set the heart on fire. (387–8)

The irony here lies in the suggestion that the coal of affection can be cooled. The biblical convention allows for no division between love and affection whereas Venus suggests that sexual passion can protect the heart from fire.

Venus continues in this vein when she revives after fainting in response to Adonis's frown. She continues to beg kisses from him and casts her thoughts in language that is more serious than she seems to be aware:

> Pure lips, sweet seals in my soft lips imprinted,
> What bargains may I make, still to be sealing?
> To sell myself I can be well contented,
> So thou wilt buy, and pay, and use good dealing:
>   Which purchase if thou make, for fear of slips,
>   Set thy seal manual on my wax-red lips. (511–16)

The kiss as a seal of love is a serious image[3] but in this passage, Venus is somewhat irreverent about the trappings of her godhead. The language of bargain and trade sets the tone rather than the solemn intensity of the biblical passage. All this is in exact accord with her anti-mythic role. Canticles provides an indication of the conventions a mythic goddess of love might have applied. She reverses these without any apparent realization of the incongruity of her arguments.

As the poem shifts from the somewhat comic mode of Venus as temptress and records her mourning for the death of Adonis, the consciousness of the goddess does not seem to advance. She is sombre enough in her prophecy but her point of view has not changed:

> Since thou art dead, lo here I prophesy,
> Sorrow on love hereafter shall attend:
> It shall be waited on with jealousy,
> Find sweet beginning, but unsavoury end;
>   Ne'er settled equally, but high or low,
>   That all love's pleasure shall not match his woe. (1135–40)

William Keach observes that 'despite her "prophecy" . . . Venus seems totally unchanged by Adonis's death' (83). Her synthesis of love, jealousy and death is flat and selfish, especially when compared to the much more moving and intense emotions reflected in the biblical passage. To the very end, then, Venus seems to ignore the deeper emotions of conventional love as reflected in the parallels from Canticles.

---

[3] A. C. Hamilton cites Castiglione's *Courtier* in his discussion of Platonic doctrine on kissing in which Bembo refers to Canticles to illustrate the doctrine that a kiss is 'the cooplinge of soules together' (10). The passage occurs near the end of the fourth book in Hoby's translation (315).

Erased Convention *in* Venus and Adonis

The conventions of love traced above in the material from Canticles call attention to serious elements of Shakespeare's traditional roots while the rhetorical texture of the verse simultaneously silences these echoes as irrelevant. The intertextual pressures exerted on the reader by the biblical text can be taken as implicit conventions available to Elizabethans which Shakespeare's narrator ignores or erases in order to focus upon Venus and Adonis as essentially mortal characters who do not seriously consider their mythic identities. This poem can thus be read as a resolution of many intertexts including Ovid's *Metamorphoses*, Lucianus's *The Syrian Goddess*, Canticles as well as ancient Sumerian poems about Inanna and Dumuzi and ancient Egyptian love lyrics. These many traditions of the myth of Venus and Adonis can take on various meanings and are shaped to some extent by yet another set of pressures determined by the modes of communication and culture that produced them. Venus and Adonis and the narrator speak through the printed text and the sounds their voices make are balanced against the textual silence of the words on the printed page.

As Shakespeare muted his mythic materials and made his poem look away from the biblical parallels that might have informed it, he was giving expression to a secularism that the Canticles tradition from Baldwin to Spenser resisted. Instead of the balance between carnal and spiritual that characterizes the tradition, Shakespeare fashioned a text that denies the numinous and concentrates on the physical. As the tradition then moved on toward Milton and *Paradise Lost* it continued to confront and reject that which Shakespeare had provided.

Chapter 4

THE SPENSERIAN CANTICLES OF ROBERT AYLETT: THE PROTESTANT TRADITION CONTINUES

ONE of the less well known links between Spenser and Milton appeared in the 1620s in the form of an epic version of the Song of Songs. Robert Aylett's *The Brides Ornaments* (1621–25)[1] provides evidence of ways in which an avowed disciple of Spenser wrote Protestant meditations with the materials that Milton later shaped into *Paradise Lost*. Aylett's work is primarily important as a literary barometer of intertextual pressures exerted on the developing consciousness of mid-seventeenth-century poets such as Milton. Whether or not Milton actually knew Aylett's verse, thematic similarities make it clear that these meditations in Spenserian stanzas connected Baldwin's mid-sixteenth century experimentation with Canticles with what became the Miltonic development of Spenser's Protestant art. Aylett's work is especially valuable as a reflection of ways in which at least one early seventeenth-century Protestant explicitly fashioned a literary project in terms of the Canticles tradition from Baldwin through Spenser.

Beyond the clearly 'Spenserian' qualities of stanzaic form, Protestant ideology, and attention to the Edenic materials of Genesis, Aylett's text is a revision of sections of the *Faerie Queene* that are central to the ideology of love as adumbrated through the Song of Songs. As some of his younger contemporaries were working out ways of articulating the sexuality that charges the biblical verses, Aylett strove to fashion an allegory that would accommodate the Protestant tendency to deny biblical carnality. While historically *The Brides Ornaments* provides evidence of traditions about Protestant poetry that Milton and Aylett shared, on the level of biblical hermeneutics, Aylett's poems, like those of Baldwin, appear to accept the authority of Origen's allegorical interpretation of Canticles. Yet this appeal to orthodoxy breaks down as Aylett's narrator is unable to follow Origen fully in

---

[1] Books 1 and 2 first appeared in 1621. I cite this work as *The Song of Songs . . . Brides Ornaments . . .* All citations to these books are to this edition unless otherwise indicated. Books 3 and 4 were published in 1625 as *The Brides Ornaments*. All available biographical information about the poet can be found in Padelford's 'Robert Aylett'.

his rejection of the carnal sense of Canticles, which was in some way related to the theologian's self-castration. Later in the century, Milton would reject the allegorizing of desire and reach toward a poetic vision that would balance the carnal and the spiritual as different aspects of the same integrated experience. This monism ultimately required that he reject monasticism as he struggled with his own problematization of Spenser's avowal of biblical sexuality in the *Amoretti*.

Much of Aylett's epic is built upon the narrator's search for salvation in love, which is analogous to Prince Arthur's romantic quest for the 'Queene of Faeries' in Spenser's epic (1.9.14ff.). In the *Faerie Queene*, Arthur's search for Gloriana is a motif that recurs at key points and helps to 'sette forth magnificence' as Spenser wrote to Raleigh.[2] Like Arthur, Aylett's narrator is in search of the Queene of Love. His meditations on Protestant values are fashioned to prepare him for the salvation that holy love should provide. The connection between the erotic and the spiritual is signalled through echoes of the Song of Songs. The effect of his situation is to provide a revision of the *Faerie Queene* that is focused on Cantos 9 and 10 of Book 1.

Aylett's work imitates various stylistic elements of Spenser as it shapes materials of medieval romance into Spenserian stanzas[3] about Protestant virtues. A first-person narrator searches for '*the glorious Court/ Of Heauenly Loue, by some call'd* Charitie' (20; st. 2) and finds a series of allegorical ladies who lead and educate him until he can meet the Queen of Love. This education corresponds to the spiritual progress presented in the 'conventional descriptions of the affective states of the elect' as enumerated by Barbara Lewalski in her *Protestant Poetics* (20). The goal of the Protestant tradition is salvation, which is secure for those who reach 'sanctification' (23). This pattern is the basis of the allegorical progress implicit in the narrator's education in *The Brides Ornaments*.

The speaker's initially fruitless quest begins to look more hopeful thanks to the intervention of a lady of the court:

> Long time I sought Loues Court most carefully,
>   And on her noble Actions set my mind,
> That, in her praise, my Muse might soare on high,
> I sought in vaine, but could no entrance find,
>   Vntill a courteous Lady then assign'd
> To keepe the Court Gate, hight Humilitie,
> Well knowing what I sought, lowly declin'd,
>   Assuring me I neuer could descrie,
> Loues honourable Court, but by Humilitie. (20; st. 4)

---

[2] 'A letter of the Authors ... To the Right noble, and Valorous, Sir Walter Raleigh', in *Faerie Queene* 737.
[3] Aylett is an exception to William B. Hunter's comment in 'Spenser and Milton' that 'although ... Milton did not leave a single Spenserian stanza, the "Spenserians" of 1610–30 did not either' (34).

As Humilitie instructs him, the narrator discovers his own pride and ambition and learns to imitate her nature. This shift in his values represents a conversion of significant import, since his long search for 'Loues Court' has been accompanied both by pride and literary ambition. The gap between the allegorical meaning of the Court and the speaker's primary concern with fame and the soaring of his muse is fundamental. Once he converts from these essentially pagan values to those of the Court (as instructed in these lines), he is ready for the next stage in his movement toward salvation.

In 'The Proeme', in full accord with Calvinist doctrine, the next step is to meet the lady Repentance. The narrator appears before her in humbled state and she asks his conscience

> *To bring my Sinnes and Follies on the stage;*
> *Who, streight-wayes, did obey her great command;*
> *And loe! my sins appear'd in number like the Sand.* (22; st. 8)

These sins are then '*exhibited plaine to bee seene*' before '*Iustice* [who] *was chiefe Iudge,*' but '*To extend Mercy shee had no permission: / They that have sinn'd must be condemn'd without remission*' (22; st. 9). It remains for '*Faith and* Hope, *two Patrons neare at hand*' (22; st. 10) to save him with advice that he appeal to Mercy. This corresponds to what Lewalski has called 'God's gift of saving faith' which 'is the vehicle for justification and adoption' (22–3). After receiving instruction from the Christian virtues of Meeknesse, Obedience and Patience, the narrator is taught by Fortitude

> *'gainst all afflictions to stand fast,*
> *For he that loueth well endureth all.* (24; st. 15)

This is part of the process of sanctification as described by Richard Rogers and William Perkins in passages quoted by Lewalski. Rogers speaks of 'life as a "combate and a conflict" against sinful lusts, unruly desires, and all manner of temptation' while Perkins 'distinguishes three principal temptations and trials of a Christian life' (Lewalski 24). The end of this spiritual progress, '*Glorification,* or the perfect restoration of the image of God in man and the enjoyment of eternal blessedness' (Lewalski 18), is represented in 'The Proeme' by Lady Laetice or Inward Joy who begins '*most graciously to smile*' upon the speaker (24; st. 16), accompanied by Zeale, Courtesie, God's Word, Prayer, and Medi[t]ation,[4] who bring him '*to* Loues *glorious presence*' (26; st. 20).

---

[4] Although the 1621 reading is 'Mediation', Aylett's 1654 edition reads 'Meditation'. Cf. *Divine* 20, st. 19. In general, the 1654 edition changes many of the spellings. This may have been Aylett's initiative but it is more probable that the printer was responsible for this. Thus, for example, there are corrections in the 1654 edition such as this one but there are also obvious errors that creep in which were not present in the 1620s . For example, on p. 3 of the 1654 edition, the translation from chapter two renders 'The *Birds* do chip, the *rain* doth cease to fall', where 1621 rendered 'doe chirpe'. Likewise, on p. 6, 1654 reads 'Thou ravisht hath mine

Aylett presents a spiritual quest for religious salvation by means of feminine figures who appeal to his narrator as attractive women before he can learn anything about their allegorical import. The movement from sexual to holy love, an underlying theme throughout *The Brides Ornaments*, is conveyed metaphorically through recurrent echoes from Canticles. These biblical quotations differ considerably from the approach of Aylett's better-known contemporaries both in relation to sexual experience and with regard to scriptural references. Aylett's narrator reduces his ladies to displaced sexual objects whose carnal attractions are constantly allegorized into Protestant ideology. Aylett's versions of poetic texts by contemporaries such as Spenser and Donne divert the narrator's carnal interests into traditional allegory, which claimed to consider only the spiritual significance of the erotic language in Canticles. He provides an illustration of Foucault's thesis that that which has often been understood as sexual repression can be more adequately described as 'a regulated and polymorphous incitement to discourse' (34).

On a superficial level, Aylett echoes Spenser's *Faerie Queene* (1.10) in his use of the Spenserian stanza as well as in the adaptation of feminine allegory to represent spiritual and theological development. Frederick M. Padelford has pointed out that the 'proem is modeled upon Spenser's House of Holiness, with the respective virtues performing essentially the same offices in each' ('Robert Aylett' 5). Aylett's adjustment of his source is apparent from the outset of his work. The 'Argument' to his translation of the Song of Songs, also written in a Spenserian stanza, is distinct from Spenser in its dependence upon a pattern of experience that relegates sexuality to the illicit and sinful. Spenser had begun *The Faerie Queene* with an account of his life that imitated a traditional view of the development of Virgil's poetic career from pastoral poetry to epic:

> LO I the man, whose Muse whilome did maske,
>   As time her taught, in lowly Shepheards weeds,
>   Am now enforst a far vnfitter taske. (Proem. 1.1–3)

Aylett's echoes of the Proem in his 'Argument' to his translation of the Song of Songs invoke a past of lust and sexual abandon:

heaat' for 'mine heart' (1621). Padelford's account of the minor differences between the editions is essentially accurate and succinct: '*The Song of Songs* is an exact reprint of the earlier edition ... The last two stanzas of the original Proem are reduced to one, and ... Books I and II are reduced a third. The *Five Divine and Moral Meditations* ... have only been reduced from 230 to 220 stanzas, and the *Five Moral Meditations* have exactly the same number – 216 – in each edition, although the later edition omits four of the original stanzas and adds four elsewhere' ('Robert Aylett' 18–19). He likewise points out that while the 'earlier volumes were all addressed to distinguished representatives of old Essex families or to prominent divines, the dedications and commendatory verses of this [1654] volume disclose friendships with mid-century scholars and writers' ('Robert Aylett' 17).

> *My Muse, that whilome, swaid by lust of youth,*
> *Did spend her strength in idle wanton toyes,*
> *Now viewes her vanity, with mickle ruth,*
> *And as awak'd doth seeke for solid ioyes.* (1)

The similarities in literary myth ('Muse') and archaic language ('whilome') are ample evidence that Aylett's narrator was looking to Spenser, but his insistence that Homer, Virgil and Spenser did not wait '*on the glorious Court / Of Heauenly Loue, by some call'd* Charitie' (20; st. 2) suggests that the speaker's rakish past and present sexual awareness are an integral part of his search for the Queen of Love. Padelford sees Aylett's 'Argument' as 'the conventional regret of the exponents of divine poetry for the youthful pursuit of worldly verse' ('Robert Aylett' 3) and concludes that 'in view of . . . the author's indebtedness to *The Faerie Queene,* it is somewhat naive to find the opening stanzas voicing regret that Spenser . . . had chosen to write of "Ladies loues, and Nobles courtesie" rather than of "Heavenly Loue," to the detriment of his poetry and the impoverishing of his soul' ('Robert Aylett' 5).

Whether or not Aylett was naive, it is certain that his narrator was addressing himself to what he chose to present as a failure on Spenser's part: an inadequate vision '*Of Heauenly Loue, by some call'd* Charitie'. That which Padelford writes off as 'conventional regret' is a motif that recurs again and again in Aylett's work. In fact, however, the vision of love that Aylett presents is considerably less intense than that of the *Faerie Queene*. Spenser's hero is more troubled by issues of trust and faith in his relationship with Una than by explicitly sexual tensions. When he awakens nervously from the dream Archimago has fashioned 'of loues and lustfull play' (1.1.47.4) in which Una, 'Now a loose Leman' (1.1.48.6), has tried to entice him, he is more suspicious and soldierly than sexually aroused:

> In this great passion of vnwonted lust,
>   Or wonted feare of doing ought amis,
>   He started vp, as seeming to mistrust
>   Some secret ill, or hidden foe of his. (1.1.49.1–4)

He represses his sexual desire and replaces it with what he considers more appropriate responses. The narrator of *The Brides Ornaments* is much more attentive to feminine beauty than Spenser's hero, even though his allegorical ladies are considerably less seductive than the false Una in Red Cross Knight's dream. As he comes in contact with the women who are to teach him, Aylett's narrator speaks in such a way as to record his libido. Although the rest of the stanza stresses her spiritual qualities, the narrator's first observation about Humilitie is that '*Shee was a louely Lady . . .*' (21; st. 5). The demand of Temperance that he cast away 'all immoderate lusts' stresses the presence of these passions, as opposed to Spenser's Red Cross Knight, who apparently had no trouble subduing his sexual desire. Ioy and Zeale '*did enflame mine inward parts*' (25; st. 18) insists the speaker. The two-edged sword of God's word must 'all sinne and lust diuide' (25; st. 19) from him, but meanwhile his imagination is unable to frame its ideology without implicit references to sexual desire. Where Spenser had Red Crosse repress his sexuality in order to achieve his goal, Aylett's narrator dwells upon the traditional motif of feminine inspiration with no conscious understanding of the sexual pressures such a figure requires.[5]

Although Aylett's treatment of Canticles is modelled after traditional allegorical readings, it seems to disregard the warnings of Church Fathers such as Origen about the reader's need to 'be rid of the vexations of flesh and blood . . . [having] ceased to feel the passion of his bodily nature' (23). Although he wrote this commentary towards the end of his life, Origen's attitude toward the flesh was more or less the same as that which had motivated his castration as a young man. There is, then, a marked difference between his discussion of the spiritual implication of an erotic passage from Canticles and Aylett's application of such detail to an account of his narrator's attempts to purify himself from carnal desire. Origen had generally explained Canticles in terms of a 'little book which has the semblance of a marriage-song . . . written in dramatic form' (58). He had then proceeded to examine the spiritual import of the feelings expressed by the biblical speakers he had isolated in specific verses. Such a procedure effectively drained his work of the sexual tensions that abound in Aylett's poetry.

Aylett's use of traditional interpretations of Canticles to convert sexual desire into allegorical discourse about Protestant ideology can be understood as an attempt to redirect the Spenserian poetic tradition toward the medieval past. His central view of love is established early in the first meditation in *The Brides Ornaments*, 'Of Heauenly Loue'. The essence of all love, he claims, is spiritual, but this perception is not always clear to

> THose learned spirits that spend their youthful prime
>   In writing Volumes large of wanton Loue. (27; st. 1)

God, the speaker insists, is 'the obiect of true Loue'. In pursuing his point about the basic spiritual nature of 'true Loue' the speaker compares love to the magnetic field of the earth:

> With Load-stone touched, to the Arctique Pole;
> All other motions violent doe proue,
> This is the obiect of true Loue: this sole
> The Center is of Loue, on which all Loue doth roll. (27; st. 3)

Aylett's narrator is participating in a discussion as to the proper object of love. The language recalls the bitter, misogynist tirade in John Donne's 'Loves

---

[5] Cf. my 'Courting Urania' 86–99.

Alchemy', whose speaker asks where love's 'centrique happinesse doth lie' and claims that 'Oh, 'tis imposture all . . . a winter-seeming summers night.' That poem concludes that women 'at their best, / Sweetnesse, and wit they'are, but, *Mummy*, possest' (126–7). Donne's speaker is thus typical of Aylett's 'learned spirits' who write passionately of 'wanton love', and lose so much time before they realize that the real 'centrique happinesse' is not woman but God. On this level, Aylett's speaker could be saying that it is pointless to begin with sexual love if one must ultimately move on to holy love in any case. The dualism that distinguishes sexuality from holiness is central. Aylett's narrator has chosen a key figure from the cultural traditions available to Christianity and ignored its roots even while the needs of his own masculine lust keep recurring beneath the surface of his text. His allegory, not unlike that of Baldwin, appropriates the language of sexuality and redirects it away from the recognition and articulation of the carnality that Donne had invoked.

As he proceeds to describe spiritual or heavenly love, Aylett's narrator abandons his simplistic position and maintains the traditional perception that all love, sexual as well as holy, can be understood as an aspect of Christ's love for his Church:

> Behold! by all these Names, he doth inuite
> Vs to embrace his mutuall heau'nly Loue,
> And calls vs Friend, Child, Sister, Spouse, Delight;
> His Seruants sends vs curteously to moue,
>   To royall Banquets and sweet beds of Loue,
> By grace adopting vs, to be Coheires
> Eu'n with himselfe, of glorie great aboue,
> No cost or paines, not his owne Blood, he spares,
> But like a Father, Husband, Friend, for vs he cares. (40; st. 54)[6]

This stanza contains various words and phrases that echo Canticles. The names we are called by God are all taken from the Song of Songs as are the terms used to describe him. The 'royal Banquets' correspond to Canticles 2.4 rendered by Aylett 'He sets me at the banquet by his side' (3), while the 'sweet beds of love' appear in Canticles 3.1, or, as Aylett summarizes at the beginning of his version of chapter 3: '*The Church her Spouse in bed doth seeke, not find*' (4). Aylett preserves the earthly language of the Song even as he insists upon the allegorical significance of the sexual imagery. His point is that, properly understood, man's sexual nature is a hint of the sweetness of Christ's love. Love is all of a kind if we understand it rightly, and its sexual roots are misapprehended if regarded as mere physical or earthly pleasure. Sexuality is thus perceived as a means of transcending man's earthliness, just as woman is a means to this transcendence. The ladies who teach the narrator to go beyond his sexual appetite are thus enshrined as semi-goddesses and the poem never confronts

---

[6] Aylett revised this stanza slightly in 1654. Cf. *Divine* 28, st. 30.

them in any deeper or more individual way. They are there to serve the spiritual needs of the masculine consciousness as represented by the narrator.

There is a significant gap between the ideals of Christianity described by Aylett's narrator and his admittedly imperfect state of salvation at any given moment. For example, soon after his description of the 'sweet names' Christ uses in the Song of Songs, the narrator suddenly remembers how committed he is to the goods of this world. He exclaims:

> Oh! that I could despise Worlds vaine promotion,
> And follow heau'nly things with all my might. (43; st. 64)
> . . .
> But though, alas, this heau'nly Loue I feele
> Abundant grace vpon mine heart to shower,
> Loue of this World my soules eyes vp so seele,
> To loue the things aboue, I haue no power:
>   And though I feele sweet flashes euery hower
> Of heau'nly Loue: I cannot loue againe
> The Head nor Members, which in earthly Bower
> Most deare and precious in his sight remayne,
> But hardly can from Enuie, Hatred, Pride refrayne. (43; st. 66)

Although the speaker is concerned with love of worldly things and not with sexual temptation, his capacity for falling into the very sins he deplores elsewhere is here made manifest. The underlying problem is that the narrator is both the presenter of an ideological position and an object of the narrative which often engages him in ironic confrontations. As Christian poet, Aylett's narrator must double as interpreter of God's word and as an individual sinner in need of grace and salvation. Origen's use of a dramatic reading of Canticles that preceded the allegorical explanation and made it almost impersonal was not a solution for Aylett. The narrative structure of *The Brides Ornaments* is not subtle enough to resolve the difficulties.

The narrator's education moves him further and further away from the initial interest he shows in the loveliness of the allegorical ladies of the court. His meditative development is predicated upon his self-perception as a sinner who would like to resist his own tendencies to excess but who feels himself incapable of doing so:

> Should my sinnes be in number as the Sand,
> And my forefathers sinnes, my sinnes exceed
> In weight and number: yet I firme would stand,
> What though eternall fire be sinnes iust meed?
>   Much is forgiu'n, where is much loue indeed;
> Wherefore mine Heart and Soule shall euer praise
> My Maker, that in me such loue doth breed,
> That doth my Soule from hellish horror raise
> Aboue the Heau'ns, to liue the life of Loue alwayes. (45; st. 75)

The reference to 'much loue' here intimates that the narrator's 'sinnes' are to some extent sexual. The line alludes to the woman 'who loved much indeed' (Luke 7.36–49) and of whom Jesus declared 'Her sins, which are many, are forgiven; for she loved much' (7.47). Perhaps there is some identification here between the narrator and the woman 'which was a sinner [who came to the house of Simon the Pharisee with] an alabaster box of ointment' (7.37) with which to anoint Jesus. Simon's scornful comment to himself about the woman suggests that her sins were sexual in nature ('what manner of woman this is that toucheth him' [7.39]). Such, at least, was the assumption of Matthew Poole about the word 'sinner' in this passage: 'That is, a remarkable Sinner, it is a Word generally so used, and applied to Women, signifies a *Prostitute*, or at least one of an ill Report as to Chastity' (2: Sff2r). In any case she was forgiven by Jesus and presumably went off to sin no more.

It is this biblical pattern that Aylett's narrator would apply to himself. He is in search of spiritual love that will make up for the sexual excesses of his youth. He speaks here of love without any sort of explicit sexual reference such as his earlier allusions to the Song of Songs provide. That which he pursues may have its roots in the sexual passion described in Canticles, but it has long since replaced the carnality of the original with allegory. Spenser's playfully ambiguous double entendre that urged his mistress to loue him since 'love is the lesson which the Lord us taught' (*Amoretti* 68) is clearly lost on Aylett's narrator in this mood. Aylett's alter ego allegorizes his women in order to disguise his sexual desire. He condemns himself as sinful because of that which he no longer admits he feels. That is, he retreats into textual allegory and seems thus to avoid contact with the real forces of his world.

Although the other meditations of *The Brides Ornaments* are only marginally concerned with sublimated sexuality, many of them reveal some tension between the professed ideology of chastity and poetic language that is either explicitly or suggestively sexual. The intensity of the first meditation about love is not, however, repeated again in either of the first two books (1621). Language conventionally used for love poetry is applied in a religious context in 'Of Humilitie' but the apparent tone always seems calm and controlled. For example, the second person of the Trinity is asked to direct the 'Muse most liuely to expresse / Humilitie, that opens wide Loues gate / To those that doe confesse their wretchednesse' (48, st. 4). Later on, the same phrase 'Loues gate' is associated with the Lady Humilitie who

> is most kind and curteous, never coy
> Vnto the vertuous; and shee opens wide
> Loues gate vnto the Humble. (52; st. 21)

Beneath the obvious surface meaning here is a possible sexual double entendre that complicates the staid message of the poem. On the surface Humilitie opens the gate to Heaven for the humble and keeps out the proud.

On the other hand there is plainly something sexually suggestive about a lady who 'opens wide / Loues gate'. This figure recurs throughout *The Brides Ornaments* as the sexual tension and desire of Canticles is allegorized into a religious treatise that never quite loses sight of its carnal origins. Whereas elsewhere, however, Aylett took pains to disguise the sexually charged language, here he seems to flaunt it. Words such as 'coy' or 'Loues gate' seem to be taken from a literary world very much aware of puns and their effects. 'Coy' could have suggested sexual double entendre in other contemporary contexts. Peter Levins had translated it as '*lasciuus, salax*' according to the *Oxford English Dictionary* which suggests that a coy mistress was not necessarily innocently shy in the sixteenth and seventeenth centuries. Aylett's Humilitie might almost be a source for Marvell's 'To his Coy Mistress'.[7] In a sense, Aylett's narrator was providing his own answer to Christopher Marlowe's passionate shepherd whose invitation to his mistress was proverbial: 'Come live with me and be my love' (211). Aylett's prayer might be a playful rephrasing of Marlowe:

> Lord! I acknowledge freely my demerit,
> It is thy Grace whereby I am, liue, moue,
> Thy humbling to the Crosse, for me, did merit,
> That I should be exalted to thy Loue,
> And live with thee in blisse eternally aboue. (60; st. 52)

This is not unlike Milton's use of Marlowe in the concluding lines of 'L'Allegro' and 'Il Penseroso'.[8]

As the narrator states explicitly in the 'Argument' to the Song of Songs, his muse seeks 'solid joys' as opposed to the 'idle wanton toys' of his lusty youth. Aylett may have seen his version of Marlowe's poem as a proper spiritualization of sexual love poetry, but the texture of his language opens his own text to sexual readings that tend to undermine the meditations. The first two books of *The Brides Ornaments* present the narrator as struggling to achieve the kind of spirituality that will gain him salvation. He admits to being

---

[7] The conventional understanding of Marvell's use of 'coy' generally ignores this ironic possibility. E.g. Alexander M. Witherspoon and Frank J. Warnke comment as follows on Marvell's poem: '"Coy" here has the older meaning of modest, reserved, inaccessible' (966). More recently, Michael Craze has limited the term to 'sexually reluctant' on the basis of references to Shakespeare, Randolph and Carew (313). In *Paradise Lost*, Milton develops the implicit conflicts in Aylett's Humilitie who is 'never coy'. Eve made love before the fall 'with coy submission, modest pride, / And sweet reluctant amorous delay' (4.310–11) while after eating the fruit, her 'eye darted contagious Fire' as Adam 'led her nothing loath' (9.1036, 9.1039). The ironies implicit in Aylett's Humilitie get played out in Milton's juxtaposition of similar acts before and after the fall. The purity of Eve's coy sexuality is distinguished from her fallen behaviour on the basis of its crude lack of delicacy. Aylett's Humilitie points in both directions.

[8] See A. S. P. Woodhouse and Douglas Bush, *A Variorum Commentary on the Poems of John Milton*, Vol. 2, Pt 1, 'The Minor English Poems' (New York: Columbia UP, 1972), 308.

tempted by 'Worlds vaine promotion' (43; st. 64), 'worlds entisements base and vaine ... gold and gaine ... Honours glitt'ring shewes' (59; st. 48), 'the lusts of sinne' (76; st. 58), 'worldly lusts' (93; st. 58), and so on. The sexual temptations that plague him are suggested in the meditation 'Of Truth' in a story about 'how a holy Man / A Harlot did diuert from filthy quest' (155, st. 52). Once the 'holy Man' has converted the Harlot, the narrator turns to himself and confesses:

> Yet often my deceitfull heart I find
> Tempting me secretly such things to doe
> Which I should not dare venture in that kind,
> If some Man present were the same to know:
> Yet Truth the closest of them all to God doth show. (155; st. 55)

He is not explicit about the nature of 'such things to doe' but the context suggests that the Harlot's 'filthy quest' is closer to the narrator than he cares to admit.

In some sense, one of the purposes of the entire poem is to put this sinful view of sexuality into the larger context of a spiritual discourse. The speaker deliberately turns his back on the Harlot's filth but again and again insists on sexual images for spiritual concerns. The final meditation of 1621, 'Of Fortitude', thus returns to the central medieval metaphor of a court of Love which inspires the courageous:

> Love conquers all: oh! What can be compar'd
> To mightie Acts of Loue? whose iealous ire
> Consumes all that her Grace doe not regard,
> Oh! what is stronger than Loues hot desire?
> None e're without her did to noble acts aspire. (196; st. 16)

The third and fourth books of *The Brides Ornaments* first appeared in print in 1625. Although Padelford was unaware of this in 1936 when he wrongly assumed that 'these books awaited publication for over thirty years' ('Robert Aylett' 4), he corrected himself shortly thereafter in an addendum to his original study ('Robert Aylett: A Supplement' 471). Aylett first alluded directly to Canticles in the course of some of these meditations. The allusions ordinarily reflect a high degree of emotional intensity, with the sublimated sexuality barely veiled by the allegorical reading of the biblical verses. The narrator seems aware of his propensity for sexual sin and makes a conscious effort to control his 'lusts' by invoking a higher spiritual love. For him then, the allusions to the Song of Songs are a key to a spiritual quest which the *Brides Ornaments* takes upon itself to explicate again and again.

The first meditation of Book Three treats 'Heavenly Knowledge'. After describing knowledge as love's treasurer [sts 1–2], the narrator provides a discussion of knowledge in images of '*wealth* and *weapons*' (1; st. 3).[9] Knowledge in our postlapsarian world comes to us through the books of nature (or 'Creatures') and the Bible. Since human studies are but '*handmaids* to their *dame Diuinitie*' (3; st. 11), the narrator devotes his attention to that sort of knowledge, comparing it to flowers, the sun and various biblical events. He then moves back to his own sense of inadequacy and finds consolation in more biblical comparisons, especially the life of Solomon, who crowned his writing with the Song of Songs: 'And swanlike sang *Christs Churches Epithalamy*' (7; st. 26). After a tribute to James I as 'another *Salomon* . . . / A *David* who doth far and wide aduance, / His gracious scepter' (7; st. 27), the narrator returns to his own fallen condition:

> Alas! of *knowledge* here we haue no care,
> But all our *youth* in follies idely spend;
> Our strength in lusts and strifes away we weare;
> In *age* we worldly profit all intend. (9; st. 32)

As he proceeds to condemn man's concern with the pleasures of this life, he points to the role of knowledge in man's search for 'heav'nly Comfort' (9; st. 33). He concludes his praise for heavenly knowledge with images of food and drink taken from Canticles which lead to a description of the Church in terms of the bride of Solomon's Song:

> For this, shee is the *Bridegroomes darling Doue*,
> And vnto her that bare her, onely deare:
> For this the daughters, when they see her loue,
> And all the *Queenes* and *Wives* make merry cheere:
>   This makes her looke than *Sunne* and *Moone* more cleere,
>   Her *navell, belly, head, necke, brests* adorne;
> With these shee to her *husband* doth appeare,
> More *beautifull*, than is the fairest *morne*;
> Or faire like *twinning Ews*, on *Gilead* washt and shorne. (10; st. 37)

This description of knowledge as an ornament for the Bride is central to Aylett's view of his entire work. Each of the meditations is meant to be seen as an adornment for the Church, Christ's bride in standard allegorical readings of Canticles. Knowledge, however, is the eleventh meditation and only here is the connection between the Song of Songs and the general theme made explicit. Aylett generalizes about the Church, using images from Canticles (chapters 4 and 6) which do not correspond exactly to any particular verse. The bride, for example, is described in various sections of the Song. Aylett had rendered the beginning of chapter 4 as follows:

---

[9] *The Brides Ornaments* [Books 3 and 4]. Since this edition does not number the stanzas, I have added these.

> HOw fayre art thou my Loue! behold, how faire!
>   Within thy locks, thy Doues eyes shine most cleere:
> Like to a flocke of Goates is thy fine Haire,
> That from the Mount of *Gilead* appeare:
>   Thy Teeth be like a flocke of sheepe, that are
> Eu'n shorne, which from their washing vp doe come;
> And e'ry one amongst them twinnes doe beare,
> Amongst them barren (loe) there is not one,
>   Thy Lips, like scarlet Ribband, round about them shone.
>
> Thy speech is comely, and thy Temples are
> Within thy locks, like a Pomegranate side:
> Thy Necke is like the Tow'r that *Dauid* reare,
> On which a thousand shields doe hang beside,
>   (All shields of mightie men in armes well tride:)
> Thy Brests are like two twinling Roes, close by
> Feeding on Lillyes neere the Riuer side:
> Vntill the day appeares and shadowes flie
> In hills of Myrrhe and Mounts of Incense let me lie. (*Song* 6)

He rendered a repetition of this motif in chapter 6 as follows:

> Yet her, the Mothers onely happinesse,
> The choice of all her Mother bare beside,
> When as the Daughters saw, they praise and blesse;
> And all the Queenes and Concubines could doe no lesse.
>
> Who is't that lookes like Morne? faire as the Moone?
> Cleare as the Sunne? as banners terrible? (*Song* 10)

The imagery in his translation of Canticles is obviously more lavish and detailed than his allusion to this material in the meditation on knowledge. As a translator, Aylett added his own clarifications to the biblical verses to direct and control the reader's imagination. In his meditation, he selected the details that would recall the biblical passage without excessive physical detail. Thus the description of the bride's person is reduced from two entire stanzas in the translation to a few lines in stanza 37.

As the meditation on Heavenly Knowledge reaches a climax, the narrator attempts to raise the level of emotional intensity by shifting to metaphors of greater sensuous appeal. The model for the entire meditation is the career of Solomon whose works trace a development from natural science ('Who knew plants natures'), to Old Testament wisdom (the '*Uanitie*' of Ecclesiastes) associated with the fall, to '*Christs Churches Epithalamy*' (7; st. 26) or Canticles read allegorically through the New Testament. The meditation likewise moves from natural to moral and theological knowledge but transcends these concerns with a presentation of knowledge as the Church's adornments. This higher vision appears as sexual appeal interpreted in explicitly spiritual terms.

The Church, presented as the bride of Canticles, is an expression of the sublimated longing of the speaker, a kind of ideal, unattainable, angel-like woman. There is, however, a serious breakdown here between the various levels of meaning. The narrator makes use of the imagery of Canticles and yet stops short of explaining the relevance of the metaphors to the meditation. The language makes suggestions without clarifying such basic questions as the antecedent of the demonstrative pronouns that the reader must read as the meditation or its subject. Thus, for example, the poem is unclear as to the spiritual reference of 'This' ('This makes her looke than Sunne and Moone more cleere') or 'these' ('With these shee to her husband doth appeare') in the passage cited above (10; st. 37).

The discontinuity between the worlds of sexual reference (e.g. 'Her navell, belly, head, necke, brests') and spiritual meaning is inconclusive, very much like the tedious discourse of the poem from meditation to meditation. The narrator in a sense complains that he cannot cut or otherwise limit the length of his work: 'In this diuine most holy contemplation, / whereof I know not how to make an end' (9; st. 34). By treating sexuality as a means of achieving a spiritual end, the narrator maintains his original state of sexual longing and lust without allowing himself to realize the sexual potential of the imagery. The allegorical understanding of the relationship between bride and groom undermines the mutuality of the original biblical verse.[10] The abstraction that presumably adorns 'Her navell, belly, head, necke, brests' converts the bride's body into an object designed to fulfill a particular function: articulation of meaning. Sexuality for Aylett is thus a force that leads him from sinful masculine lust ('*idle wanton toyes*' [*Song* 1]) to a Christian who idolizes his Church in terms of sublimated libido, and who prays for a quasi-Ovidian metamorphosis that will allow him to become the object of heavenly rape:

> Thou . . .
> Canst make this *Knowledge* in mine heart abound,
> By one sparke of diuine illumination,
> And rauish my weake soule with heav'nly admiration. (*Brides* 10; st. 38)

The metaphor of heavenly rape is an integral part of the hierarchical structure of the traditional world Aylett inhabited. The concluding prayer in

---

[10] Thus the descriptions of the woman in the Song (4.1–5; 6.4–10; 7.1–9) are balanced by parallel descriptions of the lover (2.8–9; 5.10–16). One of Aylett's contemporaries, Giles Fletcher, used one of these parallels (5.11) as the basis for a description of Jesus in *Christ's Victorie, and Triumph*: 'His haire was blacke, and in small curls did twine, / As though it wear the shadow of some light . . .' ('Christ's Victorie on Earth', st. 8). See Hunter's *English Spenserians* 51.

the meditation on 'Heavenly Knowledge' recurs in slightly different form in 'Of Zeale and Godly Iealousie'. The shift in sexual identity merely reiterates the political and social structures that saw relations between the sexes as inherently unequal. Men were assumed to be superior to women just as God was above men. Since the Hebrew Bible stressed the similarity between the marriage covenant and the bond between God and men, it was easy enough to assume that God would relate to men the way men relate to women. Aylett's allegorization of Canticles supports this reading of the Bible.

In 'Of Zeale and Godly Iealousie', Aylett's speaker employs violent images of fire, passion and anger as he elaborates upon the significance of jealousy in Canticles. This meditation presents the most intense passions of the entire poem as the speaker attempts to relate the connections between holy and human love. The basic metaphor is, of course, biblical. The verse in Canticles about love and jealousy (8.6) is rendered as follows by Aylett in his translations at the outset of *The Brides Ornaments*:

> For Loue is strong as death, and Iealousie
> Cruell as graue; her coles be brands of fire,
> Whose raging flames consume most violently:
> No water can asswage her direfull ire,
>   Nor any floods can drowne her hot desire:
> No, though a man all that he hath would sell,
> And let himselfe for wages out to hire,
> Yet house and substance all shee would refell,
> Yea eu'n contemne: No worldly thing can Loue compell. (*Song* 13)

In the meditation on 'Iealousie' he returns to most of these images with only slight changes:

> Oh! *Loue* as strong as *Death* and *Jealousie*,
> Cruell as *graue*: Thy flames like coales of fire
> Consume and burne vp all most violently,
> No Streames or Flouds can quench her sacred ire,
>   Should we sell all we haue, we could not buy her. (*Brides* 14; st. 12)

The significance of the biblical metaphor is spelled out a few verses later:

> *God* often by an *Anthropopathy*,
> By which his nature best wee vnderstand,
> Ascribes vnto himselfe this *Iealousie*,
> As being link'd in *Hymens* holy band;
>   Vnto his *Church*, his *undefiled*: And
> His *Church* againe, to shew her feruent *Loue*,
> And *Ioy* thee takes in her new ioyned hand,
> Like *loue-sicke Bride* the *Bridegroome* oft doth proue,
> And him with *zeale* inuites her to imbrace and *Loue*. (*Brides* 15; st.15)

114

Jealousy then is a key to the emotional intensity of the meditation. God's love for his Church and for man's soul is akin to the possessiveness of human love. He is possessive in his insistence that no other gods be worshipped, and this is expressed from the point of view of women as well as men:

> The Daughter *zeale* is like the Mother free,
> Them both from *Heau'n* th'*Almightie* doth inspire,
> And therefore neither will affronted bee,
> With *Riualls*, Heathen *Gods* most base *Idolatree*. (*Brides* 14; st. 12)

From the male perspective, it is Christ who is jealous:

> No *Keeper* in *Christs* Vineyard must command,
> Hee will his Vineyard prune and dresse alone,
> Whereby his *Jealousie* wee vnderstand,
> His *Vine* the *Bridegroome* will haue drest of none,
> The *Bride* out of his presence neuer will be gone. (*Brides* 15; st. 17)

In this way the reference in Canticles to jealousy is interpreted on a spiritual level, connecting the feelings which seem merely human on the surface of the biblical text to something much more extended and complex.

The violence implicit in this divine jealousy has its counterpart in the passions of the speaker who goes well beyond the staid meditative calm of most of *The Brides Ornaments*. Aylett's narrator formally recognizes this early in the meditation:

> All other holy *Graces* disposition,
> By rules of *Art* I formerly define;
> But *Zeale* so feruent is no definition
> Can her containe, or bound in any line. (*Brides* 12; st. 5)

At the very outset of the meditation, the speaker introduces images of fire and violence that recall John Donne's Holy Sonnet 'Batter my heart, three person'd God'. Aylett begins:

> OH that some holy fire enlightening,
>   My Soule now rauish would with thoughts diuine,
>   Whilst I of *Iealousie*, *Loues* daughter sing,
> And godly *Zeale*, which like the *Sunne* doth shine. (*Brides* 11; st. 1)

The violence of 'rauish' brings to mind Donne's sestet in which the speaker, 'betroth'd unto your enemie' implores God to 'divorce' him:

> for I
> Except you 'enthrall mee, never shall be free,
> Nor ever chast, except you ravish mee. (344)

Although Aylett may have seen Donne's sonnet in manuscript, the metaphor is part of a shared tradition that associates sexual violation with the spiritual world. Aylett's image is, of course, much less striking than Donne's, yet the desire for violence expressed in the meditation is no less disturbing in its refusal to integrate sexual fulfilment into the spiritual life of the believer. The absence of any ongoing human interaction in the imagination of Aylett's narrator helps to transfer libido to the world of religious and meditative discourse. Nevertheless this sexually inspired energy enters the poem here by expanding upon biblical metaphors of marital relations between God and Israel. The conjugal problems of Israel as God's unfaithful wife were extended to articulate issues of power and control that the poets addressed in terms of ravishment. Aylett's speaker is thus anxious to be treated as a sexual object by God as a means of expressing his devotion.

Such a religious mythology, however, leads Aylett's narrator away from a more personalized, interactional religious model based on what Spenser established as 'married love'. The line that connects Spenser's *Amoretti* with Milton's praise of wedded love in *Paradise Lost* (4.750–70) is part of a movement toward spiritual fullness that included sexual fulfilment as part of a larger world of unified Puritan vision. Aylett's work provides a convenient summary of the literary and cultural tradition[11] that a poet such as Milton inherited in the 1620s and 1630s but outgrew in the 1640s.[12] It distinguishes between permitted and forbidden sexual pleasures in terms of a very sharp line:

> Oh *blessed fire*! if kindled aright,
> It burne with Loue of Heauen, and holy things,
> Retaining in our hearts, both day and night,
> His sweet imbraces, who is *King* of *Kings*,
> Loathing the worlds vaine wanton wicked dallyings. (*Brides* 18; st. 27)

---

[11] This tradition has both positive and negative ways of presenting sexuality. The positive images include an image of Truth as a naked woman: 'Here the glad Soules the face of beauty kisse, / Powr'd out in pleasure, on their beds of blisse . . . / That Angels sing, to tell their untould joyes; / Their understanding naked Truth, their wills / The all, and selfe-sufficient Goodnesse fills, / That nothing here is wanting, but the want of ills.' (Giles Fletcher, 'Christ's Triumph After Death,' st. 33–4, in Hunter's *English Spenserians* 102–3). Fletcher's brother Phineas avoids the carnal level of the allegory more completely than Aylett. Thus when he alludes to the woman who goes out into the night to seek her lover (Canticles 5.2–8), it is clear that he is referring to a search for Christ: 'in bed I sought by night, / But found not him in rest, nor rest without him. / . . . thy Turtle Dove / Seek on his cross: there, then, thus Love stands nail'd with love' ('[Vast Ocean of light.]' in Hunter's *English Spenserians* 391).

Negative presentations of sexuality abound in the Spenserian tradition. Spenser's 'Bower of Bliss' (*Faerie Queene* 2.12) is the model for Giles Fletcher's presentation of sexual temptation in 'Christ's Victorie on Earth': 'whear whiter Ladies naked went, / Melted in pleasure, and soft languishment, / And sunke in beds of roses, amourous glaunces sent' (st. 52, in *English Spenserians* 64). In a similar vein, Phineas Fletcher presents Sin as sexual enticement in *The Locusts, or Apollyonists* (st.13, *English Spenserians* 322).

[12] Padelford points out that if Aylett 'seems faintly prophetic of Milton, it is but one of many indications that Milton was consciously working in the tradition of the sacred epic and that he gave ultimate expression to the genre in *Paradise Lost, Paradise Regained*, and *Samson Agonistes* – a fact that seems completely to have escaped Miltonic scholars' ('Robert Aylett' 15–16).

Aylett's evocation of Spenser is thus a conservative attempt to ignore the newer kinds of social and cultural developments in the love ethic reflected in the use of the Song of Songs by other seventeenth-century poets. When he translated and attached Canticles to the first books of his long epic, Aylett established the biblical poem as a key to the significance of his meditations on the allegorical ladies at the court of the Queen of Heavenly Love or Charity. Language taken directly from Canticles helps to register the spiritual significance of the sexual tropes. The women are thus means used by the narrator to convey his ideas and as such they rarely portray independent characters. For Aylett, Spenser provided a narrative pattern in which to present Protestant ideology. Spenser's mythic binding of love and marriage in the *Amoretti*, which was to reshape western love poetry for hundreds of years, was of no apparent interest to his seventeenth-century imitator who was content to maintain his women on their pedestals that enshrined them as objects for the edification and gratification of the masculine narrator.

Aylett should be seen as a reflection of the contemporary interest in Spenser that would eventually lead to the work of Milton. His view of Spenser is superficially similar to Milton's and as such provides an important cultural link between the two major poets. Like other Spenserians such as Giles and Phineas Fletcher, Aylett took up the archaic surface of Spenser. He attempted to fashion a medieval love ethic that would articulate Protestant ideology with no concern about the possibilities for radical change implicit in the tradition. Aylett dressed his Calvinist doctrine in medieval imitations that share a superficial archaic surface with *The Faerie Queene* and steadfastly disregard the ways in which others were to shape Canticles into a text about the crisis in seventeenth-century English stability. When Aylett reissued *The Brides Ornaments* with only minor changes in 1654 he was reiterating positions about love, sexuality, religion and politics that corresponded to Calvinist orthodoxy first presented almost a century earlier.

Aylett and Milton both saw a need to deal with the initial chapters of Genesis as an expression of what served as a common view of Christian doctrine. For Aylett the hexaemeral material provided an example or background for the presentation of particular virtues. Thus 'Of Humilitie' presents 'Edens Garden' (*Song* 52; st. 22), 'Of Repentance' refers to the two edged sword which guards the Tree of Life after the fall (st. 42) and 'Of Hope' recalls God's promise 'to the Woman, that her seed, / Though Serpent bruis'd his heel, should break the Serpents head' (st. 17). In each case, however, the material he shared with Milton led Aylett in a conservative, somewhat reductive direction. Instead of Milton's complex woman, Aylett envisioned a 'simple Eue' about whom his narrator sighs:

> Oh! had Humilitie true Knowledge brought
> To *Eue*, before shee did commit this sinne! (*Song* 52; st. 23)

Aylett's meditations represent a claim to the role of seventeenth-century Spenserian poet with aspirations not unlike those of Milton. The elements of allegory, Spenserian stanza, Protestant meditation, and hexaemeral tradition make it clear that like Milton in *Reason of Church-Government*, he must have hoped: 'That what the greatest and choycest wits of *Athens*, *Rome*, or modern *Italy*, and those Hebrews of old did for their country, I in my proportion with this over and above of being a Christian, might doe for mine' (*Complete Prose* 1: 812).

As a very minor poet who aspired to the Spenserian epic mantle, Aylett sheds light on values and attitudes of Milton's generation that more talented writers obscure. Aylett points to ways in which Spenser's influence was felt and interpreted which, although quite distinct from the political and cultural directions that Milton followed, made use of similar materials and traditions. This is the case with regard to Aylett's use of Canticles. The biblical poem represents for him a political world similar to his own proto-medieval ideal. The allegory allows him to ignore the carnal imagery when convenient with little or no attention to the comparatively nonsexist mutuality of the Hebrew lyrics. The narrator's allegorized romantic quest for the Queen of Love takes poet and reader away from the tensions of seventeenth-century politics. Although this practice is in direct opposition to the use of Canticles by others, it articulates views commonly held in the early seventeenth century in England.

Aylett's approach to Spenser provides a view of a political and poetic mode available to Milton as well. The return to a reading of Canticles that is in accord with Origen's allegorizing stands in contrast to the direction that Milton would take, just as the political and cultural world of the *Bride's Ornaments* is largely detached from consciousness of the changes that the times were imposing. Although most written testimony from the period insists upon an allegorical reading of Canticles, there is evidence of various kinds of carnal reading of the biblical text. George Scheper quotes from the Assembly *Annotations* on one erotic passage in Canticles (5.4): 'It is shameful to mention what foul ugly rottenness some have belched here . . .' Scheper likewise cites the disapproval of the theologian Nathanael Homes: 'away, say we, with all carnal thoughts, whiles we have heavenly things presented us under the notion of Kisses, Lips, Breasts, Navel, Thighs, Leggs. Our minds must be above our selves, altogether minding heavenly meanings' (558). Despite the purpose of these commentators, they provide clear evidence that some of their contemporaries were interpreting Canticles in a carnal fashion. Aylett's practices continue and extend the traditional allegory explored by Baldwin during the previous century. Like Baldwin, Aylett maintained a balance between the dichotomies of oral and written, carnal and allegorical, but by the middle of the seventeenth century, this balance had become much more precarious. The final chapters of this study will examine in detail just how the Canticles tradition shifted significantly, first in the works of a sect known as Ranters, and finally in Milton.

Milton's presentation of love and sexuality in *Paradise Lost* can be read in terms of the contrast between the allegorical approach to Canticles in Aylett and the carnal interpretations referred to by Scheper and given expression by the Ranters. Aylett's allegory is based upon that of Origen which must have appealed strongly to Milton in the 1630s while he was contemplating remaining celibate. In the 1640s, however, Milton decided to marry and, in *Doctrine and Discipline of Divorce*, reserved Origen's castrating knife for those who opposed his views on divorce: 'And if then [after reading Matthew 19.12] he please to make use of *Origens* knife, he may doe well to be his own carver' (*Complete Prose* 2: 334). Instead of reading Canticles allegorically in *Paradise Lost*, Milton had Adam take over its language in his love song to Eve at the beginning of Book 5. This song is, of course, replete with ironies, some of which depend upon the spiritual implications of allegorizing texts like Aylett's. In the end, however, Milton's verse balances traditional allegorizing with the oral version of a carnal interpretation of Canticles not unlike Homes's rejected thoughts or the Ranters. Milton had no use for the fears of sexuality expressed by Homes. He saw Eros as an integral part of the human condition which led to Agape when properly experienced. He bent the Spenserian tradition away from a focus on woman as enshrined allegorical object which essentially looked back to a world-view more in accord with the past than the present. Nonetheless, Aylett's work reflects the poetic world that nurtured Milton in his youth. It testifies to the existence of a tradition that links Milton's biblical epic to Spenser, even as it clarifies just how far *Paradise Lost* had to go before it could transcend this facet of the Spenserian tradition.

Chapter 5

RANTER SEXUAL POLITICS: CANTICLES IN THE ENGLAND OF 1650

DURING the century or so that elapsed after the publishing of Baldwin's *Canticles*, English society knew many periods of political stress that were reflected in literary and religious activity of all kinds. We have seen in some detail how Baldwin's work can be understood as fomenting or even effecting the political and social events of the late 1540s, and have traced the direct and indirect pressures of his poems on works by Spenser, Shakespeare and Aylett. The political, religious and social crises of mid-seventeenth-century England are, like the beginnings of the English reformation in Baldwin's time, reflected in the use of language from Canticles by writers whose millenarian and antinomian beliefs were at the fringes of the Puritan movement. The larger issues that Englishmen were fervently debating concerned the nature of political reality and constitutional rights, the extent and scope of the Protestant reformation, as well as social and economic tensions that included in some cases an assault on public sexual mores not unlike the so-called sexual revolution of the late twentieth century. People who became known as Ranters expressed views about each of these issues, and, by their dramatic use of language, they in effect used the hermeneutic tools of more conservative Puritans to call for a revolution that was almost universally condemned by their contemporaries. Their allusive references to biblical language in general and to the Song of Songs in particular epitomize attitudes to politics, religion and social mores, and provide striking illustrations of ways in which a crisis in language has unmistakable effects on the culture which produces and uses it.

The metaphorical world of the people who were styled 'Ranters'[1] seems to

---

[1] This group received little critical attention before the highly influential work of historians such as Norman Cohn and Christopher Hill. A. L. Morton first published his full length study of the Ranters in 1970. As a result of their work, many others have focused various kinds of attention on groups like the Ranters. More recent studies like those of Jerome Friedman and James Turner extend the discussion. As opposed to these studies, that of J. C. Davis raises serious questions about the existence of the group 'as a movement'. He argues that 'the Ranters were a public mask, almost dissociated from real people, but, nevertheless, performing a public rôle and function. As with witchcraft, once fear and anger had been

have encouraged simultaneous consideration of the material and the spiritual. Their written works provide some evidence of this but it is crucial to recognize that much of Ranter discourse probably developed in what were primarily oral contexts. Many of the written texts manifest indications of an underlying orality. This goes beyond the clear-cut situations in which the written text presents a narrative about a meeting during which certain words were spoken. There was a need for an aura of secrecy about those aspects of Ranter activities most threatening to more conservative Puritans. This fostered the development of a style that conveyed different messages to readers and listeners of varying familiarity with their ideas and practices. Use of Canticles thus became both a measure of the ways in which these people expressed themselves as well as a tool for presenting the various messages and meanings they wanted to convey so as to articulate a balance between a series of antinomies such as secrecy and revelation, carnality and spirituality, and, implicitly at least, orality and textuality.

Within the context of these balances, the Ranter tracts provide an indication of a slight yet significant shift in attitude toward an understanding of and approach to Canticles. Whereas earlier writers would occasionally allow sexual aspects of the biblical poems to appear momentarily as part of the tension necessary to produce requisite spiritual and poetic insights, the Ranters can be read as primarily concerned with the carnal level of these texts. Their balance seems to make use of the spiritual readings that had accrued to the Song of Songs in order to deepen and extend the significance of sexual activity. Canticles provided the Ranters with a series of important texts used to articulate their view of the world. Although other biblical quotations also recur frequently in Ranter discourse, references to Solomon's Song appear in contexts that are clearly important yet which do not reveal their significance in an ordinary or straightforward manner. Although the allusions can be taken allegorically, understood sexually, they help to intimate doctrines about the relationship between sexual experience and spiritual liberty. In some sense, then, both the natural and spiritual levels of the intertexts from Canticles are essential for an understanding of Ranter discourse. This view of the Ranters depends on a careful sifting of the evidence available to us about them.

---

aroused and the mechanisms of discipline were in place, victims had to be found' (136). Although few historians have been willing to accept Davis's views (cf. Hawes 45–7, Holstun 211–16) his cautions about how to read the extant documents are worth considering, if only as a means of weighing the evidence more closely. Nigel Smith has pointed out that even if one accepts Davis's 'subtle and astute attempt to show that the Ranters were not a movement... if the Ranters were a fiction, they were one of their own as well as of others' making' (*Perfection Proclaimed*, 8–9n). Thus, whether real historical force or merely 'a public mask', Ranter texts and approaches to other texts remain striking and impressive. The literary and hermeneutical implications of the textual practices developed in Ranter documents are the primary concern of this chapter.

Kisses of their Mouths

The Ranters first surfaced on the English scene in the late 1640s. In his seminal study of these people, A. L. Morton discusses their political radicalism, yet finds 'in them all the signs of a revolution in retreat, an abandonment of the rational hope that had inspired men like Overton and Walwyn, a realisation that they were calling upon their last resources when everything else had failed' (18). Such a position neglects the intense mood of millenarian anticipation that the Ranters shared with other more orthodox Puritans.[2] Earlier in the century, Thomas Brightman's commentary on Canticles had predicted that 'if you desire the time of this conversion [of the Jews]: God hath very much concealed the moments of time from us . . . But as neer as we can attain to it by conjectures, (and those not light, as they seem to me) it is to be expected about the yeer 1650' (1051).[3] Brightman's student, Nathanael Homes (or Holmes) wrote a commentary on Canticles which he published in 1652 with the rest of his works. Homes was a millenarian and involved in the movement to readmit the Jews to England.[4] The connection between millennial expectation and an interest in Canticles helps to explain the spiritual excitement of a whole range of seventeenth-century English Protestants that includes the Ranters at one extreme. Although the theology of Ranter leaders, such as Joseph Salmon, went considerably beyond the naive anticipation of an immediate end to time and the world, most of their contemporaries were unwilling to relinquish a belief in imminent apocalypse. As mid-century approached, English millenarians were girding themselves for the last days and their language reflects this tendency. Ranter discourse is thus very far from conveying a mood of defeat. The social and political significance of their doctrines is in some sense secondary to the intense involvement in denying the significance of the entire material universe that ultimately informs these tracts.

The extant Ranter texts introduce a series of methodological problems that must be confronted before going on to illustrate the significance of particular

---

[2] See Nigel Smith's introduction to his very important *Collection of Ranter Writings* (9–10). In citing Ranter texts I shall indicate the pagination of the original work and then provide bracketed references to Smith's anthology whenever he has reprinted the text under consideration.

[3] Although Brightman's works had originally appeared in Latin early in the century, this citation is from a translation published in 1644. The original Latin read: 'Si quaeris ad quod tempus erit haec prima conversio, Momenta temporum celavit nos Deus ut plurimum. Hujus tamen certam in scripturis designationem arbitror, cui dies appropinquans clariorem lucem afferet, Dan.12,4. &c. Sed quantum conjecturis assequi possimus, iisque non levibus, ut mihi videntur, expectanda est ad annum MDCL' (Thomae Brightmanni, *Commentarius in Cantica Canticorum Salomonis, Analysi & Scholiis illustratus* . . . [Basileae, 1614], 119r [wrongly paginated '120' in Huntington Library copy]).

[4] See Fixler, 238. For correspondence between Homes and Manasseh ben Israel, see Lucien Wolf, 'Introduction,' *Manasseh Ben Israel's Mission to Oliver Cromwell* . . . (London: Macmillan, 1901), xxv–xxvi, lxxx–lxxxii. More recently, David S. Katz discusses Homes and Brightman in his *Philo-Semitism* (98–107).

doctrines. In one sense, attention to the Ranters demands of its students a recognition of the essential orality of the material treated. We must assume that most mid-century English readers who knew about the Ranters in any detail, had access to oral reports about the group that were never recorded in print. There are, in fact, at least three different categories of primary source about the Ranters. Some provide open attacks and, in so doing, summarize the views they wished to condemn. These can hardly serve as objective sources. Other works, written by Ranters themselves, must be examined carefully to ensure that the author was in fact a Ranter at the time the piece was written. In a great many of the extant works the writer refers to himself as a 'late fellow Ranter'.[5] Such texts are at least partially suspect because the speaker is often interested in discrediting the group whose tenets he no longer accepts. This kind of writing is complicated to evaluate because while it presents material from the perspective of personal experience, and thus provides a first-hand account of events, it is nevertheless of limited accuracy because of the stated desire to illustrate the errors of the writer's previous ways.[6] The third category consists of works written by Ranters convinced of the truth of their arguments at the moment of writing. This includes books by Laurence Clarkson, Abiezer Coppe and Joseph Salmon, and in these the air of secrecy in the written discourse often suggests that the writer is hiding as much as he is revealing. Only this third category can be taken as direct evidence for Ranter positions and ideas, even though the other kinds of material can provide significant testimony.[7] Presumably contemporaries who wanted to hear more about Ranter ideas would have been forced to contact the writers and attend the meetings for themselves. Today we must be wary not to assume that the surviving texts provide us with more than a series of fragments about the essence of the group's ideas.

This distinction between different categories of written evidence implies an additional factor that introduces further complication. Although we must

---

[5] E.g. Gilbert Roulston on the title page of *The Ranter's Bible, Or, Seven several Religions by them held and maintain'd* . . . (London, 1650).

[6] Thus J. M. identified himself as '(a deluded Brother) lately escaped out of their snare' on the title page of *The Ranters Last Sermon* . . . (London, 1654).

[7] The methodological distinctions here are often disregarded by scholars who have made important contributions to recent study of the Ranters. For example, James Turner's seminal *One Flesh* mixes references to works by Ranters and anti-Ranters in an extended discussion of the group's practices. In a reference to a paper of mine on which the present chapter is largely based, Turner uses the ex-Ranter M. Stubs to substantiate a reference to supposed 'communal orgies' (84–5, n. 75). As I shall indicate further on, I suspect that he is correct that such activities probably took place, but the blurring of distinctions between the nature of the various sources is unfortunate. Turner's language implies as much but fails to clarify. Thus his reference to 'the authentic Ranters Abiezer Coppe and Laurence Clarkson' (88) implicitly distinguishes between the other sources and these 'authentic' examples of what he terms his 'composite portrait of the Paradisal eroticist' (85). Nevertheless, in his account of Coppe and Clarkson, Turner integrates references from their Ranter works with what they wrote subsequently (88, 92) with no attempt to make methodological distinctions between them.

depend almost exclusively upon written documents for evidence about ideas in earlier civilizations, it is neither feasible nor possible to find an exact literary pedigree for each one. Such an admission, however, should not be regarded as a temporary excuse to be used only when written evidence is lacking. The survival of published documents about particular religious and theological ideas is largely the result of chance. If we assume that a particular text depicts an idea or movement definitively, we disregard the primarily oral provenance of most such imaginative forces in the Middle Ages and Renaissance. It is therefore important to consider the theoretical implications of the non-written or oral aspect of a movement such as the Ranters. Since there is, however, no available evidence that is not written, it will be necessary to arrive at an estimate of the orality of Ranter discourse on the basis of those written texts that have survived.

An important ploy used by various Ranter leaders involved subversion of traditional approaches to biblical texts so as to make their radically different new readings appear to be reasonable understandings of Scripture. Although this stratagem served to justify their ideological positions, it also legitimized a biblical hermeneutic that was tied to the original Hebrew and Greek texts in only an associative or impressionistic fashion. It also led the way to the doctrine of the 'inner light', which Quakers viewed as no less reliable than the Bible. One instance of such subversion appears in Joseph Salmon's treatment of the nuptial metaphor in the Bible. Biblical prose and verse present relations between God and 'his people' in terms of a marriage, in which Israel is expected to be a faithful wife to God, and any worship of other gods is described as whoredom and fornication.[8] In his *Antichrist in Man*, Salmon referred to '*fornication* with the *great whore*, the wisdom of the flesh; attributing all *power, glory, salvation* and *happines* to selfish wisdome' (12). The 'carnall wisdom' that he rejected as fornication is traditional religion. He explained that

> it is a property of a *Strumpet* to pretend what she doth not intend to her *Lovers*: behold a Character of the *Mother of Harlots*, thy fleshly wisdom . . . she alwaies pretends, what she never intends: So that here, all is well in the history, but meer deceit and delusion in the *mystery*; this *whore*, she will present a glorious shew, but there is nothing but wickednes and harlotry intended . . . Now therefore know, O Christian! that this *whore* appears to thee in all thy spiritual *performances*, and *sacrifices* to the *Lord*. (13–14)

In some sense then, the traditional Puritan, certain of his religious way, was condemned by Salmon as a fornicator, while, according to Laurence Clarkson's *A Single Eye*, a Ranter who engaged in extra-marital sex 'in light

---

[8] E.g. Exodus 34.11–17, Deuteronomy 31.16–22, Hosea chapters 1–4 and Ezekiel 16.23–9. All biblical citations in this chapter are to the Authorized Version. I have not, however, changed any of the Ranter biblical references which occasionally differ slightly from this translation.

and love, is light, and lovely . . . for love in light is so pure, that a whore it cannot indure, but estranges it self from darknesse from whence whoredom has its first original' (10 [Smith, *Collection* 170–1]).[9]

The most explicit theoretical statement about the relationship between language and the spiritual mindset of the Ranters comes in tracts by Abiezer Coppe. Whereas Laurence Clarkson tried to protect himself from persecution for his views by keeping *A Single Eye* somewhat anonymous, Coppe openly acknowledged the tracts he wrote as a Ranter. Nevertheless, he was much more secretive about his views and ideas. He vacillated between a strong drive to tell all and an equally powerful sense of the secrecy of his message.

Abiezer Coppe was definitely a Ranter in 1649 when he published *Some Sweet Sips of Some Spirituall Wine* as well as his *A Fiery Flying Roll* and *A Second Fiery Flying Roule*. Nigel Smith describes *Some Sweet Sips* as 'fiercely critical of formalised religion . . . and excitedly Antinomian, but also stressing the sublimity of God in man and in nature. It is Coppe's first deeply pantheistic statement' (*Collection* 12). Coppe's discourse establishes recurrent motifs that seem to be urging a traditional approach to religious spirituality as opposed to carnal experience. There are places, however, where this façade disappears momentarily and then the reader discovers the unmistakable political point of the reference. For example, Coppe reinterprets the allegory of Hagar and Sarah which Paul had fashioned to distinguish between Jewish Law and Christian freedom (Galatians 4.21–31) into undisguised praise for Libertinism:

> Isaac is the heire, (the son of the *freewoman*, not *Ismael* the son of the *bondwoman*[ )][10] . . . but the son of the *freewoman* who is free, and very free too – is also free from persecuting any – so, and more then so, the son of the *freewoman* is a Libertine – even he who is of the *freewoman*, who is borne after the Spirit. (17–18 [Smith, *Collection* 55])

Chapter IV concludes with an equally clear rejection of Anglican hierarchies and Presbyterian elders:

> Thus saith the Lord, I will recover my Vineyard out of the hands of all *Husbandmen* and be *Pastor* my Self, and my people shall know no Arch-Bishop, Bishop, &c. but my Self. This you will believe and assent to (dear hearts, at first

---

[9] Clarkson acknowledged writing this pamphlet published under the initials L. C. in *The Lost Sheep Found* (26 [Smith, *Collection* 181]). There he described his previous life and beliefs along with a great many details about his Ranter experience, including his refusal to admit to having written *A Single Eye* when confronted by a committee of Parliament (30 [Smith, *Collection* 184]). Testimony from *The Lost Sheep Found* must, of course, be regarded as similar to works of other 'late fellow Ranters' and does not have the same testimonial validity as *A Single Eye* which was written when Clarkson was still a believing Ranter.

[10] I follow Smith's addition of the closing parenthesis which is missing in Coppe's text. Where Clarkson or Coppe used brackets, I have supplied { } in order to distinguish between later editorial comment (such as Smith's or my own) and Ranter use of unusual typography.

dash;) But they shall know no Pastor (neither) *Teacher, Elder,* or *Presbyter,* but the Lord, that Spirit. (21 [Smith, *Collection* 56])

The radical nature of the political position here becomes most clear with the rejection of 'the *Sword* of the *Lord Generall*' (i.e. Cromwell) at the very end of the chapter (21-2 [Smith, *Collection* 56]).

In his pamphlets *Some Sweet Sips of Some Spirituall Wine* and *A Fiery Flying Roll,* Coppe encouraged his readers to go beyond the conventions of language and religion in anticipating a new order. Established words and symbols take on new meanings and subvert the old forms with hints at something new. The actual words, however, are always ambiguous and incomplete, and thus suggest that the printed text contains only a small part of the message of the prophet. The written word serves to undermine its own conventional world and prepares the reader for an experience that the writer cannot (or will not) articulate in full.

Coppe's 'Epistle I' in *Some Sweet Sips* begins with a series of paradoxes that underscore the difficulty of understanding the message. It contains 'some things hard to be understood, which they that are *Unlearned,* and unstable, wrest: as they doe also the other Scriptures, unto their own destruction' (1, [Smith, *Collection* 47]). The language is to be biblical but without citation of 'Book, Chapter, and Verse' because 'the *Father* would have it so; And I partly know his designe in it; And heare him secretly whispering in me the reason thereof: Which I must (yet) burie in silence, till—' (2 [Smith, *Collection* 47]). This motif of secrecy suggests that God will soon allow his prophet to reveal the truth, but at no point does Coppe clarify his idea. In fact, his very words imply that language itself is part of the old way which is to be abandoned. A voice in his text advocates a series of shifts, each of which connotes an increase in spirituality: 'Here is the voyce of one crying; Arise out of *Flesh,* into *Spirit*; out of *Form,* into *Power*; out of *Typs,* into *Truth*; out of the *Shadow,* into the *Substance*; out of the *Signe,* into the thing *Signified*' (2-3 [Smith, *Collection* 47-8]). The new order that is intimated here is one that cannot be captured in '*Form*' or '*Typs*' or '*Signes.*' Coppe wanted to go beyond the limitations of conventional religion and language in order to apprehend spiritual reality with no intermediary. Although this longing to transcend the earthly may seem to conform to Puritan orthodoxy, the voice sets up a whole series of antinomian heresies. Since the aim is to move from sign to signified, there is a point in the text that words and language itself must be abandoned as mere signs. The meaning of language is thus related to its words or signs, but the voice commands the listener to arise 'out of the *Signe,* into the thing *Signified*' and thus intimates that one can apprehend the signified without sign or language. The relationship between word and meaning is seriously questioned.

This prepares the way for Coppe and his fellow Ranters to establish their own procedures for subverting biblical language with no sense of commitment to traditional understandings of meaning. While his frequent references to libertinism suggest a positive orientation to carnal experience, he continually rejects the flesh. He explains that the spiritual condition of a particular action is determined by the spirit of the doer, not by the action itself. Thus he can be pure in doing something which would be wrong for a less spiritually prepared person. Later in *Some Sweet Sips* he explains to his '*Cronies at Oxford*' that 'there be five Tenses or Times: there is a Time to be merry {*To be merry in the Lord*} and that is the Present Tense with some, to others the Future' (37 [Smith, *Collection* 62]). His merrymaking is in the present while others must wait until some point in the future before they can begin. Elsewhere he describes this merrymaking as a return '*Home, to the Inside, heart, Graine. To the finest wheate-flower, and the pure bloud of the grape; To the fatted calfe, ring, shoes, mirth, and Musicke, &c. which is the Lords Supper indeed*' (46 [Smith, *Collection* 66]).

The intertext from Canticles is therefore very much like the Ranter position it is meant to articulate. It seems to have a traditional allegorical meaning yet the speaker in Coppe's text undermines the validity of such an interpretation both directly and implicitly. He establishes himself as part of God and includes the whole spectrum of English Christianity from '*The Kings . . . and the Bishops* & the *Priests*' to 'the *Seekers, and the Family of Loves*' (8 [Smith, *Collection* 50]), in his personal disclaimer that simultaneously denies and claims divinity: 'I am, or would be nothing. But by the grace of God I am what I am' (7 [Smith, *Collection* 49–50]). Although other Ranter texts allude more directly to the sexual level of Canticles, in *Some Sweet Sips*, Coppe was secretive about such clear articulation.

On the other hand, he cautioned, 'arise, but rise not till the *Lord* awaken thee. I could wish he would doe it by himselfe, immediately: But if by these, mediately. His will be done' (3 [Smith, *Collection* 48]). That is, it would be better for the reader to perceive these truths without the intervention of the written text, which is also a collection of signs. If this perception is not possible, however, the speaker is resigned to God's will. This, of course, returns the reader to the secrecy motif, since one can hardly understand what is signified by means of signs that ultimately refuse to reveal their significance.

On one level it is clear that this motif of secrecy is a reflection of Coppe's implicit objections to a reasoned discourse fully revealed to the public. It is a consequence of translating oral sermons into written prose that was, by definition, potentially available to anyone able to read. The form of the discourse thus reflects its political and ideological perspectives. Views expressed about sexuality and the Jews turn out to be part of an antinomian system of biblical references that reduces all human experience to the inner world of the Ranter's imagination. As the actions that accompany the ideology become manipulative, they also become increasingly dehumanized.[11]

---

[11] Cf. Norman Cohn (especially 281–6) who suggests a connection between revolutionary millenarianism and twentieth-century phenomena such as Nazism and Communism. James

Kisses of their Mouths

Basic to Ranter doctrine is an insistence on liberty that most contemporaries must have regarded as blasphemous and licentious. The explicit testimony that we have is often colourful and sensational. Gilbert Roulston, who referred to himself as 'a late Fellow-RANTER' on the title page of *The Ranters Bible*, described a Ranter gathering which supposedly took place on 16 November 1650:

> *A great Company of these new Generations of Vipers, called* Ranters, *were gathered together near the Soho as Westminster, where they exercised themselves in many royatous and uncivil actions; and after some hours spent in feasting and the like, they stript themselves quite naked, and dansing the* Adamites Curranto, *which was, That after 2. or 3. familist Giggs, hand in hand, each man should imbrace his fellow-female, in the flesh, for the acting of that inhumane* Theatre of carnal copulation, *which is so gloriously illustrated in the sacred Scriptures, to be one of the greatest sins, in bringing them to the very brinks of perpetual damnation; in defence of which abominable and lascivious act, they hold it a tenent lawful, to lie with any woman whatsoever: These are a sort of* Ranters, *called by the name,* Of the Familists of Love, *who would have all things common, and hold it a* Paradice *to live so, because their Discipline allowes, to court naked, in which they blush no more, then* Adam *at his first Creation, Gen. 2.5.* (2)

Their emphasis on sexual freedom evidently made the Ranters simultaneously attractive and repellent to most Englishmen. Morton reports that 'Parliament set up a Committee to inquire into the Ranters and other heretical groups' (102), but also quotes George Fox who claimed in his *Journal* that Justice Hotham had 'said, if God had not raised up this principle of light and life [i.e. Fox's Quakerism], the nation had been overspread with Ranterism and all the Justices in the nation could not stop it with all their laws, because they would have done and said as they commanded them and yet kept their principle still' (110). Fox's testimony must be taken in its context and understood to reflect a sustained effort on his part to distinguish between early Quakers and Ranterism. Many contemporaries grouped them together because, aside from sexuality, their ideologies were often strikingly similar.

The testimony of the many anti-Ranter tracts is quite explicit about the sexual practices of the group, but as Morton suggests, there is something very

---

Holstun rejects Cohn's view of the Ranters 'as instances of group psychosis' (210) and cites Christopher Hill's reading of Cohn in terms of 'the rhetoric of the cold war era' (210). Clement Hawes is careful to distinguish his own theoretically complex account of 'manic rhetoric [which] provides a transindividual framework for the seemingly inescapable metaphor of vision . . . a collective way of seeing and not seeing, rather than a merely individual pyschic mode' (14) from what he sees as Cohn's reduction of 'the ideologies of popular protest to the terms of individual psychopathology' (45). I would nevertheless argue that despite the significant critical insights of Holstun's article and the brilliant analysis of Ranter texts in Hawes's extended study, Cohn's claims about the dangers of apocalyptic thought and rhetoric retain a certain degree of validity.

unreliable about these documents: 'Much of the evidence is, of course, hearsay and grossly prejudiced. We may well doubt the report that at a meeting in Shoemakers Alley their time was spent "in drunkenness, uncleanness, blasphemous words, filthy songs, and mixt dances of men and women stark naked"' (81). The radical Digger, Gerrard Winstanley, was perhaps less prejudiced a source, yet he too was bitter about Ranter sexuality. In his *Vindication of those . . . called Diggers*, Winstanley complained about 'the immoderate use of creatures, or the excessive community of women called Ranting, or rather Renting' (title page). This pamphlet was evidently written after permissive sexual practices had caused the Digger leader to force the uninhibited Ranters out of his radical commune. Other less sophisticated attacks are filled with accusations about sexual orgies and similar practices, much of which may have been highly exaggerated.

The works of former Ranters likewise abound with references to sexual license. Morton refers to a work of Laurence Clarkson to show 'that at times a ritual nudism may have been practised as a symbol of their liberation from the bondage of the moral law' (81). A typical example of an attack on the Ranters by 'a late fellow-Ranter' appears in *The Ranters Declaration*:

> On the 9 of this instant *Decemb.* a great Company of the new Generation of *Ranters*, assembled together near the *White Lyon* in *Pelicoat-lane* [sic], where they entred into a large dispute, concerning the exaltation of their jolities, affirming, that that man who tipples deepest, swears the frequentest, commits adultery, incest, or buggers the oftenest, blasphemes the impudentest, and perpetrates the most notorious crimes, with the highest hand, and rigedest resolution, is the dearest darling to be gloriously placed in the tribunal Throne of Heaven, holding this detestable Opinion, (equalizing themselves with our blessed Redeemer) that it is lawful for them to drink healths to their Brother *Christ*, and that in the bonsing off of their liquor, each Brother ought to take his Fellow-Female upon his knee, saying, *Let us lie down and multiply*, holding this lascivious action to be the chief motive of their salvation, *&c.* (2)

When the complaints of both the anti-Ranters and the 'late-fellow Ranters' are compared with statements of practising members of the sect, it becomes clear that while many of the details referred to by detractors may have been exaggerated, there was probably more involved here than what Morton calls 'ritual nudism'. Thus Laurence Clarkson's *A Single Eye* was nearly explicit about the spiritual importance of extra-marital sexual activity. In order to communicate his idea of monistic wholeness, Clarkson preached a gospel of spirituality predicated on the subversion of Puritan orthodoxy. One must become 'that lovely pure one who beholds nothing but purity, wheresoever it goeth, and whatsoever it doth, all is sweet and lovely . . . so that Devil is God, Hell is Heaven, sin Holiness, Damnation Salvation, this and only this is the First Resurrection'. To experience 'the second Resurrection' however, these general antinomies were to have been acted upon:

therefore till acted that so called Sin, thou art not delivered from the power of sin . . . So that I say, till flesh be made Spirit, and Spirit flesh, so not two, but one, thou art in perfect bondage: for without vail, I declare that whosoever doth attempt to act from flesh, in flesh, to flesh, hath, is, and will commit Adultry: but to bring this to a period, for my part, till I acted that, so called sin, I could not predominate over sin; so that now whatsoever I act, is not in relation to the Title, to the Flesh, but that Eternity in me. (13–14 [Smith, *Collection* 173])

Clarkson was insisting on the spiritual significance of sexual activity, and used religious language to make his antinomian point. Nouns such as 'spirit', 'flesh' and 'sin' thus take on double meaning as the spirituality of the actor is supposed to distinguish between 'Adultry' and 'Eternity'.

Clarkson's discourse in *A Single Eye* is as close as Ranter texts get to unambiguous accounts of their sexual ideology. The anti-Ranter tracts provide more explicit accounts of supposed Ranter meetings. Thus the anonymous *Ranter's Religion* lists the following as the one of the chief of the sect's 'horrid Blasphemies':

They affirme that all Women ought to be in common, and when they are assembled altogether (this a known truth) they first entertaine one another, the men those of their own sex, and the Women their fellow females: with horrid Oathes and execrations, then they fall to bowzing, and drinke deep healths (Oh cursed Caitiffes!) to their Brother God, and their Brother Devill; then being well heated with Liquor, each Brother takes his she Otter [?] upon his knee, and the word (spoken in derision of the sacred Writ) being given, *viz. Increase and Multiply*: they fall to their lascivious imbraces, with a joynt motion, &c.' (5)

The account of this anonymous critic is not far removed in spirit from Clarkson's own recollection in *The Lost Sheep Found*:

I was moved to write to the world what my Principle was, so brought to publick view a Book called *The Single Eye*, so that men and women came from many parts to see my face, and hear my knowledge in these things, being restless till they were made free, as then we called it. Now I being as they said, *Captain of the Rant*, I had most of the principle women came to my lodging for knowledge, which then was called *The Head-quarters*. (26 [Smith, *Collection* 181]).

The similarity, however, is primarily the result of the desire of both writers to discredit the Ranters. By 1660 Clarkson was no longer a Ranter and was doing his best to earn the approval of the Muggletonians. That which *The Ranter's Religion* and *The Lost Sheep Found* deride as 'lascivious imbraces' and 'filthy lust' appears very different in *A Single Eye*. There remains considerable rhetorical force in the language of *A Single Eye* that avoids the crude mockery of the anti-Ranter texts by juxtaposing implicitly sexual references with spiritual or transcendent terms: 'so that now whatsoever I act, is not in relation to the Title, to the Flesh, but that Eternity in me' (14 [Smith, *Collection* 173]). This tactic is similar to the practice of other Ranters such as

Joseph Salmon and Abiezer Coppe whose works were somewhat more careful to preserve the balance between secrecy and revelation.

The women with whom Clarkson had sexual relations were theoretically taking part in an act that was not significant in itself, but meaningful instead in terms of its import for the male speaker. Ten years later, Clarkson looked back at his career as a Ranter and ignored anything that was elevating and admirable about the experience. Instead he focused upon the degradation and manipulativeness of his sexual exploits. In one memorable passage in *The Lost Sheep Found*, a pamphlet that should be read with critical scrutiny because of his rhetorical purposes in publishing it, he recalled his misuse of the kind of preaching he had described in his previous pamphlet:

> So coming to *Canterbury* there was some six of this way, amongst whom was a maid of pretty knowledge, who with my Doctrine was affected, and I affected to lye with her, so that night prevailed, and satisfied my lust, afterwards the mayd was highly in love with me, and as gladly would I have been shut of her, lest some danger had ensued, so not knowing I had a wife she was in hopes to marry me, and so would have me lodge with her again, which fain I would, but durst not, then she was afraid I would deceive her, and would travel with me, but by subtilty of reason I perswaded her to have patience, while I went into *Suffolk*, and setled my occasions, then I would come and marry her, so for the present we parted, and full glad was I that I was from her delivered . . . and then I heard the maid had been in those parts to seek me, but not hearing of me, returned home again, and not long after was married to one of that sect, and so there was an end of any further progress into Kent. (22–3 [Smith, *Collection* 178–9])

The personal revelations discovered here must, of course, be taken as part of Clarkson's general purpose in this tract. He wished to discredit his earlier experiences in the eyes of his readers; thus he avoided the excited spirituality of *A Single Eye*. Nevertheless, it is not likely that the manipulative psychology portrayed here is totally untrue to what Clarkson felt in 1650. It would seem to corroborate what Winstanley claimed in 1649 as he warned women:

> Therefore you women beware, for this ranting practice is not the restoring, but the destroying power of the creation . . . This Ranting power, or god, is full of sutletie to deceive others of what they can, and is a nurse of hardnesse of heart against others, when he hath deceived them, for this is his nature, to gets what he can from others, labours to eat up other and make them poore, and then to laugh and rejoyce in others poverty. (G2v–G3r)

Clarkson's comments in 1660 about the manipulative nature of his earlier sexual exploits are part of the satirical, perhaps even ironical tone of *The Lost Sheep Found*. *A Single Eye* is highly mystical and concerned with Ranter spiritual intensity, while the later pamphlet deliberately vilifies that which seemed glorious in 1650. He implicitly condemned that which he had written earlier. Although the texts of believing Ranters are much more insistent upon the spirituality of their sexuality, this very claim carried within it the basis for the manipulative character of Clarkson in *The Lost Sheep Found*.

Clarkson and Coppe both referred to the Song of Songs as a biblical intertext for blending the spiritual and the sexual. By making text and world into signs of something within, they may have become blind to the dynamics of human interaction that they were developing. In any case, their texts are filled with allusions to Canticles that intimate spirituality and direct the reader away from a concern for the mutuality of sexual relations.[12]

In Clarkson's *A Single Eye*, Canticles is invoked as part of the argument about the holiness of adultery. Solomon's Song provides a means of establishing Clarkson's central thesis about darkness and light, an ongoing commentary on Isaiah: 'I will make darkness light before them.'[13] The following passage juxtaposes Isaiah and Canticles to show that the imaginative intentions of a man's sexual acts determine their spiritual signification:

> Observe not the act nakedly, as the act, for we find the Prayer and Prayses of some to be pure, though to others impure: impure to those acting, in relation to the title his apprehension, his Conscience in the improvement of them is defiled and condemned for a Swearer, a Drunkard, an Adulterer, and a theef.
>
> When as a man in purity in light, acts the same acts, in relation to the act, and not the title: this man {no this man} doth not swear, whore, nor steal: so that for want of this light, of this single pure eye, there appeareth Devil and God, Hell and Heaven, Sin and holynesse, Damnation and Salvation; only, yea only from the esteemation and dark apprehension of the Creature.
>
> *I will make darknesse light, rough ways smooth*; not half light and half darknesse, not part rough and part smooth; but as it is said, *Thou art all fair my Love, there is no spot in thee*. Observe, all fair my Love; in thee only is beauty and purity, without defilement: my love my dove is but one, thou one, not two, but only one, my love: Love is *God* and God is Love; so all pure, all, light, no spot in thee. (10 [Smith, *Collection* 170])

The implicit message here is that the love described in Canticles ('Thou art all fair, my love: there is no spot in thee'[14]) is a justification for all acts, as long as they are done 'in light and love'. Clarkson did not treat the nature of the inner imagination which must ascribe spiritual meaning to action. If 'Love is *God* and God is Love,' then the sexual acts of the Ranters turn out to be 'Prayer and Prayses', with the text from the Song of Songs as a crucial nexus between holy and sexual.

When Clarkson wanted to please Lodowick Muggleton and his followers ten

---

[12] In addition to my own work, other scholars such as Nigel Smith (*Perfection* 43, 57), Christopher Hill (*English Bible* 367) and Clement Hawes (62) have pointed to the use of Canticles in Ranter texts.

[13] Isaiah 42.16. The later reference to 'rough ways smooth' is from Luke 3.5, itself a quotation from Isaiah 40.4 where the Authorized Version renders 'plain' instead of 'smooth.'

[14] Song of Songs 4.7.

years later in *The Lost Sheep Found*, he explained that Solomon had been central to his errors: 'and indeed *Solomons* Writings was the original of my filthy lust, supposing I might take the same liberty as he did, not then understanding his Writings was no Scripture' (26 [Smith, *Collection* 181]). Muggleton would express a similar view about the source of Ranter sexual practices:

> for whoever is in Solomons spirit; doth not know the true God, nor the right devil, for Solomon knew neither of them, though he was a wise man in things of nature, but ignorant of spiritual and heavenly wisdom; for Solomons wisdom hath the Ground-work of much lust of the flesh and idolatry; for the Ranters practice was grounded upon Solomons practice, who knew so many women, so the Ranters thought they might have the same liberty, seeing wise Solomons Writings were owned for Scripture-record; thus they continued many of them in their practice of lust till many of them were weary of it, as Solomon was when he was old, and then they left off that practice, and turned Quakers; and so fell to be the greatest idolaters of any, as Solomon did to his Heathenish Wives, drew his heart away from the worship of Moses, to worship idols.
>
> So is it with those Ranters that are turned Quakers, they are become absolute Heathen idolaters, for when they were Puritaines, so called, they were zealous for the letter of the Scriptures, and did practice a good life as near as they could to the letter, but after they fell to the practice of lust, being encouraged by Solomons writings, they left that legal worship and civil practice the law tied them unto, and followed Solomons practice of lust. (63–4)

Muggleton's impression of the relevance of Solomon (and his Song) on Ranter practices speaks for itself. Although this may, perhaps, represent no more than a prejudiced view of a rival doctrine, it is significant that both he and Laurence Clarkson, his former Ranter convert, explicitly connected Solomon and the Ranters. By attacking Solomon and his works, the Muggletonians were discarding what they regarded as a dangerous, corrupting text from the biblical canon. Their sense of the power of Canticles to corrupt believers is additional evidence of the importance of a simultaneously sexual and spiritual understanding of this biblical book in the minds of the Ranters and their critics.

For Coppe, too, the Song of Songs was important in establishing his implicit argument for libertinism. Alluding to the Song in *Some Sweet Sips*, he described his work as 'a great pounding at the doors, – But it is not I but the voice of my *Beloved*, that knocketh, saying, Open to me, and let me come *In*' (2 [Smith, *Collection* 47]). Similar allusions appear in the context of a call to the reader to awaken:

> Are you asleepe? for shame rise, its break aday, the *day* breaks, the *Shaddows* flie away, the *dawning* of the *day* woes you to arise, and let him *into* your *hearts*. It is the voyce of my beloved that knocketh, saying, Open to me my *Sister*, my *love*, my *dove*, for my head is filled with dew, and my locks with the drops of night. (10 [Smith, *Collection* 51])

Kisses of their Mouths

This is followed almost immediately with a passage that at first glance seems to be based on an allegorical reading of Canticles: 'The day *star* is up, rise up my *love*, my *dove*, my faire one, and *come away*, The day *star* woeth you, it is the voice of my beloved that saith open to me – I am risen *indeed*, rise up my love, open to me my faire one' (11 [Smith, *Collection* 52]). There are two passages from Canticles that are most obviously relevant here. In one the speaker urges his beloved to awaken and enjoy the spring: 'My beloved spake and said unto me. Rise up, my love, my fair one, and come away ... Until the day break, and the shadows flee away, turn my beloved' (2.10, 17). In the other the beloved recounts an incident in which her lover knocks on her door at night and then disappears before she can unlock it: 'Open to me, my sister, my love, my dove, my undefiled: for my head is filled with dew, and my locks with the drops of the night' (5.2).

The contemporary reader's initial response to these references might have been to regard Coppe as a self-proclaimed prophet who claimed to speak in the name of Christ, the bridegroom of Canticles in standard Christian commentaries. The spiritual awakening intimated by allusion to the language of the lover in the Song of Songs ('Rise up, my love . . .') appears almost too obvious until one asks about the precise nature of the newly evoked state of consciousness. It turns out that the biblical texts are to be understood in a sexual sense, since the terms used here ultimately lead back to libertinism. The argument of the prophet moves from one set of Christ-like activities to another. In his *Fiery Flying Roll*, Coppe explained that God is 'UNIVERSALL love . . . whose service is perfect freedome, and pure Libertinisme' (1 [Smith, *Collection* 86]). This tortuous and circuitous reading of Coppe recalls the secrecy motif that made it possible for him to publish his views at all. He depended upon the reader's difficulties to shield him from the attacks of the uninitiated. The combination of an explicitly sexual understanding of Canticles and an immediate anticipation of apocalypse provided Coppe with a striking means to articulate his own sense of God in himself.

Some Sweet Sips refers to the Song of Songs in other passages as well in order to communicate a message that nonetheless remains quite unclear much of the time. Chapter III of Epistle II begins with an appeal to the reader to awaken to a new world of natural beauty and light:

> WEll, once more; Where be you, ho? Are you *within*? Where be you? What! sitting upon a *Forme*, without doors, (in the Gentiles *Court*,) as if you had neither life nor soul in you? Rise up, rise up, my Love, my fair one, and *come away*; for lo, the Winter is past, the raine is over and gone, the flowers appear on the earth, the time of the singing of birds is come, and the voice of the Turtle is heard in our land, And {let him that hath an eare to heare, heare what the Spirit saith} the figtree putteth forth her green figges, and the vines with the tender grape give a good smell: *Arise* my love, my fair one, and *come away*, Cant. 2.10,11,12,13.

The day breaks, the *shadowes* flie *away*. *Rise* up, my Love, and come away.

Come with me from *Lebanon*, with me from *Lebanon*, from the top of *Amana*, look from the top of *Shenir*, and *Hermon*, from the Lyons dens, from the mountains of the Leopards. Come with me, *Rise*, let us be going.

Awake, awake, put on thy beautifull garments. Awake thou that sleepest and arise from the dead, and Christ shall give thee *light*. Awake, awake thou that sleepest in security, in the cradles of carnality. Arise from the dead. (15–16 [Smith, *Collection* 53–4])

Here the traditional garb consists of the references to Canticles that seem to conform to standard allegorical interpretations of the biblical poem as a love song between Christ and the church. This, however, would make the speaker in Coppe's text into a Christ figure urging the Church to relinquish its hold on dead flesh and embark upon some new spiritual venture associated with natural splendour and beauty.

Although there is no explicit indication in *Some Sweet Sips* of the sexual level of the intertexts from Canticles, there is a curious irony to the constant rejection of the carnal. The occasional references to libertinism suggest that the accusations of 'late fellow Ranters' about the sexual nature of Ranter practices may have been justified to some extent. Coppe's insistence upon the pejorative nature of the carnal must be understood in the context of his total vision. It is part of his policy to subvert language in order to suggest the real nature of truth.

This aspect of Coppe's work is much less hesitant about articulating the relationship between spirituality and lust. There is tension between the spirituality which is praised and the carnality which is deprecated, especially in Coppe's discussion of the necessity to confound a sense of righteousness with what he called 'base things'. In his *Second Fiery Flying Roule* he insisted upon a relationship between his 'wanton kisses' and those of Canticles:

And then again, by wanton kisses, kissing hath been confounded; and externall kisses, have been made the fiery chariots, to mount me swiftly into the bosom of him whom my soul loves, {his excellent Majesty, the King of glory.} Where I have been, where I have been, where I have been, hug'd, imbrac't, and kist with the kisses of his mouth, whose loves are better then wine, and have been utterly overcome therewith, beyond expression, beyond admiration.

(13 [Smith, *Collection* 108])

Obviously, the kisses here allude to those of Solomon's Song: 'Let him kiss me with the kisses of his mouth: for thy love is better than wine' (1.2). In a sense then, Coppe is suggesting that sexual experience is a way to holiness. The kisses of Canticles lead toward heaven, but they are rooted in a natural reading of the sexual imagery that abounds in the Song. Coppe rejected the allegorical conventions that firmly discouraged sexual readings of Canticles and intimated that sexual experience could be a source for spiritual arousal and development. As for Clarkson, the emphasis is on sexuality with no concern for the individual Ranter's relationship with his or her 'fellow creature'. Coppe is almost exclusively concerned with himself as he describes his approach to Ranter women: he describes various sexual escapades: 'and clip't, hug'd and kiss'd them, putting my hand in their bosomes, loving the she-Gipsies dearly ... yet I can if it be my will, kisse and hug Ladies, and love my neighbours wife as my selfe, without sin' (11, misnumbered 9 [Smith, *Collection* 106–7]). The breakdown of language into signs whose meaning can only be found within the imagination, combines to undermine the spirituality described.

Additional evidence for the connection between Canticles and Ranter sexual practice can be found in an anonymous song recently discovered and published by Anne Laurence:

> As I was walking on a day, itt thus did come to passe
> A gallant Citty I expied Jerusalem new itt was
> A gallant Citty to behold wherein was pastures greene,
> A waterie fountaine was therein 2 bankes it run between,
> The gates therof they were nott shutt by day nor yet by night,
> And ere the neerer I did come the more itt shined bright
> And fain I would enter therein and gott the gates within,
> Where Ball my nagge might have a dras-(?)* or therin I might swim
> And e're the More I sought to gett into these Meadows greene,
> A while for to refresh myself or sleepe those Hills between,
> The more the gates were closed too, which did mee much annoy,
> But if I had gott in thereto I'm sure I had gott a Boy.
> But since thus basely from this place I am repulsed soe
> The nought but cry and call for Plagues to wheresoere I goe,
> O God confound them suddainly their Creditts bring to thrall,
> And all that is to bee consum'd, O God consume itt all. (59)
>   * Possibly 'draught'.

The speaker's desire to 'sleepe those Hills between' corresponds to the words of the beloved in Canticles: 'he shall lie all night betwixt my breasts' (1.13). The speaker presents Jerusalem as a woman with whom he wants to make love and have a child. Although the sexual imagery is quite direct, the use of Canticles combines the holy and the sexual in a vision that incorporates both into a strange amalgam of ambiguity. The city appears as a pastoral sexual paradise that is somehow closed to the speaker. His only recourse is to ask God to 'consume it all', perhaps as an expression of jealousy and frustration. The speaker in the poem stresses apocalypse, an important concern of the Ranter community which expected the end of the world during the late 1640s and early 1650s. Like similar texts by Coppe and Clarkson, this poem refers to the nexus between Canticles, sexuality and spirituality within the Ranter community, while simultaneously calling for the apocalyptic destruction expected at the end of days.

Another indication of the dangers of Ranter dehumanization can be found in Abiezer Coppe's claim to have been converted from Judaism. On the title page of *Some Sweet Sips* he referred to himself as 'כף אביעזר [aviʿezer caf] A Late converted JEW'. By having his name printed in Hebrew letters, Coppe upset the normal conventions of reading. The author claimed that he had recently converted from Judaism to Christianity and apparently expected that the visually shocking use of Hebrew letters might lend greater credence to his message.

There is, however, no evidence at all that Coppe had ever been a Jew. Alexander Gordon asserts that 'he was first a presbyterian' (*Dictionary of National Biography*, s.v. 'Coppe, Abiezer'), but makes no reference to Jewishness. In fact, the title page of *Some Sweet Sips* seems to imply that the same relationship that traditionally obtained between Judaism and Christianity now holds between Christianity and the new religion of Coppe and his followers. The conventions of traditional Christianity are drained of their ordinary signification and simultaneously charged with a new level of meaning. The reader soon discovers that unlike his original assumption about the Jewishness of Coppe, the text implies that he, the reader, is one of 'the bewildered Israelites' (1 [Smith, *Collection* 47]) mentioned in the full title of the tract. Coppe's use of Hebrew letters and Roman capitals for 'Jew' operates within a double convention. On the one hand the Jews had been officially banned from England for centuries, and thus provided Englishmen with dehumanized symbols for the unregenerate. On the other, the conversion of the Jews was a crucial part of the millenarian myth shared by most Englishmen. As for Andrew Marvell's coy mistress, 'the conversion of the Jewes' signified the beginning of the end of time. Coppe combined these conventions in his own version of the myth that guardedly articulated his own messianic pretensions.

In *A Fiery Flying Roll*, evidently published a few months later, Coppe went one step further in referring to himself as part of his discourse. He translated his Hebrew first name (literally 'father of help') into its literal Latin equivalent, *auxilium patris*, and instead of referring to himself as a converted Jew, he described a vision that began with his own personal destruction: 'First, all my strength, my forces were utterly routed, my house I dwelt in fired; my father and mother forsook me, the wife of my bosome loathed me, mine old name was rotted, perished' (A2v [Smith, *Collection* 82]). This experience is parallel to the conversion in *Some Sweet Sips* because it fills in the gaps about the speaker's identity in the earlier pamphlet. There the conversion is extra-textual and as such leaves unanswered questions that are to some extent thematized in *A Fiery Flying Roll*, where the rotting of Coppe's 'Old name' is part of the conversion pattern.

Coppe's surname, however, appears in Hebrew characters in both pamphlets. Although there is no textual explanation of the significance of the name, the millenarian expectation of the conversion of the Jews is clearly relevant. In their commentaries on Canticles, Brightman and Homes both looked forward to such a conversion, and Homes went so far as to work actively for the readmission of the Jews to England.[15] Coppe was less interested in real Jews, since for him they too were signs or types whose inner meaning signified the imminence of the millennium. Perhaps he elaborated upon this when he spoke to the initiated, but in print Coppe cloaked everything in secrecy. Near the end of the first epistle in *Some Sweet Sips*, Coppe made explicit reference to the closed nature of his discourse:

> If I here speake in an unknown tongue, I pray that I may interpret when I may. Only take one Clavall hint. That which is here (mostly) spoken, is inside, and mysterie. And so farre as any one hath the mysterie of God opened to him, *In Him*, can plainly reade every word of the same here. The rest is sealed up from the rest, and it may be the most, – from some. (5 [Smith, *Collection* 49])

Further on, he elaborated: 'Thus you have one Claval hint; if the Lord come *in*, it may be an instrumentall key to open the rest. But the Spirit alone is the incorruptible Key' (7 [Smith, *Collection* 49]). The epistle closes: 'And yours; all of ye that are the Lords, by what names or titles soever distinguished, Yours – כף אביעזר *The Key* *Christ* was Re-baptized – The Lord is my *King*, and my Shepheard, or *Pastor, &c.* – The Eternall God, whose *I Am*, is *Independent,– &c.*' (8 [Smith, *Collection* 50]).

Coppe's utilization of Hebrew characters for his name suggests that it may have some special biblical significance. In the Song of Songs, the word כף (kaf) can mean 'key' in a phrase that literally denotes 'handles of the lock' (5.4). In a representative seventeenth-century explanation of these words, Theodore Haak translated a Dutch commentary that saw the handles as a means of facilitating the implicitly sexual union of bride and bridegroom: 'understand here the bolts, wherewith the door was bolted within, keeping Christ without doors, and hindering him from coming in; which now being oiled with the oil of myrrhe; that is, her heart being anointed with the oil of grace, and so all locks and bolts, that is all impediments and hinderances being removed, the Bridegroom might come in unto her without molestation, to enjoy the fruits of his grace, which she had received of him' (Nnnnn 1r). In these terms, Coppe was himself the key or handle that would introduce Christ into the world. Since much of the language of both pamphlets refers directly or indirectly to Canticles, Coppe's name can be read as a key to the significance of these allusions, just as it seems to be a key to the hidden or mystical meaning of the text.

It is fitting that the Hebrew name can thus function as a sign for the interrelation of Canticles, sexuality and the Jews. All of these functioned for Coppe as indications of an imminent apocalypse in which he fully expected to play a crucial role. His methodology serves to break down all apparent meanings and to establish his own sense of the universe in their place. The way in which his discourse distinguishes between the sign and the signified,

---

[15] See the work of historians such as Michael Fixler (238) and David S. Katz (104–7).

however, led him in the direction of dehumanization. His women and his Jews became objects to be manipulated by and through his imagination. One paradoxical effect of this discourse was to deny the significance of the world outside the consciousness of the imagining 'creature'. References to women ('fellow creatures') and Jews turn out to be part of a mindset that views events and people as signs that must be understood to signify something beyond themselves.

These texts thus point to an implicit dualistic conflict at the heart of the impassioned Ranter cries for spiritual oneness. While their doctrines suggest that all experience is godly when imagined so, the interpretation of language, acts and people as signs of greater ends reduces human experience to a series of empty forms which are drained of inherent significance. In some sense, the act of reading Canticles provides a paradigm of the radical millenarian politics and theology which disappeared from the mainstream of English culture after the 1650s. The linking of public sexuality and imagery from Canticles on one hand and a view of people as apocalyptic signs on another, led the Ranters to embrace the world while denying the significance of its flesh. The 'inner light' of these radicals thus undermined the relations between people and helped to make possible the reduction of human dignity in the name of ideology.

Texts by Ranters such as Clarkson, Coppe and others thus shift the ways in which the balance between their open and closed modes of revelation and secrecy present the language of Canticles. As they placed the underlying carnal sense of the biblical verses at the centre of their delicate balance between flesh and spirit they were extending the practices of earlier writers. The secrecy that underlies the writing likewise serves to stress the necessary balance required to apprehend the message. The oral world of Ranter meetings is implicitly necessary to make the deliberate fragments of written text coherent. In this way they articulated an approach to biblical materials that had a lasting effect on themselves and their contemporaries.

Chapter 6

ADAM'S REVISED RANT WITH EVE

MILTON implicitly recapitulates all the developments in the Renaissance tradition of Canticles from Baldwin through the Ranters. Although his most complex and interesting treatment is to be found in *Paradise Lost*, there are also traces of Canticles in his fifth sonnet (written in Italian). Like Spenser before him, Milton seems to have written in the tradition of Guido Cavalcanti as he alluded to the stilnovist version of the woman who simultaneously inspires love and awe. The Italian materials and language of the sonnet anticipate Milton's use of Canticles in his epic. When Adam serenades Eve in language that evokes the Song of Songs at the beginning of Book 5, he sets in motion a series of interpretive questions that recall Baldwin's balances, Spenser's 'wedded love', Aylett's allegory and Ranter sexuality in an ironic mode that, unlike the straightforward sexuality of Shakespeare's *Venus and Adonis*, threatens to upset the delicate equilibrium of the epic. The echoes from Canticles are simultaneously carnal and spiritual as they engage most of the other dyadic conflicts discussed in earlier chapters between oral and written, present and future, lyric and apocalyptic. The resolution between these various tensions is ultimately balanced at the end of Book 12, but this result depends upon a development that takes place as the poem proceeds. The balance in Book 5 is quite tentative as Adam tries to express his love for Eve in language from Canticles that echoes Coppe and Clarkson in addition to Baldwin, Spenser and Aylett.

MILTON'S FIFTH SONNET: ECHOES OF CANTICLES AND CAVALCANTI

Many of the most traditional motifs in Milton's fifth sonnet are often ascribed to the influence of Petrarch despite the fact that the great fourteenth-century Italian poet was not the first to work out themes such as the angelic lady with eyes like the sun. Although there can be no question about the relevance of poems by Petrarch and his successors for Milton's Italian sonnets, their intertextual significance must be qualified by reference to predecessors such as Dante and some of his earlier contemporaries. As practitioners of the *dolce stil nuovo* or sweet new style, these poets had developed a philosophy of love that extended what Maurice Valency terms the 'earthly perfection' (240) of the troubadours to a star or an angel with explicit spiritual powers associated with charity. One of the more famous of these, Guido Cavalcanti, helped to set the characteristic tone of the *stil novisti* by writing sonnets to a lady who inspired him so intensely that one aspect of his love for her was fear and awe. Simultaneously angel and woman, the stilnovist's inspiration was thus responsible for poetry that analysed the ways in which the male poet desired yet feared his lady. Milton, like Spenser, could have read from the sixteenth-century anthologies of Tuscan verse by Bernardo di Giunta which made Cavalcanti's work readily available in England. In addition, the Italians that he certainly had read, such as Petrarch or Bembo, were very conscious of Dante's older friend (labelled 'primo de li miei amici' in *Vita Nuova* [3.14]) and even echo him in their poems.[1]

Milton's fifth sonnet, like Spenser's *Amoretti* 3, shares with Cavalcanti the biblical motif that juxtaposes love and awe.[2] The biblical subtext presents a woman 'fair as the moon,' and 'clear as the sun' yet 'terrible as an army with banners' (Song of Songs 6.10). Milton's consciousness of the unresolved duality of his lady who is both angel and woman, fair and terrible owes something to the stilnovist practice of Cavalcanti.[3] This aspect of love represents the core of a myth with biblical roots that was developed by the stilnovists in the form of the 'donna angelicata' and which Milton inherited as part of what he elsewhere called 'lingua di cui si vanta Amore' (the language of which Love boasts) ('Canzone', *Complete Poetry* 90).[4] The lady whose loveliness is terrifying as she ascends from the desert and makes her way into the gardens is explicitly part of Cavalcanti's poem but is likewise present as an intertextual echo in Milton, amplified through Spenser's *Amoretti.*

Milton's sonnet explores a world of love that begins with the awed wonder of the stilnovist but which concludes with resolutions of the lover's conflicts that fashion a new means of overcoming the threats and dangers of the mythic lady who is fair yet terrible. As the speaker's rhetoric takes him through a landscape that associates extremes of hot and cold with the desert, intertextual echoes of various traditions resound to establish the pain and the strangeness of his condition. The conclusion, however, resolves the stilnovist

---

[1] In 'Poesie Italiane di Milton', Sergio Baldi cites a sonnet by Bembo (3) as a source for many of Milton's Italian phrases (113). Bembo's sonnet concludes with the phrase 'lato manco' which echoes Cavalcanti's Sonnet 13 ('Voi che per li occhi mi passaste 'l core' [Cavalcanti, ed. Nelson 20–1]) and even uses the same rhyme word ('fianco') as the source. I am indebted to the assistance of Professors Rinaldina Russell and David Anderson on this matter in particular and for advice on Italian in general. All errors are, of course, my own responsibility.

[2] See Chapter 2, 69–72.

[3] See my Introduction (21–3) for more on the *dolce stil nuovo* as well as an analysis of Cavalcanti's sonnet and its text.

[4] Unless otherwise indicated, all citations from Milton's poetry in my text are to John T. Shawcross's *Complete Poetry*.

indeterminacy in terms of another landscape with related connections between man and the cosmos. The poet's account of the way his lady's eyes strike him like the sun's rays on a traveller in the desert registers the threatening blaze of the lady's effect upon him:

> Per certo i bei vostr'occhi, Donna mia,
> Esser non può che non sian lo mio sole
> Sì mi percuoton forte, come ei suole
> Per l'arene di Libia chi s'invia.

In truth your fair eyes, my lady, / could not but be my sun; / they powerfully strike me as the sun him / who dispatches his way through the sands of Libya. (91–2)

The brilliant attractiveness of his lady's eyes is, perhaps, more threatening than alluring, yet this is the primary point of the quatrain. The beauty of her eyes burns him fiercely and thus carries with it more of the terrible quality of love than its pleasures. This merciless brilliance represents the lady who is simultaneously inviting and threatening. The second quatrain of the octave and the first tercet of the sestet then proceed to develop the motif of the lover's sigh which Cavalcanti had made the universal response of whoever saw his lady:

> Mentre un caldo vapor (nè senti' pria)
> Da quel lato si spinge ove mi duole,
> Che forse amanti nelle lor parole
> Chiaman sospir; io non so che si sia:
> Parte rinchiusa, e turbida si cela
> Scossomi il petto, e poi n'uscendo poco,
> Quivi d'attorno o s'agghiaccia, o s'ingiela.

while a fervent steam (not felt before) / from that side proceeds where is my grief, / that perhaps lovers in their words / call a sigh; I know not what it may be: / the hidden part, and turbid thus concealed, / has shaken my breast, and then a bit escaping, / there from being enclosed has either frozen or congealed. (92)

Although Sergio Baldi has traced this description of the sigh to Petrarch, Bembo, Tasso and others, Cavalcanti's struggles are also relevant. The stilnovist's sighs are an integral part of his physiology of love which locates the emotional experience in a series of references to bodily functions that are explicitly connected with love. Valency points out that 'These lovers sigh constantly, and their sighs dispirit them, for the sigh is an exhalation of the breath of life, it comes from the heart. For this reason, sighs may be wet with tears, since the soul weeps internally, exuding radical moisture. Cavalcanti wrote [in 'S'io prego questa donna' 9–11]: "My sorrowful and fearful soul goes weeping among the sighs which it finds in the heart so that they issue forth bathed in tears"' (238). In a private correspondence, Professor

Rinaldina Russell has indicated to me that 'the Italian poet often dramatizes the lover's suffering by personifying various aspects of his emotive condition – *sospiri*, *spiriti* or *spiritelli* that cause his losing color, freezing, fainting etc.; sighs run to his eyes and become tears'.

Milton's sigh is one of conflict and difficulty, and proceeds directly from the speaker's perceptions of his condition as hopeless. As with the sun-like eyes, the landscape here is disturbing. The desert heat of the first quatrain elicits the sigh which 'turns frosty and congeals' as it escapes the lover. Although this movement from fire to ice is undeniably Petrarchan,[5] the theme is anticipated by the sighs of Cavalcanti and other stilnovists. Guinizelli describes the brilliance of his lady who is the morning star in human shape: She has a 'face like snow tinged with red, shining eyes that are gay and full of love'.[6] In a somewhat different mood, Cavalcanti responds to a sonnet of Bernardo da Bologna by promising to send a river full of nymphs despite the pain of a sigh that makes a light of him, a burning heart in a shipwreck.[7] Milton's sigh reformulates the effects of Guinizelli's snow and shining eyes within the body of the lover–speaker. The speaker shudders and shakes as he tries to account for what he is feeling, but the effort at articulating this provides its own release and relief.

Whereas Cavalcanti's sonnet begins with excitement and wonder at the lady (and her dual nature) and concludes with a widening sense of distance between the male speaker and his beloved, Milton resolves the pain and misery of his desert landscape with an implicit literary garden that intimates a joining of the different kinds of love reverberating in the intertextual echo chamber.[8] The lady's blazing eyes suggest the spiritual and sexual attraction of the bride coming up from the wilderness, but instead of Cavalcanti's realization that he cannot apprehend her, Milton's speaker cries all night, and then finds Dawn returning with Roses in her hair:

> Ma quanto a gli occhi giunge a trovar loco
>   Tutte le notti a me suol far piovose
>   Finchè mia Alba rivien colma di rose.

but as much as reaches my eyes to find its place / makes all the nights rainy to me alone / until my dawn returns overflowing with roses. (92)

---

[5] Cf. *In Vita* 134 'Pace non trovo, e non ho da far guerra; / e temo, e spero; et ardo e son un ghiaccio' (Petrarca 166). Sir Thomas Wyatt translated 'I FYNDE no peace and all my warr is done; / I fere and hope, I burne and freise like yse' (21).

[6] 'Viso di neve colorato in grana / occhi lucenti gai e pien d'amore' (Kay 53).

[7] 'Avegna che la doglia i' porti grave / per lo sospiro, ché di me fa lume / lo core ardendo in la disfatta nave, / mand' io a la Pinella un grande fiume / pieno di lammie', [XLIVb] 'Risposta di Guido' in *Rime* 174–5.

[8] This accords with John T. Shawcross's view of Milton's sonnets: 'On the one hand, the Christian context raises the love to an ideal and ethereal level, and on the other, the hints of a divine love suggest the common metaphor between human love and divine love' ('Milton's Italian Sonnets' 27–8).

In the reversal at dawn, Milton's persona finds fulfilment in the image of the rose. This traditional symbol of love and poetry appears in various stilnovist poems such as Cavalcanti's 'Fresca rosa novella' (Contini 491–2; *Rime* 3–8) or Guido Guinizelli's 'Io voglio del ver la mia donna laudare' (Contini 472). More important for Milton is that the return of dawn with roses intimates the Homeric 'Rosy-fingered dawn' and provides a kind of solution to the larger conflicts in the poem. For all his tears, Milton's persona discovers that the experience of misery takes him forward toward a sense of poetic achievement. The intense spirituality that arises from sensuous detail stretched to its intellectual limits is communicated intertextually by echoes of Cavalcanti, Guinizelli and various others, in addition to Petrarch.

Milton's sonnet moves from desert sun through the traditional hot and cold lover's sighs to rain-tears and roses. By the conclusion of the poem he has reshaped his Italian traditions and resolved them by recapitulating their diachronic development from Guinizelli through Cavalcanti and Dante to Petrarch. Guinizelli's use of snow for colour and his comparison of his lady to roses leads to Cavalcanti's 'fresh new rose' and thence to Dante and Petrarch. The stilnovist spirit of intellectual blending of woman in her dual aspect of 'donna angelicata' is heightened by the literary garden that produces roses from desert sands. Milton's language suggests some of the conflicting attitudes towards love in these poets, but transforms all of it into a comment on poetic inspiration. His 'Alba rivien colma di rose' thus includes the stilnovists as well as Homer, Dante and Petrarch in its resolution of the lover's misery into poetic achievement. This is the humanism that Milton practised in his later English works as well. The materials of his tradition are revised and redirected for the poet's own purposes, which are no less concerned with poetic practice and technique than with the nominal theme of love.

In a curious way then, Milton reverses the rhetorical shifts of Cavalcanti. His speaker finds resolution of the mythic tension between sexual desire and numinous awe in a conscious embracing of textuality. His 'Alba ... colma di rose' thus looks forward to the inspiration he asks of Urania in *Paradise Lost*. That is, while the sonnet appears to develop a standard Petrarchan ploy designed to win a lady's favours by means of an exaggerated compliment, the experience it recounts seems to rejoice in the textual rewards of dawns filled with roses whose echoes are unavoidably literary but also spiritual. The lady becomes the speaker's means of finding a source of textual inspiration that the poet would continue to seek out even in later poems. By directing his attention away from the rhetoric of desire Milton is merely recognizing the inevitability of its textualization. Rather than settle for a text that subverts sexual desire into verbal discussion, he shifts his attention to the source of inspiration. His sonnet thus becomes part of its author's deliberate search for poetic inspiration. John T. Shawcross sees the lover's grief as a figure with religious significance:

> In terms of divine love, the poet says that he is so pervaded by the light of God (his intensity of love for God, I presume, is meant) that he produces only things evanescent (like *The Passion*); in his grief from God's seemingly negative treatment of his desire comes that which will produce the flowers of divine love, again the poems which we are reading. ('Milton's Italian Sonnets' 31)

In a sense, then, it was Cavalcanti and the myth of Canticles with its traditional juxtaposition between carnal and holy that led Milton, via Petrarchan sighs and tears, in the direction of his Heavenly Muse.

REVISED RANT IN *PARADISE LOST*

Milton's *Paradise Lost* extends his use of Canticles beyond faint echoes of his Italian sonnet. Not unlike the discussion of the Italian sonnet, the guiding spirit of my reading is once again that of John T. Shawcross who has argued cogently for the simultaneously spiritual and erotic nature of Milton's epic:

> The need for joint action between God and man is explicit in Sonnet 7 as well as other early poems. But the basic equation which underlies this inspiration is the mystic union of God and man in terms of sexual intercourse . . . We can not help being struck by the sexual overtones of the metaphor of inspiration: the poem itself is the creation of God and the poet; it simulates an act of generation . . . it deals with creation which is bodily, conceptual, and physical; and it suggests constant generation through impregnation of its readers with its 'message'. (*With Mortal Voice* 12, 20)

Shawcross's clarification of the psycho-sexual roots of the language and theme of *Paradise Lost* has established an important matrix for this and other studies.

When Milton has Adam use a carnal approach to Eve in his love song in Book 5, he is establishing a curious parallel between the Ranter approach to sexuality and the Song of Songs and that of *Paradise Lost*. In some sense Adam is insisting upon the validity of Ranter positions in a prelapsarian world. That is, some of the views presented by men such as Coppe and Clarkson seem to be unobjectionable to Adam. The implicit criticism of the Ranters to be found in *Paradise Lost* is their assumption that Adam's fall is irrelevant. Much that must have been objectionable for Milton in the views of a Clarkson or a Coppe became acceptable in the prelapsarian world represented in the epic before the middle of Book 9.

Christopher Hill has made it clear that Milton should be read in the context of the radical political ideas that were an important part of his public world during the Interregnum. Hill stresses Milton's revolutionary background in the epics where he sees the poet 'grappling with problems set by the failure of God's cause in England' (*Milton* 345). He points to a great many parallels between the Ranters and Milton that suggest the importance of examining the nature of their contemporary relations.[9] The character of Satan provides an area of thematic and ideological congruity between the Ranters and *Paradise Lost* 'with . . . emphasis on fate, chance and necessity . . .[and] denial of the divine providence which Milton is asserting' (397). On another level, he might perhaps have seen Ranter antinomianism in Satan's soliloquy that concludes 'Evil be thou my Good' (*Complete Poetry, Paradise Lost* 4.110). None of this is problematic since the use of Ranter materials is confined to Satan. Hill does not extend his probings of the intertextual space occupied by *Paradise Lost* and certain Ranters beyond what can be seen as Milton's conscious adaptation of a particular ideological line for rhetorical purposes. He summarizes: 'I am suggesting only that one possible source for Milton's conception of the rebel angels is the people he had encountered, whose activities had done (in his view) harm to the cause he believed in, although their ideas started from premises alarmingly close to his' (398).

Joan S. Bennett has extended this consideration of Miltonic interest in radical seventeenth-century political and theological discourse to a prelapsarian aspect of *Paradise Lost*. She deals primarily with antinomians less radical than the Ranters whom she understands Milton to have rejected: 'Some antinomians – the Ranting sort – Milton condemned, as in his sonnet 12: "License they mean when they cry liberty"'. Nevertheless, her discussion of Adam and Eve as 'the first persons who had to deal with this dilemma of total spiritual liberty' (389) could be seen as an indication of Milton's partial sympathy for all antinomian views. Milton's sonnet need not blind us to the sympathies he may have felt with well meaning sectarians who were guilty of confusing license and liberty, but whose political and religious tendencies were not wholly unlike his own.

James Turner's *One Flesh* is a rich and fruitful study of the relationship between sexuality and seventeenth-century views of the Bible in general and Genesis and Canticles in particular. Like Bennett, his work develops insights and suggestions of Christopher Hill, as he explores the many ways in which Milton's prose and verse can be read in terms of biblical sexuality. Turner's views of the connections between Canticles, the Ranters and Milton anticipates many of my interests in this chapter. His treatment of the divorce tracts points to ways in which Milton's prose can be read as a response to the Song of Songs:

> Milton's doctrine and discipline of divorce may be summarized as follows: marriage must retain its prelapsarian bliss 'in some proportion', and to do this it must not be grounded in mere procreation – whereby woman becomes a department of the domestic economy, a kind of brood mare – but in 'a mutual fitnes to the final causes of wedlock, help and society', in a 'due conversation' suffused with erotic gestures of the sort that pass between the lovers in the Song of Songs. (215)

---

[9] In his recent book on the English Bible, Hill generously cites my own 'Milton and the Ranters', an earlier version of this chapter.

His chapter on *Paradise Lost* (230–309) brilliantly concludes his reading of what his book's subtitle terms 'Paradisal Marriage and Sexual Relations in the Age of Milton'.

When Milton had Adam sing a love song to Eve in language that refers back to biblical intertexts similar to those found in Ranter writings, he was in some sense granting his hero an approach to love that underlines the similarities of his own revolutionary sympathies. Although Milton the libertarian who defended personal and intellectual freedom in the 1640s was not as radical as some of the sectaries who embraced his doctrines, his ideals and principles had much in common with them. This is not to identify Milton with the antinomian views of a Clarkson or the fierce cursing of a Coppe but it is to suggest that despite some of his obvious objections to such positions and practices, he had a basic sympathy for their underlying spirit. It is thus useful to read Milton's presentation of the prelapsarian human condition as a refining of some Ranter views of God and human nature as reflected in interpretations of Canticles.

During the two decades that separated the publication of Ranter works by Coppe and Clarkson from that of *Paradise Lost*, the English political scene changed radically. Coppe's expectation of imminent apocalypse in 1649 had lost much of its urgency long before the Restoration made it clear that the hopes of many English Protestants for the establishment of God's kingdom on earth had been premature. *Paradise Lost* shifts the imminent expectation of the Interregnum to a sense of an inner paradise that somehow consoles its readers for the loss of Eden. A comparison between Milton's Eden and the promises of Coppe and Clarkson suggests that like the Ranters, Adam and Eve enjoyed a liberty that assumed innocence.[10] When Satan's machinations ruined them, he also foredoomed the entire revolution, but with an important difference. Adam's similarities to the Ranters end with the Fall. The 'Paradise within . . . happier farr' (12.587) has no equivalent in Ranter practice which in some sense had tried to deny the fallen condition.

Although none of the Ranter texts that have been preserved provide explicit support for reports of ritual nudity and public sexual acts such as those described by Gilbert Roulston in *The Ranter's Bible*,[11] these suggestions are not in conflict with the views they did profess. Especially striking is the comparison between the Ranters and Adam, since the liberty that a man such as Abiezer Coppe claims is that of unfallen Adam, or rather, of Christians who see themselves as beyond sin because of Christ and thus capable of

---

[10] Achsah Guibbory claims that Milton's 'most interesting and unusual example of the true rites of worship appears in his depiction of the prelapsarian love of Adam and Eve'. She goes on to suggest that the 'effort to sanctify sexual love might recall the more radical sects, particularly the Ranters who encouraged sexual promiscuity for men as a sign and privilege of their state of grace. But Milton emphatically disassociates himself from the promiscuous Ranters as he glorifies monogamous marriage' (202).

[11] This account is cited above in Chapter 5, 128.

committing any act in purity. For Milton's Adam, however, Roulston's testimony contains nothing that is objectionable. Only after his fall would nudity and unabashed sexuality become sinful.

There are, then, certain parallels between Milton's Adam and the Ranter presentation of holiness and sexuality through Canticles. These in some sense provide a Miltonic revision of revolutionary radical ideas in a biblical context that eliminates the most obvious objections to Ranter practice. Thus the various indications of Ranter public adultery are irrelevant in Eden since Adam's only sexual partner is Eve. On the other hand, Adam's love for Eve is articulated in terms that suggest quite clearly a passage from Canticles. This can be read as one of the earliest indications in the epic of Adam's confusion between two kinds of love. On one hand he is committed to agape, love of God, and the consequent obedience demanded of humanity. Nevertheless he is also in the grip of eros, deeply, even irrationally, in love with Eve. Although there is nothing tainted about the coexistence of these two loves, a dynamic tension develops between them which provides motivation for the fall in Book 9.

At the beginning of Book 5 of *Paradise Lost*, Adam awakens Eve from the dream Satan has whispered into her ear and in so doing evokes the same intertext from Canticles that Coppe used to develop his metaphor of spiritual awakening. Adam sings:

> Awake
> My fairest, my espous'd, my latest found,
> Heav'ns last best gift, my ever new delight,
> Awake, the morning shines, and the fresh field
> Calls us, we lose the prime, to mark how spring
> Our tended Plants, how blows the Citron Grove,
> What drops the Myrrh, and what the balmie Reed,
> How Nature paints her colours, how the Bee
> Sits on the Bloom extracting liquid sweet. (5.17–25)

The connections between this passage and Canticles (2.10–13 and 7.11–12) are well known to Milton scholarship.[12] Adam's use of Solomon's words seems to say something about the biblical poem just as it tells us about the love he feels. The significance of Milton's use of the biblical intertext is,

---

[12] H. J. Todd pointed out that 'Addison has observed the similarity of this address to that of Solomon, Cant. ii.10, &c.' (2: 374). Editions by Merritt Y. Hughes (113) and Alastair Fowler (Carey and Fowler 675) also have appropriate comments about the allusion. Howard Schultz claims that if Milton meant Satan's 'Why sleepst thou *Eve*?' (5.38) as 'an allusion to the Song of Solomon, he achieved it by contrast, for he carefully inverted the pictures, changing the dove for a nightingale, keeping only the sensuous delights' (24). Diane McColley (92–8) discusses the relevance of the reference in terms of the vast tradition of medieval and Renaissance commentary. She stresses the typological force of the material from Canticles and points out that 'the Song of Songs is, after all, an impassioned love poem; and one finds in Milton's use of it none of the strain to disembody or reembody the divine lovers that one finds in the allegorical annotations' (97).

however, further complicated by the specific use of the same intertext by Coppe as well as by the general Ranter interest in Solomon's Song as a biblical warrant for their rites and views.

In a mythic sense Adam can be understood to have inspired Solomon to compose Canticles thousands of years later.[13] Solomon's Song is, then, somehow about the relations between Adam and Eve. Thus, when the lover in Canticles invites the beloved to 'go forth into the field' to 'see if the vine flourish' (7.11–12), he is invoking Adam's song to Eve. On a human level this makes Canticles a text about man's love for woman and her no less impassioned response. Just as Milton's epic is quite explicit about sexuality and lovemaking before the fall, so it provides an interpretation of Canticles that seems equally straightforward about sexuality in the biblical text.

This is not, however, to reject a spiritual or allegorical reading of Canticles.[14] In his divorce tracts Milton had been quite definite about the way sexual and romantic love provide a model for spiritual love: 'and in the Song of Songs, which is generally beleev'd, even in the jolliest expressions to figure the spousals of the Church with Christ, [wisest Salomon] sings of a thousand raptures between those two lovely ones farre on the hither side of carnall enjoyment'. He cites this as an instance by which 'we may imagine how indulgently God provided against mans lonelines'.[15] Milton had no use for the fears of sexuality expressed by most Protestant biblical commentators on Canticles.[16] He saw eros as an integral part of the human condition which led to agape when properly experienced. Similarly, *Paradise Lost* intimates that the sexual love of Adam for Eve is part of a process that leads eventually to the sacrifice of the Son and the resultant Christian redemption. Adam's erotic

---

[13] Cf. James Turner's comment: 'Thus when Adam hangs "enamour'd" over the sleeping Eve and whispers "Awake, the morning shines . . ." he echoes (Milton would say anticipates) the morning invitation of the Song of Songs, and thereby unwittingly dispels the nocturnal parody of a similar passage that Satan had put into Eve's dream' (233). Turner generously cites an early unpublished version of my work with regard to Milton and the Ranters (85 n. 75, 91 n.100).

[14] In his *Reinvention of Love*, Anthony Low generally reads the Song of Songs in traditionally allegorical terms. His definition of 'the biblical marriage trope' cites a series of biblical references including Canticles and sees the trope as 'a rich system of metaphors connected with human love, divine love, and Christian community' (2). His traditional association of the bride of the Song of Songs with the Church is precisely the assumption that my study tries to avoid. Although his chapters on Milton do not treat the allusive language of the opening of Book 5, they recognize the relevance to Milton of a literal approach to lovemaking and to Canticles: 'As Milton was presumably aware, there is a tradition that interprets the Song of Songs literally as well as allegorically' (165).

[15] *Tetrachordon*, in *Complete Prose Works* 2:597. There is a similar reference to Canticles (8.6–7) in Milton's *Doctrine and Discipline of Divorce*: 'but this pure and more inbred desire of joyning to it self in conjugall fellowship a fit conversing soul (which desire is properly call'd love) is stronger then death, as the Spouse of Christ thought, many waters cannot quench it, neither can the flouds drown it' (*Complete Prose Works* 2:251).

[16] Cf. the words of Nathanael Homes cited above (p. 118).

desire is a type of Christ's love for the Church and humanity. The intertext from Canticles thus suggests the typological methodology of reading that informs all of *Paradise Lost*. The type prefigures the antitype, yet is no less real and earthly as it does so. It is the sign that Coppe wanted to go beyond but which Milton recognized was essential to human existence and understanding.

Adam's predicament at the outset of Book 5 nevertheless can appear to be problematic in terms of his choice of language in his love song to Eve. At the very moment that Eve has responded in her dream to Satan's temptation, Adam conflates the language of eros with that of agape. The reader of *Paradise Lost* could assume that there is a significant parallel here between Adam and Eve's unfallen state in the garden and their eventual decisions to disobey. Just as she has anticipated her fall by eating the fruit in her Satanically inspired dream, he will later choose his erotic desire for her over his commitment to God. One could thus argue that the language of Canticles here is bitterly ironic as it attaches a post-Restoration view of Ranter revolutionary practice as explicitly fallen even before the fall.

Such a reading, however, threatens to undermine the entire fabric of the epic's carefully considered verse which associates Ranter doctrines and interpretations of Canticles with Edenic innocence. If Adam is already nearly sinful as he sings to Eve in Book 5, much of the revolutionary struggle of the poem disintegrates. The Narrator's praise of 'Wedded love' (4.741–75) unequivocally insists upon the sexual nature of prelapsarian Edenic love. The 'rites / Mysterious of connubial love' (742–3) are explicitly erotic and spiritual at the same time. This is an essential part of the baroque vision of *Paradise Lost* which does not begin to unravel before the fall in Book 9.

A carnal reading of Canticles is likewise part of the picture. The balance between oral and written, between lyric and apocalyptic, between men and angels was not necessary before the fall. The richly sexual imagery of Canticles is part of what the Narrator claims that 'God declares / Pure' (4.746–7) and then insists:

> Farr be it, that I should write thee sin or blame,
> Or think thee unbefitting holiest place,
> Perpetual Fountain of Domestic sweets. (4.758–60)

After Eve and Adam eat of the fruit, it will be necessary to deal with the break up of this idyllic world. The fall will create a need to reconsider the monism of Milton's paradise and to work out the details of the machinery then necessary to balance the different dyadic aspects of the divides between holy and profane, written and oral, spiritual and sexual.[17] Before the fall, however,

---

[17] This recapitulation of the formulations of my introduction should be accompanied here by an acknowledgment of the enabling importance of work by Harold Fisch and Jason Rosenblatt in terms of the relevance of Hebraic materials and rabbinic thinking for the study of

Adam's Revised Rant with Eve

sexual passion is holy and the language of Canticles simultaneously connotes God and the flesh.[18]

The tone of Adam's love song is intensified further when Eve responds with an account of a similar song that she has heard in her dream. Satan's Cavalier parody of Adam's song, analysed by Howard Schultz (22–4) represents the manipulative, sexist approach to love of all kinds. Adam ignores the Satanic perversions of the dream song which substitutes idolatry for the spiritual potential of his own poem. Satan's song thus tempts Eve with a bogus type of spiritual temptation:

> Here, happie Creature, fair Angelic *Eve*,
> Partake thou also; happie though thou art,
> Happier thou mayst be, worthier canst not be:
> Taste this, and be henceforth among the Gods
> Thy self a Goddess, not to Earth confind. (5.74–8)

Adam's love song to Eve is ironic on different levels. It is a passionate song to Eve which, when reconsidered after the fall, anticipates Adam's failure to realize the difference between the values of human and divine love in Book 9. At this level the irony may be partially established by the reader's consciousness of the traditional fulfilment of the lover's love for his beloved in Canticles, that

---

Renaissance England in general and of John Milton in particular. Fisch's *Jerusalem and Albion* and his essay on Hebraic style in *Paradise Lost* have long been recognized as ground-breaking attempts to account for the influence of Hebraic materials on seventeenth-century English culture. I have not yet been able to examine his most recent study, *The Biblical Presence in Shakespeare, Milton, and Blake: A Comparative Study* (Oxford: Clarendon Press, 1999). Rosenblatt's recent book adjusts some of Fisch's insights and establishes an important thesis about comedy and tragedy in *Paradise Lost*: 'alongside the Pauline comedy is the Hebraic tragedy of Torah degraded into law, underscored by the damage wrought in historical time by the central biblical texts of book 12' (234). Although my claims about the relevance of rabbinic balance between orality and textuality to an understanding of the Song of Songs in the Renaissance in general and to Milton specifically do not depend on either Fisch or Rosenblatt, their work has in some sense enabled my own.

[18] Achsah Guibbory reads the prelapsarian sexuality in the epic as an aspect of 'a holy rite, bringing the body fully into the worship of God and sanctifying sex as a way of connecting with God' (206). She connects this to a reading of Canticles that has both the Hebrew Bible and Milton integrate sexuality and spirituality: 'The integration of sexual and spiritual, body and soul, that distinguishes the Hebrew Song of Songs above all other books of the Bible, characterizes Milton's description of paradisal life. Departing from dominant Christian traditions, his celebration of the sacredness of sexual love is part of the Hebraic ethos that Rosenblatt has shown characterizes the Edenic books of *Paradise Lost*' (208). My view of the biblical text distinguishes between its diachronic secularization of the earlier, primarily oral, pagan traditions and the restoration of the full synchronic pattern by later allegorizations (see Introduction, 12–19). My reading of Milton and his use of Canticles underscores the tensions between the different strains that Guibbory sees as integrated. This, however, is merely an anticipation of what she describes as 'the tension between monist and dualist attitudes' and 'the difficult, conflicted representation of the relation between love and worship – and of Eve – in the poem' (211).

is Christ's love for the Church. The unity between oral and written understandings of the text will break down after the fall and set up imagined conflicts between the oral perception of the lover in the biblical text and the written allegorical traditions about the ways in which this language connotes Christ and the Church.

On another level, the irony results from an awareness of the ways in which Canticles was seen by Ranters such as Coppe and Clarkson. The vision of these radical antinomians is spiritualized by Adam in Book 5 when he internalizes their attempt to see sexuality and holiness as part of a unified process. A revision of Ranter doctrine in the context of unfallen Adam suggests that as long as love for Eve leads Adam toward God, as does the Son's love for the Church, sexual eros is holy and commendable. There is no necessary distinction between the sexual and the holy for Adam before he eats the fruit. Nevertheless the possibility of confusion remains an option throughout the epic. Indeed, it is this that makes Satan's task feasible and finally successful.

A view of Adam as Ranter could thus read the love song to Eve in the context of Coppe's entreaties to his reader: 'Rise up, rise up, my Love, my fair one, and *come away* . . .' (*Some Sweet Sips*, 15 [Smith, *Collection* 53]) or of Clarkson's argument: '*Thou art all fair my Love, there is no spot in thee* . . . Love is *God* and God is Love; so all pure, all, light, no spot in thee' (*A Single Eye* 10 [Smith, *Collection* 170]). That is, in addition to the sexual aspects of the Ranter rites, there were clear entreaties for spiritual awakening as well. If Adam is akin to Coppe and Clarkson, he is also conscious of the spiritual implications of his words that will inspire Solomon. As long as he perceives the values of holy and sexual love as consistent there is no way that he can fall.

When Adam surrenders this monistic unity for the dialectically opposed worlds of Satan and God, he falls like Clarkson into total Muggletonian rejection of Solomon and a reconsideration of his love for Eve in selfish, manipulative terms. After eating the fruit, Adam regards Eve as a sexual object:

> For never did thy Beautie since the day
> I saw thee first and wedded thee, adorn'd
> With all perfections, so enflame my sense
> With ardor to enjoy thee, fairer now
> Then ever, bountie of this vertuous Tree. (9. 1029–33)

Later on, he can only recall her part in his deliberate fall. His understanding of love has lost the mixture of eros and agape that characterized it before the fall. His excuse for eating the fruit is selfless love for Eve, but only a little while after the act he begins to scold and blame her:

> Is this the Love, is this the recompence
> Of mine to thee, ingrateful *Eve*, exprest
> Immutable when thou wert lost, not I,
> Who might have liv'd and joyd immortal bliss,
> Yet willingly chose rather Death with thee:
> And am I now upbraided, as the cause
> Of thy transgressing? not enough severe,
> It seems, in thy restraint: what could I more?
> ...
>   and perhaps
> I also err'd in overmuch admiring
> What seemd in thee so perfet, that I thought
> No evil durst attempt thee, but I rue
> That errour now, which is become my crime,
> And thou th' accuser. Thus it shall befall
> Him who to worth in Woman overtrusting
> Lets her will rule; restraint she will not brook,
> And left t' her self, if evil thence ensue,
> Shee first his weak indulgence will accuse. (9.1163–70,77–86)

The various conclusions to *Paradise Lost* establish the ways in which postlapsarian men and women can hope to fashion an Edenic substitute: 'A Paradise within thee, happier farr' (12.587). Although this involves a complicated process by which Adam and Eve must learn the nature of their newly fallen world, it is primarily predicated upon a reconciliation between them which marks Milton's correction or refinement of Coppe's discourse with 'Mrs. T. P.' As between Adam and Ranter men, there are parallels and major distinctions between Eve and this Ranter woman.

Near the end of *Some Sweet Sips*, Abiezer Coppe claims to quote from his correspondence with a woman to whom he refers as 'Mrs. T. P.' who has written to him of her role as a Ranter. Although her letter to him and his response can be read primarily as an exchange of ideas between two sectarian believers, the language sets up a lively conversation between a woman and a man which conveys a good deal more than philosophical and religious positions:

> It hath pleased *The Father* of late, so sweetly to manifest his love to my soule, that I cannot but returne it to you, who are the Image of my *Father*.
>
> I should rejoyce, if the Father pleased also, to see you, and to have some Spirituall communion with you, that I might impart those soul-ravishing consolations which have flowne from the bosome of the Father, to our mutuall comfort. What though we are weaker vessels, women, &c. yet strength shall abound, and we shall mount up with wings as Eagles; we shall walke, and not be weary, run, and not faint; When the *Man Child Jesus* is brought forth *In Us*.
> (39–40 [Smith, *Collection* 64])

Further on she recounts a dream in which she learns to become intimate with various creatures that she had previously regarded with revulsion:

> I was in a place, where I saw all kinde of Beasts of the field; wilde, and tame together, and all kinde of creeping wormes, and all kinde of Fishes – in a pleasant river, where the water was exceeding cleere, – not very deep – but very pure – and no mud, or setling at the bottom, as ordinarily is in ponds or rivers. And all these beasts, wormes and Fishes, living, and recreateing themselves together, and my selfe with them; yea, we had so free a correspondence together, as I oft-times would take the wildest of them, and put them in my bosome, especially such (which afore) I had exceedingly feared, such that I would not have toucht, or come nigh: as the Snake, and Toade, &c. – And the wildest kinde, and strangest appearances as ever I saw in my life. At last I tooke one of the wildest, as a Tiger, or such like, and brought it in my bosome away, from all the rest, and put a Collar about him for mine owne, and when I had thus done, it grew wilde againe, and strove to get from me, And I had great trouble about it. (41 [Smith, *Collection* 64–5])

It is clear that Mrs T. P. sees herself as a kind of prophetess. Her visions are partially shaped by the biblical account of Peter's trance in which he saw 'all manner of four-footed beasts of the earth, and wild beasts, and creeping things, and fowls of the air' (Acts 10.12). Whereas the biblical narrative treats of God's commandment to Peter with regard to the eating of non-kosher food ('What God hath cleansed, that call not thou common' [Acts 10.15]), Mrs T. P. interprets her vision in terms of spiritual freedom: 'And it was shewen me, that my having so free a commerce with all sorts of appearances, was my spirituall libertie, – and certainly, did I know it, it would be a very glorious libertie, and yet a perfect Law too' (42 [Smith, *Collection* 65]). She is likewise conscious of her weakness in attempting to collar and control the 'Tiger, or such like' that had previously roamed wild and free:

> Now concerning my taking one of them from all the rest (as distinct,) and setting a collar about it – this was my weaknesse, and here comes in all our bondage, and death, by appropriating of things to our selves, and for our selves; for could I have been contented to have enjoyed this little, this one thing in the libertie of the Spirit – I had never been brought to that tedious care in keeping, nor that exceeding griefe in loosing, – waite therefore upon God for a further understanding in this thing, And when you have it, I make no question but I shall partake of it. – (42–3 [Smith, *Collection* 65])

Despite the authority with which she accounts of her prophetic role, Mrs T. P. expresses a certain degree of concern lest Coppe regard her as a threat. She covers herself by clarifying her acceptance of traditional feminine inferiority: 'What though we are weaker vessels, women, &c.' She also concludes by asking for Coppe's view of her inspiration as she waits 'therefore upon God for a further understanding in this thing, And when you have it, I make no question but I shall partake of it'.

Near the beginning of his response, Coppe refers to Mrs T. P. in the language of Canticles: 'And it is the voyce of my *Beloved*, that saith, drinke oh friends! yea, drinke abundantly oh Beloved!' He then goes on to resist her tendency to denigrate herself as a woman by insisting upon the equality of the sexes: 'Deare friend, why doest in thy letter say, {what though we be weaker Vessels, women? &c}. I know that Male and Female are all one in *Christ*, and they are all one to me. I had as live heare a daughter, as a sonne prophesie' (46 [Smith, Collection 66]). He calls upon her to accept the freedom signified by her dream and to join with him in a spiritual union filled with various other biblical references. Clement Hawes reads this interchange as a straightforward testimony to Coppe's commitment to gendered equality, an egalitarian moment which demonstrates 'the genuine political promise inherent in the manic topoi of fluid and interchangeable gender identity' (72). He also cites James Holstun who reads Coppe's comment as 'an extraordinary inversion of the metaphors of gender hierarchy' (72 [Holstun 220]).

As we have seen in the previous chapter, however, Coppe regularly ignored the human complexities of his 'wanton kisses' which signify a spirituality in and beyond sexuality, just as he ignored the real Jews whose readmission to England would soon become a serious political issue. In the light of Coppe's use of allegory to hint at yet avoid explicit articulation of his ideas, it is worth reading his comments to Mrs T. P. with great care. The pattern of biblical references that follow his praise of 'interchangeable gender identity' is very similar to that which introduces his 'wanton kisses'. That is, his carnal reading of Canticles leads toward sexual acts which then signify a meaning in the mind of the male participant which was not necessarily in accord with that of the female 'fellow creature'. Mrs T. P.'s self deprecation for desiring to own the wild creature in her dream is sexually suggestive: 'At last I tooke one of the wildest . . . and brought it in my bosome away.' She may have something in common with Clarkson's 'maid of pretty knowledge' who expected sexual intimacy to lead to a wedding and did not suspect that her Ranter lover was already married.[19] The sexual politics revealed in Clarkson's *Lost Sheep Found* are, perhaps, indicative of the practice of other Ranters. In any case, Coppe's letter to Mrs T. P. rehearses the earlier discussion of 'wanton kisses' which suggests that the talk of equality is at least partially motivated by sexual desire.

The exchange between Mrs T. P. and Coppe parallels the relationship between Adam and Eve in *Paradise Lost*. Mrs T. P. and Eve share such elements and themes as learning from visions and dreams, responding to toads, and sexually charged transcendence of fears and taboos. Each submits her vision of the night to a male companion for interpretation and spiritual support. On another level, the male creators of these characters are themselves

---

[19] See Chapter 5, 131.

involved in a struggle to define their own positions and personalities in response to a feminine entity. Finally, the implicit dynamics of the relations between Coppe and Mrs. T. P. point to the very different set of relations between Adam and Eve.

Both Mrs T. P. and Eve view their dreams or visions as direct inspiration from God. This is part of the underlying assumption each woman makes even before she begins to provide details of her experience. For Mrs T. P. this is merely part of her introductory comment: 'That of late the Father teacheth me by visions of the night – It will be too large to communicate by letter, yet because to one is given a revelation; to another an interpretation. I cannot but repeat one, which was thus – I was in a place, where I saw all kinde of Beasts ...' (40–1 [Smith, *Collection* 64]). Although Eve gives no such credence to the dream she recounts at the beginning of Book 5, she is quite explicit about the divine source of the vision to which she refers in a brief conversation with Adam after Michael has instructed him in Books 11 and 12:

> Whence thou returnst, and whither wentst, I know;
> For God is also in sleep, and Dreams advise,
> Which he hath sent propitious . . . (12.610–12)

Although both Eve and Mrs T. P. are similar in their willingness to see themselves as prophetesses, Eve is much more circumspect in the account of her earlier dream whose Satanic source has been clarified earlier by Milton's Narrator:

> him [Satan] there they found
> Squat like a Toad, close at the ear of *Eve*;
> Assaying by his Devilish art to reach
> The Organs of her Fancie, and with them forge
> Illusions as he list, Phantasms and Dreams. (4.799–803)

This Satanic dream, which Eve recounts in dismay just after Adam's love song to her from Canticles, is another aspect of the way in which *Paradise Lost* rewrites Ranter discourse as part of prelapsarian experience. That which is theologically objectionable is ascribed to Satan. He is the source of Eve's vision and thus the inspiration for the temptation to which she yields in her dream:

> the pleasant savourie smell
> So quick'nd appetite, that I, methought,
> Could not but taste. (5.84–6)

The familiarity with creatures such 'as the Snake, and Toade' in Mrs T. P.'s vision is transformed into a dream whispered by Satan 'like a Toad' in which the Adam-like tempter prefigures Satan himself in the form of a serpent in the actual temptation scene in Book 9.

Mrs T. P.'s letter is quite sensuous as she refers to her 'true love in the Spirit of one-nesse'. She tells Coppe that 'it hath pleased *The Father* of late, so sweetly to manifest his love to my soule, that I cannot but returne it to you, who are the Image of my *Father*'. 'I have been at the Holy Land,' she exclaims, 'and have tasted of the good fruit; not only seen that fruit which the Spies brought, but surely I have tasted' (40 [Smith, *Collection* 64]). Her intimacy with the wildest creatures was, she says, her 'spirituall libertie . . . a very glorious libertie' (42 [Smith, *Collection* 65]). This passionate sensuousness pulsates with sexuality that is only partially subdued in Eve's account of her dream. She begins by referring to the 'gentle voice' (5.37) she heard which she thought was Adam. The voice she hears pays Petrarchan tribute to her beauty in terms of the implicit sexual desire of Heaven for her:

> Heav'n wakes with all his eyes,
> Whom to behold but thee, Natures desire,
> In whose sight all things joy, with ravishment
> Attracted by thy beauty still to gaze. (5.44–7)

The fairness of the tree of knowledge ('Much fairer to my Fancie then by day' [5.53]), the 'dewie locks [which] distill'd / *Ambrosia*' (5.56–7) of her interlocutor, his reference to her as 'a Goddess' (5.77), the 'pleasant savourie smell' (5.84) of the fruit, all lead her to taste and fly 'To this high exaltation' (5.90). Milton has rewritten the desire of Mrs T. P. into an implicitly sexual temptation which avoids the tone of Canticles used by Adam in his earlier love song. Satan's suave approach to Eve awakens her senses and alludes to sexual pleasure without ever making this apparent. As Eve reaches her 'high exaltation' she suddenly falls back to sleep.

As *Paradise Lost* rewrites the desire of Ranter discourse, it translates the implicitly manipulative sexuality of Coppe and Clarkson into Satanic flattery and temptation. The agency of Coppe and Mrs T. P. is replaced by Satan and the resultant approach to love and desire is then juxtaposed against the Solomonic tone of Adam's song. Coppe made Canticles into the initial part of his response to the passionate letter of Mrs T. P.: 'And it is the voyce of my *Beloved*, that saith, drinke oh friends! yea, drinke abundantly oh Beloved!' The balance between the carnal and the spiritual here points toward sexual manipulation that then connotes a detachment of the individual Ranter in a final kind of apocalypse: 'O my beloved! Be thou as a Roe, or young Hart – Even so Lord Jesus, Amen, come quickly, Amen. I see him comming (to some *come*) in the clouds, with great power and glory, Amen, *Halelujah*' (60 [Smith, *Collection* 72]). In Milton's epic, Adam and Eve turn away from the apocalypse as they proceed to leave Paradise 'hand in hand'. Adam's love song accepts the carnality of Canticles but applies it to a love that is mutual and lyric rather than manipulative and apocalyptic.

There is one additional interesting parallel between *Some Sweet Sips* and

Paradise Lost. Both Coppe and Milton exercised close rhetorical control over the ways in which Mrs T. P. and Eve speak and relate to their men. Whether or not Mrs T. P. was a real person with whom Coppe corresponded, he consciously indicated that her letter was 'AN Extract of an Epistle sent to A. C. from Mrs T. P. . . .' (39 [Smith, *Collection* 64]). That is, Coppe presents her letter in such a way as to shape and direct *Some Sweet Sips*. Although this is no less the case for *Paradise Lost* as Milton directed the poetic texture of Eve's language and behaviour, the epic does have an added level of complication as the epic narrator can be understood to act as an additional source of control which is not a conscious part of Coppe's text. Milton's narrator adds to the love discourse in the epic as he thematizes the relations between Adam and Eve in the praise of 'Wedded Love' discussed above as well as in terms of his own courtship of the Heavenly Muse.[20] This places the discourse about Eve's dreams in a context of a broad series of love relations that explore a set of connections between love and desire that include interaction between Adam and Eve, the narrator's desire for and fear of his Muse as well as the ways in which the narrator's choice of language to describe love is simultaneously an account of the actions of his characters and an expression of his own inspired love for holy song. On this level, the narrator's choice of Canticles to express Adam's love for Eve becomes a medium for expressing tensions between lover and beloved as well as between singer and muse.

The relationship between Adam and Eve can be understood as a refinement of this aspect of Ranter rhetoric. Like Mrs T. P., Eve has a dream which she finds troubling to some extent. Adam's Solomonic love song precedes Eve's account of her dream (in contrast to Coppe's references which explain and extend the dream) and his innocent explanation finds positive significance in what Eve experienced as threatening and troubling. *Paradise Lost*, however, then goes on to flesh out a complicated interaction between Adam and Eve that includes their bickering about separation, the actual eating of the fruit and the aftermath of the Fall. The final reconciliation between the couple takes place as a result of Eve's willingness to confront her error and beg for Adam's forgiveness. This 'heroism' changes his strident and nearly comic rejection of her into a reaffirmation of his love. *Paradise Lost* thus returns to the text of Canticles in terms of a sexuality that deals with love and not with 'wanton kisses'. The excesses of the Ranter world are reintegrated into a presentation of human love that allows for sexuality as an important aspect of human life before and after the fall, but avoids the pitfalls of Ranter doctrine that enlisted a carnal view of Canticles as a means of achieving closure in the form of Apocalypse. While Ranter discourse makes lust a means of anticipating the End, *Paradise Lost* balances Michael's instruction to Adam in Books 11 and 12 with another dream experienced by Eve. History and Apocalypse allow

---

[20] For more on this aspect of the relations between narrator and muse, see my 'Courting Urania' 86–99.

Adam's Revised Rant with Eve

Adam to prepare for the rest of his life with Eve while she takes similar resolution from her dream. Together they are prepared for the beginning of the rest of their lives in a lyrical expression of bitter-sweet love:

> They hand in hand with wandring steps and slow
> Through *Eden* took thir solitarie way. (12.648–9)

CONCLUSION

FROM Baldwin to Milton, this study has examined English Renaissance texts that depend upon readings of the Song of Songs in the presentation of themes, characters and relationships on the one hand, and upon the articulation of these and other concerns in language on the other. Each of the preceding chapters has treated a specific set of literary texts which range in canonicity from the most universally accepted poets (Spenser, Shakespeare and Milton) to lesser-known texts (Baldwin, Coppe and Clarkson) to the relative obscurity of the long neglected (Aylett). The line of development has moved on different planes. Central to the argument has been a balance in a series of dyadic tensions between orality and textuality, secrecy and revelation, lyric and apocalyptic, and carnal and spiritual. Understanding this kind of equilibrium depends upon the historical and theoretical discussion of reading Canticles presented in the Introduction. The balance between the various tensions could be described as stereoscopic in the sense that they all require the presence of both extremes in order to make sense of either. Thus textually established positions of the Church about the importance of reading Canticles allegorically and not literally must be juxtaposed (or balanced) against the oral practice of literal reading which can be established on the basis of a few written texts such as Chaucer or the Ranters. On a similar level, we have seen many examples of lyrical texts which can be read apocalyptically, secret texts that are simultaneously open and closed, and, of course, Canticles itself with its ancient pedigree for both carnal letter and allegory.

The line from Baldwin to Milton has been consistently Protestant with the exception of Shakespeare. The spiritual figure of a biblical text which integrates sexuality into its view of the holy is a major concern of most of the writers discussed. As Shakespeare explored a secular sexuality that erased or simply ignored the underlying spirituality, he pointed the way for a very different sort of project from that of the other writers presented in this study. From Baldwin to Milton, these explicitly Protestant writers kept sexuality in mind as an important focus in their treatment of Canticles, but they likewise tried to integrate their interest in kisses, oral and written, into the otherness of the spirit.

LIST OF WORKS CITED

Asals, Heather. 'Venus and Adonis: The Education of a Goddess'. *Studies in English Literature* 13 (1973): 31–51.
Astell, Ann W. *The Song of Songs in the Middle Ages*. Ithaca and London: Cornell UP, 1990.
Aylett, Robert. *The Brides Ornaments*. [Books 3 and 4] London, 1625.
——. *Divine, and Moral Speculations in Metrical Numbers, upon Various Subjects*. London, 1654.
——. *The Song of Songs, which was Salomons Metaphrased in English Heroicks by way of Dialogue. With certayne of the Brides Ornaments* [Books 1 and 2], *viz. Poeticall Essayes upon a Diuine Subiect. Wherunto is added a Funerall Elegie, consecrate to the memorie of the euer honoured Lord, Iohn, late Bishop of London*. London, 1621.
The Babylonian Talmud, Vol. 14 [Seder Kodashim], I. Epstein, ed. and trans. London: Soncino Press, 1960.
Baldi, Sergio. 'Poesie Italiane di Milton'. *Studi Secenteschi* 7 (1966): 103–30.
Baldwin, William. *The Canticles, or Balades of Salomon, Phraselyke Declared in English Metres*. London, 1549.
Baroway, Israel. 'The Imagery of Spenser and the Song of Songs'. *Journal of English and Germanic Philology* 33 (1934): 23–45.
Bennett, Joan S. '"Go": Milton's Antinomianism and the Separation Scene in *Paradise Lost*, Book 9'. *PMLA* 98 (1983): 388–404.
Bialik, Hayim N. and Yehoshua H. Ravnitsky. *The Book of Legends Sefer ha-aggadah: Legends from the Talmud and Midrash*. Tr. William G. Braude. New York: Schocken, 1992.

Bibles:
Authorized Version. *The Holy Bible: A Facsimile in a reduced size of the Authorized Version published in the year 1611*. Intro. A. W. Pollard. Oxford and New York: Oxford University Press, 1911.
Coverdale Bible. *The Holy Scriptures, Faithfully and Truly Translated by Myles Coverdale, Bishop of Exeter*. Biblia: The Bible that is, the holy Scripture of the Olde and New Testament, faithfully and truly translated in to Englishe. 1535. Repr. London: Samuel Bagster, 1838.
Etienne [Stephanus], Robert [?] Bible. OT. Latin. 1537. Re-issue of 1532 [?] *Biblia Breues in eadem annotationes, ex doctiss. interpretationibus, & Hebræorum commentariis. Interpretation propriorum nominum Hebraicorum. Index copiosissiumus rerum & senteniarum vtriusque testamenti*. Lugduni. Ex officina Guilelmi Boulle. In uico Mercuriali. 1537.

List of Works Cited

Geneva Bible. *The Geneva Bible: A Facsimile of the 1560 edition*. Madison, Milwaukee and London: U of Wisconsin P, 1969.
Great Bible. *The Byble in Englyshe, that is to saye the content of al the holy scrypture, both of ye olde, and newe testament with a prologe thereinto, made by the reuerende father in God, Thomas [Cranmer] archbysshop of Canterbury*. Prynted by Edward Whytchurche, 1540.
Matthew Bible. *The Byble which is all the holy Scripture: In whych are contayned the Olde and Newe Testament truly and purely translated into English by Thomas Matthew*. 1537.
Vulgate. *Bibliorom Sacrorum Iuxta Vulgatam Clementina*. Nova Editio. Aloisius Gramatica, Typis Polyglottis Vaticanis, 1959.

Booth, Stephen, ed. *Shakespeare's Sonnets*. New Haven and London: Yale UP, 1977.
Boyarin, Daniel. 'The Song of Songs: Lock or Key? Intertextuality, Allegory and Midrash'. *The Book and the Text: The Bible and Literary Theory*. Ed. Regina M. Schwartz. Cambridge, MA and Oxford: Basil Blackwell, 1990. 214–30.
Boyarin, Jonathan. 'Introduction'. *The Ethnography of Reading*. Ed. Jonathan Boyarin. Berkeley: U Cal P, 1993. 1–9.
Brightman, Thomas. *The Workes of that Famous, Reverend, and Learned Divine, Mr. Tho. Brightman. . .* London, 1644.
Bruns, Gerald. 'The Hermeneutics of Midrash'. *The Book and the Text: The Bible and Literary Theory*. Ed. Regina M. Schwartz. Cambridge, MA and Oxford: Basil Blackwell, 1990. 189–213.
Campbell, Lily B. *Divine Poetry & Drama in Sixteenth-Century England*. Cambridge: University Press; Berkeley and Los Angeles: U California P, 1959.
———. ed. *Mirror for Magistrates*. Cambridge: University Press, 1938.
Carey, John, and Alastair Fowler, eds. *The Poems of John Milton*. London: Longmans, 1968.
Castiglione, Baldassare. *The Book of the Courtier*. Trans. Sir Thomas Hoby. 1561. London: J. M. Dent, 1975.
Cavalcanti, Guido. *The Poetry of Guido Cavalcanti*. Trans. ed. Lowry Nelson, Jr. Vol. 18, Series A. Garland Library of Medieval Literature. New York and London: Garland Publishing. 1986.
———. *Pound's Cavalcanti: An Edition of The Translations, Notes and Essays*. Ed. David Anderson. Princeton, NJ: Princeton UP, 1983.
———. *Rime*. Ed. Domenico De Robertis. Torino: Giulio Einaudi, 1986.
Cavanaugh, Sister Francis Camilla. *Critical Edition of 'The Canticles or Balades of Salomon Phraselyke Declared in English Meters' by William Baldwin*. Dissertation, St. Louis U, 1964. Ann Arbor: University Microfilm International, 1965.
Chaucer, Geoffrey. *The Riverside Chaucer*. Gen. ed. Larry D. Benson. 3rd edn. [based on *The Works of Geoffrey Chaucer*, ed. F. N. Robinson] Boston: Houghton Mifflin, 1987.
Clarkson [or Claxton], Laurence. *The Lost Sheep Found: Or, the Prodigal returned to his Fathers house, after many a sad and weary Journey through many Religious Countreys*. London, 1660.
———. *A Single Eye: All Light, no Darkness; or Light and Darkness One . . .* London, 1650.
Cohn, Norman. *The Pursuit of the Millennium: Revolutionary Millenarians and Mystical Anarchists of the Middle Ages*. Revised and expanded edition. New York: Oxford UP, 1970.

List of Works Cited

Contini, Gianfranco, ed. *Poeti del Duecento*. La Letteratura Italiana: Storia e Testi. Vol. 2. Milano: Riccardo Ricciardi Editore, 1960.

Coppe, Abiezer. *A Fiery Flying Roll: A Word from the Lord to all the Great Ones of the Earth, whom this may concerne: Being the last WARNING PIECE at the dreadfull day of JUDGEMENT* . . . London, 1649.

———. *A Second Fiery Flying Roule: To All the Inhabitants of the earth; specially to the rich ones* . . . London, 1649. Although this pamphlet has its own title page, it is bound together with *A Fiery Flying Roll* in the British Library copy [Thomason Tracts].

———. *Some Sweet Sips of some Spirituall Wine, sweetly and freely dropping from one cluster of Grapes, brought between two upon a Staffe from Spirituall Canaan (the Land of the Living; the Living Lord.) To Late Egyptian, and now bewildered Israelites*. London, 1649.

Craze, Michael. *The Life and Lyrics of Andrew Marvell*. London: Macmillan; New York: Harper & Row, 1979.

Dante Alighieri. *The New Life: La Vita Nuova*. Trans. William Anderson. Baltimore: Penguin, 1964.

———. *Purgatorio*. Trans. Allen Mandelbaum. 1982; repr. New York: Bantam, 1984. Vol. 2 of *The Divine Comedy of Dante Alighieri*. Notes by Laury Magnus, Allen Mandelbaum and Anthony Oldcorn, with Daniel Feldman. 3 vols. 1980–84.

———. *Vita nuova Rime*. Ed. Fredi Chiappelli. 4th edn. Milano: Mursia, 1973.

Davis, J. C. *Fear, Myth and History: The Ranters and the Historians*. Cambridge: Cambridge UP, 1986.

DeNeef, A. Leigh. *Spenser and the Motives of Metaphor*. Durham, NC: Duke UP, 1982.

di Giunta, Bernardo, ed. *Sonetti è canzoni di diversi antichi autori toscani in dieci libri raccolte*. Firenze, 1527.

———. *Rime di diversi antichi autori toscani in dieci libri raccolte*. Vinegra [Venice], 1532.

Donne, John. *The Complete Poetry of John Donne*. Ed. John T. Shawcross. New York: New York UP; London: U of London P, Ltd, 1968.

Dronke, Peter. *Medieval Latin and the Rise of European Love-Lyric*. 2 vols. Oxford: Clarendon P, 1965–66.

———. *The Medieval Lyric*. London: Hutchinson U Library, 1968.

———. 'The Song of Songs and Medieval Love-Lyric'. Ed. W. Lourdaux and D. Verhelst. *The Bible and Medieval Culture*. Mediaevalia Lovaniensia 1/7. Leuven (Belgium): Leuven UP, 1979. 236–62.

Dubrow, Heather. *Captive Victors: Shakespeare's Narrative Poems and Sonnets*. Ithaca and London: Cornell UP, 1987.

Eco, Umberto. *The Name of The Rose*. Trans. William Weaver. New York: Harcourt Brace Jovanovich, 1983.

Engammare, Max. *Qu'il me baise des baisiers de sa bouche: Le cantique des cantiques à la renaissance, étude et bibliographie*. Travaux d'Humanisme et Renaissance 277. Genève: Librairie Droz, 1993.

Faur, José. *Golden Doves with Silver Dots: Semiotics and Textuality in Rabbinic Tradition*. Bloomington: Indiana UP, 1986.

Fisch, Harold. 'Hebraic Style and Motifs in *Paradise Lost*'. Ronald D. Emma and John T. Shawcross eds. *Language and Style in Milton: A Symposium in Honor of the Tercentenary of* Paradise Lost. New York: Ungar, 1967. 30–64.

Fisch, Harold. *Jerusalem and Albion: The Hebraic Factor in Seventeenth-Century English Literature*. New York: Schocken, 1964.

Fixler, Michael. *Milton and the Kingdoms of God*. Evanston, IL: Northwestern UP, 1964.

Flinker, Noam. 'Courting Urania: The Narrator of *Paradise Lost* Invokes his Muse'. *Milton and the Idea of Woman*. Ed. Julia M. Walker. Urbana and Chicago: U of Illinois P, 1988. 86–99.

——. 'Milton and the Ranters on Canticles'. *A Fine Tuning: Studies of the Religious Poetry of Herbert and Milton.*. Ed. Mary Maleski. Medieval and Renaissance Texts and Studies 64. Binghamton, NY: Medieval and Renaissance Texts and Studies, 1989. 273–90.

——. 'Ranter Sexual Politics: Canticles in the England of 1650'. *Identity and Ethos: A Festschrift for Sol Liptzin on the Occasion of his 85th Birthday*. Ed. Mark Gelber. Bern: Peter Lang, 1986. 325–41.

Foucault, Michel. *The History of Sexuality*. Vol. 1: *An Introduction*. Trans Robert Hurley. 1978; New York: Random House Vintage Books, 1980.

Fox, Michael V. *The Song of Songs and the Ancient Egyptian Love Songs*. Madison, WI, and London: U of Wisconsin P, 1985.

Frazer, Sir James George. *Adonis, Attis, Osiris: Studies in the History of Oriental Religion*. 3rd edn. Vol. 1. 1914. London: Macmillan; New York: St. Martin's Press, 1963. 2 vols.

Friedman, Jerome. *Blasphemy, Immortality, and Anarchy: The Ranters and the English Revolution*. Athens, OH and London: Ohio UP, 1987.

Geller, M. J. 'Introduction'. *Figurative Language in the Ancient Near East*. Ed. M. Mindlin, M. J. Geller and J. E. Wansbrough. London: School of Oriental and African Studies, U London, 1987. ix–xiii.

Gibbs, Donna. *Spenser's Amoretti: A Critical Study*. Aldershot, Hants., UK, and Brookfield, VT: Scolar Press [Gower], 1990.

Goodblatt, David. 'The Babylonian Talmud'. Ed. Jacob Neusner *The Study of Ancient Judaism*. Vol. 2 [The Palestinian and Babylonian Talmuds]. New York: Ktav Publishing House, 1981. 257–336. Pagination is both continuous from the first volume (no brackets) and separate for the second volume (indicated in brackets): [2:120–99].

Gresham, Stephen. 'William Baldwin: Literary Voice of the Reign of Edward VI'. *Huntington Library Quarterly* 44 (1981): 101–16.

Grossman, Marshall. *The Story of All Things: Writing the Self in English Renaissance Narrative Poetry*. Durham and London: Duke UP, 1998.

Guibbory, Achsah. *Ceremony and Community from Herbert to Milton: Literature, Religion and Cultural Conflict in Seventeenth-century England*. Cambridge: Cambridge UP, 1998.

Haak, Theodore. *The Dutch Annotations upon the Whole Bible . . .* London, 1657.

Hamilton, A. C. 'Venus and Adonis'. *Studies in English Literature* 1 (1961): 1–15.

Handelman, Susan A. *The Slayers of Moses: The Emergence of Rabbinic Interpretation in Modern Literary Theory*. Albany: State University of New York Press, 1982.

Hardison, O. B., Jr. '*Amoretti* and the *Dolce Stil Novo*'. *English Literary Renaissance* 2 (1972): 208–16.

Harrison, Robert Pogue. *The Body of Beatrice*. Baltimore and London: Johns Hopkins UP, 1988.

Hawes, Clement. *Mania and Literary Style: The Rhetoric of Enthusiasm from the*

Ranters to Christopher Smart. Cambridge Studies in Eighteenth-century English Literature and Thought, 9. Cambridge: Cambridge UP, 1996.

Herbert, George. *The Works of George Herbert*. Ed. F. E. Hutchinson. Oxford: Clarendon P, 1941.

Hester, M. Thomas. '"If thou regard the same:" Spenser's Emblematic Centerfold'. *American Notes and Queries* 6 (1993): 183–89.

Hill, Christopher. *The English Bible and the Seventeenth-century Revolution*. London: Penguin, 1994.

———. *Milton and the English Revolution*. New York: Viking Press, 1978.

———. *The World Turned Upside Down*. London: Temple Smith, 1972.

Holstun, James. 'Ranting at the New Historicism'. *English Literary Renaissance* 19 (1989): 189–225.

Hughes, Merritt Y., ed. *John Milton: Complete Poems and Major Prose*. New York: Macmillan, 1957.

Hunter, William B., ed. *The English Spenserians: The Poetry of Giles Fletcher, George Wither, Michael Drayton, Phineas Fletcher, and Henry More*. Salt Lake City: U of Utah P, 1977.

———. 'Spenser and Milton'. *A Milton Encyclopedia*. Gen. ed. William B. Hunter. 9 vols. Lewisburg, PA: Bucknell UP; London: Associated University Presses, 1978–83. 8: 34–36.

Johnson, William Clarence. *Spenser's Amoretti: Analogies of Love*. Lewisburg: Bucknell UP; London and Toronto: Associated University Presses, 1990.

Josephus, Flavius. *Josephus with an English Translation*. Trans. Ralph Marcus. 9 vols. London: Wm Heinemann; Cambridge, MA: Harvard UP, 1951. *Jewish Antiquities*, Books 9–11 in vol. 6.

Kalmin, Richard L. *The Redaction of the Babylonian Talmud: Amoraic or Saboraic?* Cincinnati: Hebrew Union College Press, 1989.

Kaske, Carol V. 'Spenser's *Amoretti* and *Epithalamion* of 1595: Structure, Genre, and Numerology'. *English Literary Renaissance* 3 (1978): 271–95.

Kaske, R. E. 'The Canticum Canticorum in the Miller's Tale'. *Studies in Philology* 59 (1962): 479–500.

———. 'Chaucer's Marriage Group'. *Chaucer the Love Poet*. Ed. Jerome Mitchell and William Provost. Athens: U of Georgia P, 1973. 45–65.

———. 'Panel Discussion'. *Chaucer the Love Poet*. Ed. Jerome Mitchell and William Provost. Athens: U of Georgia P, 1973. 91–106.

Katz, David S. *Philo-Semitism and the Readmission of the Jews to England, 1603–1655*. Oxford and New York: Oxford UP, 1982.

Kay, George, ed. *The Penguin Book of Italian Verse*. 1958. Repr. with additional poems. Baltimore: Penguin, 1965.

Keach, William. *Elizabethan Erotic Narratives: Irony and Pathos in the Ovidian Poetry of Shakespeare, Marlowe, and their Contemporaries*. New Brunswick, NJ: Rutgers UP, 1977.

Kermode, Frank. 'The Argument of Marvell's "Garden"'. *Essays in Criticism* 2 (1952): 225–41. Repr. in *Seventeenth-Century English Poetry: Modern Essays in Criticism*. Rev. ed. Ed. William R. Keast. London and New York: Oxford UP, 1971. 333–347.

Kerrigan, John, ed. *The Sonnets and A Lover's Complaint* (William Shakespeare). New Penguin Shakespeare. Harmondsworth: Penguin, 1986.

List of Works Cited

King, John N. *English Reformation Literature: The Tudor Origins of the Protestant Tradition*. Princeton: Princeton UP, 1982.

——. *Spenser's Poetry and the Reformation Tradition*. Princeton: Princeton UP, 1990.

Kostić, Veselin. *Spenser's Sources in Italian Poetry: A Study in Comparative Literature*. Faculte de Philologie de L'Universite de Belgrade. Monographies, Tome 30. Belgrade, 1969.

Kraemer, David. *The Mind of the Talmud: An Intellectual History of the Bavli*. New York and Oxford: Oxford UP, 1990.

Kramer, Samuel Noah. *The Sacred Marriage Rite: Aspects of Faith, Myth, and Ritual in Ancient Sumer*. Bloomington and London: Indiana UP, 1969.

Lambert, W. G. 'Devotion: The Languages of Religion and Love'. *Figurative Language in the Ancient Near East*. Ed. M. Mindlin, M.J. Geller, J. E. Wansbrough. London: School of Oriental and African Studies, U London, 1987. 25–39.

Laurence, Anne. 'Two Ranter Poems'. *Review of English Studies* 31 (1980): 56–59.

Leclercq, Jean. 'Epilogue, Bernard and Dante: The Bride and Beatrice'. *Monks and Love in Twelfth-century France: Psycho-Historical Essays*. Oxford: Clarendon P, 1979. 137–44.

Leick, Gwendolyn. *Sex and Eroticism in Mesopotamian Literature*. London and New York: Routledge, 1994.

Lever, J. W. 'The Poems.' *Shakespeare Survey* 15 (1962): 18–22.

Lewalski, Barbara Kiefer. *Protestant Poetics and the Seventeenth-century Religious Lyric*. Princeton, NJ: Princeton UP, 1979.

Littledale, Richard Frederick. *A Commentary on the Song of Songs*. London: Joseph Masters; New York: Pott and Avery, 1869.

Lord, Albert B. *The Singer of Tales*. Cambridge, MA: Harvard UP, 1964.

Low, Anthony. *The Reinvention of Love: Poetry, Politics and Culture from Sidney to Milton*. Cambridge: Cambridge UP, 1993.

Lucianus Samosatensis (attributed). *The Syrian Goddess* [*De Dea Syria*]. Trans. Harold W. Attridge and Robert A. Oden. Society of Biblical Literature. Missoula, MT: Scholars Press, 1976.

Luther, Martin. 'Lectures on the Song of Solomon'. *Luther's Works*. Ed. Jaroslav Pelikan. St. Louis: Concordia Publishing, 1972. 115: 191–222.

McColley, Diane Kelsey. *Milton's Eve*. Urbana: U of Illinois P, 1983.

Marlowe, Christopher. *The Complete Poems and Translations*. Ed. Stephen Orgel. Harmondsworth and Baltimore: Penguin, 1971.

Marot, Clément. *Œuvres*. Ed. Georges Guiffrey. Vol. 4. Geneve: Slatkine Reprints, 1969.

Martz, Louis L. '*The Amoretti*: "Most Goodly Temperature"'. *Form and Convention in the Poery of Edmund Spenser: Selected Papers from the English Institute*. Ed. William Nelson. New York and London: Columbia UP, 1961. 146–68, 180.

Marvell, Andrew. *The Poems and Letters of Andrew Marvell*. Ed. H. M. Margoliouth. Rev. Pierre Legouis and E. E. Duncan-Jones. 3rd edn. 2 vols. Oxford: Clarendon P, 1971.

Matter, E. Ann. *The Voice of my Beloved: The Song of Songs in Western Medieval Christianity*. University of Pennsylvania Press Middle Ages Series. Philadelphia: U Pennsylvania P, 1990.

Midrash Rabbah. Trans. H. Freedman and Maurice Simon. 10 vols. London: Soncino P, 1939.

List of Works Cited

Milton, John. *The Complete Poetry of John Milton.* Ed. John T. Shawcross. Rev. edn. Garden City, NY: Doubleday, 1971.

——. *Complete Prose Works of John Milton.* Gen. ed. Don M. Wolfe. 8 vols. New Haven: Yale UP, 1953–82.

Morton, A. L. *The World of the Ranters: Religious Radicalism in the English Revolution.* London: Lawrence & Wishart, 1970.

Moulton, Richard G., ed. *The Modern Reader's Bible.* New York, Macmillan, 1907.

Muggleton, Lodowick. *A Looking-Glass for George Fox the Quaker, and other Quakers; Wherein they may see themselves to be Right Devils* . . . London, 1668 [corrected on title page from 1667].

Neusner, Jacob. *Oral Tradition in Judaism: The Case of the Mishnah.* New York: Garland Press, 1987.

Ong, Walter J., S.J. 'Oral Residue in Tudor Prose Style'. *PMLA* 80 (1965): 145–54.

——. *Orality and Literacy: The Technologizing of the Word.* London: Methuen, 1982.

——. *Ramus: Method and the Decay of Dialogue: From the Art of Discourse to the Art of Reason.* Cambridge: Harvard UP, 1958.

Origen. *Origen: The Song of Songs, Commentary and Homilies.* Trans. and annotated R. P. Lawson. Ancient Christian Writers, 26. New York: Newman P, 1957.

Ovide Moralisé: Poème du Commencement du Quatorzième siècle, Publié d'apres tous les Manuscrits Connus. Ed. C. de Boer (avec la collaboration de Martina G. de Boer et de Jeannette Th. M. Van 'T Sant). Vol. 4. 1915. Wiesbaden: Dr. Martin Sändig oHG, 1967. 4 Vols.

Padelford, Frederick M. 'Robert Aylett'. *Huntington Library Bulletin* 10 (1936): 1–48.

——. 'Robert Aylett: A Supplement'. *Huntington Library Quarterly* 2 (1938–39): 471–8.

Palliser, D. M. 'Popular Reactions to the Reformation during the Years of Uncertainty 1530–70'. *The English Reformation Revised.* ed. Christopher Haigh. Cambridge: Cambridge UP, 1987. 94–113.

Partridge, Eric. *A Dictionary of Slang and Unconventional English.* Ed. Paul Beale. 8th edn. London: Routledge & Kegan Paul, 1984.

——. *Shakespeare's Bawdy.* 3rd edn. 1968. Repr. London and New York: Routledge, 1993.

Petrarca, Francesco. *Canzoniere.* Ed. Maria A. Camozzi. Milano: Fratelli Fabri, 1969.

Poole, Matthew, ed. *Annotations upon the Holy Bible. Wherein the Sacred Text is Inserted, and Various Readings Annex'd, Together with the Parallel Scriptures.* 4th edn. 2 vols. London, 1700.

Pope, Marvin H. *Song of Songs: A New Translation with Introduction and Commentary.* Anchor Bible, 7C. Garden City, New York: Doubleday, 1977.

Prescott, Anne Lake. 'The Thirsty Deer and the Lord of Life: Some Contexts for *Amoretti* 67–70'. *Spenser Studies* 6 (1985 [act. pub. 1986]): 33–76.

Priest, Paul. 'Dante and "The Song of Songs"'. *Studi Danteschi* 49 (1972): 79–113.

The Ranters Bible. Or, Seven several Religions by them held and maintained . . . Published by Mr. Gilbert Roulston, a late Fellow-Ranter. London, 1650.

The Ranters Declaration, with Their new Oath and Protestation . . . Licensed according to order, and published by M. Stubs, a late fellow-Ranter. London, 1650.

The Ranters Last Sermon . . . London, 1654.

The Ranters Religion. Or, A faithfull and infallible Narrative of their damnable and diabolical opinions, with their detestable lives & actions . . . Printed for R. H. London, 1650.

Rosenblatt, Jason P. *Torah and Law in* Paradise Lost. Princeton: Princeton UP, 1994.

Salmon, Joseph. *Antichrist in Man: Or A Discovery of the Great Whore that sits upon many waters.* London, 1647.

Sandys, George. *Ovid's Metamorphosis: Englished, Mythologized, and Represented in Figures.* 1632. Ed. Karl K. Helley and Stanley T. Vandersall. Lincoln, NE: U of Nebraska P, 1970.

Scheper, George L. 'Reformation Attitudes toward Allegory and the Song of Songs'. *PMLA* 89 (1974): 551–62.

Schultz, Howard. 'Satan's Serenade'. *Philological Quarterly* 27 (1948): 17–26.

Scott, Janet G. 'The Sources of Spenser's "Amoretti"'. *Modern Language Review* 22 (1927): 189–95.

Sefati, Yitschak. *Love Songs in Sumerian Literature: Critical Edition of the Dumuzi-Inanna Songs.* Bar-Ilan Studies in Near Eastern Languages and Culture. Ramat Gan, Israel: Bar-Ilan UP, 1998.

——. 'An Oath of Chastity in a Sumerian Love Song (*SRT* 31)?' *Bar-Ilan Studies in Assyriology: Dedicated to Pinhas Artzi*, ed. Jacob Klein and Aaron Skaist. Ramat Gan, Israel: Bar-Ilan UP, 1990. 45–64.

Shakespeare, William. *The Poems.* Ed. F. T. Prince. The Arden Edition of the Works of William Shakespeare. London: Methuen; Cambridge, MA: Harvard UP, 1960.

——. *The Riverside Shakespeare.* Text. ed. G. Blakemore Evans. Boston: Houghton Mifflin, 1974.

Shawcross, John T. 'Milton's Italian Sonnets: An Interpretation'. *University of Windsor Review* 3 (1967): 27–33.

——. *With Mortal Voice: The Creation of* Paradise Lost. Lexington: UP of Kentucky, 1982.

Sidney, Sir Philip. *An Apologie for Poetrie.* Ed. Evelyn S. Shuckburgh. Cambridge: Cambridge UP, 1915.

Smith, Nigel, ed. *A Collection of Ranter Writings from the 17th Century.* London: Junction Books, 1983.

——. *Literature and Revolution in England, 1640–1660.* New Haven and London: Yale UP, 1994.

——. *Perfection Proclaimed: Language and Literature in English Radical Religion 1640–1660.* Oxford: Clarendon P, 1989.

Spenser, Edmund. *The Faerie Queene.* Ed. A. C. Hamilton. London and New York: Longman, 1977.

——. *Works: A Variorum Edition.* Ed. Edwin Greenlaw et al. 9 V. in 10. Baltimore: Johns Hopkins UP, 1932–49; repr. 1961.

——. *The Yale Edition of the Shorter Poems of Edmund Spenser.* Ed. William A. Oram, Einar Bjorvand, Ronald Bond, Thomas H. Cain, Alexander Dunlop and Richard Schell. New Haven and London: Yale UP, 1989.

Stern, David. *Parables in Midrash: Narrative and Exegesis in Rabbinic Literature.* Cambridge, MA, and London: Harvard UP, 1991.

Stewart, Stanley. *The Enclosed Garden: The Tradition and the Image in Seventeenth-Century Poetry.* Madison, WI, and London: U of Wisc. P, 1966.

Strack, Hernann L. and Paul Billerbeck. *Kommentar zum Neuen Testament aus Talmud und Midrasch.* 5 vols. in 6. München: C. H. Beck'sche Verlagsbuchhandlung, 1922–56.

List of Works Cited

Tanna DeBe Eliyyahu: The Lore of the School of Elijah. Ed. and trans. William G. Braude and Israel J. Kapstein. Philadelphia: Jewish Publication Society, 1981.

Tasso, Torquato. *Rime d'amore*. Ed. Franco Gavazzeni, Marco Leva, Vercintgetorige Martignone. Modena: Panini, [1993].

Thompson, Charlotte. 'Love in an Orderly Universe: A Unification of Spenser's *Amoretti*, "Anacreontics," and *Epithalamion*'. *Viator: Medieval and Renaissance Studies* 16 (1985): 277–335.

Todd, H. J., ed. *The Poetical Works of John Milton*. 3rd edn. London, 1826.

Turner, James Grantham. *One Flesh: Paradisal Marriage and Sexual Relations in the Age of Milton*. Oxford: Clarendon P, 1987.

Udall, Nicholas, trans. *The Apophthegmes of Erasmus*. Boston, Lincs.: Robert Roberts, 1877.

Urbach, Ephraim. 'Concerning the Language and Sources of the Book "Seder Eliyyahu"' [Hebrew]. *Leshonnenu* 21 (1957): 183–97.

Valency, Maurice. *In Praise of Love: An Introduction to the Love-Poetry of the Renaissance*. New York: Macmillan, 1961.

Wilcher, Robert. *Andrew Marvell*. Cambridge: Cambridge UP, 1985.

Williams, Gordon. *A Glossary of Shakespeare's Sexual Language*. London and Atlantic Highlands, NJ: Athlone P, 1997.

Wimsatt, James I. 'Chaucer and the Canticle of Canticles'. Ed. Jerome Mitchell and William Provost eds, *Chaucer the Love Poet*. Athens, GA: U of Georgia P, 1973. 66–90.

——. 'Panel Discussion'. In *Chaucer the Love Poet*. Ed. Jerome Mitchell and William Provost. Athens: U of Georgia P, 1973. 91–106.

Winstanley, Gerrard. *A Vindication of those, Whose endeavors is only to make the Earth a common treasury, called Diggers: Or, Some Reasons given by them against the immoderate use of creatures, or the excessive community of women called Ranting; or rather Renting*. London, 1649.

Witherspoon, Alexander M. and Frank J. Warnke, eds. *Seventeenth-century Prose and Poetry*. 2nd edn. New York, Chicago, Burlingame: Harcourt, Brace & World, 1963.

Wood, Anthony à. *Athenae Oxonienses*. Ed. Philip Bliss. 3rd edn. Vol. 1. 1813. Anglistica & Americana 22. Hildesheim: Georg Olms Verlagsbuchhandlung, 1969. 4 vols.

Wyatt, Sir Thomas. *Collected Poems of Sir Thomas Wyatt*. Ed. Kenneth Muir. 1949. Cambridge, MA: Harvard UP, 1963.

Zumthor, Paul. 'The Text and the Voice'. *New Literary History* 16 (1984): 67–92.

INDEX

Adam, 50, 57 n16, 62, 109 n7, 119, 128, 140, 145–53, 155–8
Adonis, 88–99
agape, 79, 119, 148–50, 152
Akiba, 5, 6 &n9, 18 &n20, 25
allegory, 6 n10, 7, 18–20, 23, 27, 29, 31–33, 37, 39, 40, 43–5, 50, 53, 55, 60, 62, 63 n18, 65, 67, 72, 75, 77–81, 83, 86, 90, 93, 100–107, 110, 111, 113, 114, 117–19, 127, 134, 135, 148 n12, 149, 152
Anacreon, 68
Anderson, David, 70 n6, 141 n1
apocalypse, 1, 2, 6, 10–12, 18, 19, 24, 29, 31–3, 65, 83, 87, 91, 122, 128 n11, 134, 136, 138–40, 147, 150, 157, 158, 160
Asals, Heather, 91
Astell, Ann W., 20
Aylett, Robert, 65, 88, 100–20, 140, 160

Baldi, Sergio, 141 n1, 142
Baldwin, William, 31–65, 66, 69, 72–87, 88, 92, 99, 100, 118, 120, 140, 160; *Mirror For Magistrates*, 35
Baroway, Israel, 66, 67, 69, 73–6, 78–80
Bennett, Joan M., 146
blazon, 55 &n14, 69, 77
Book of Common Prayer 34, 36
Booth, Stephen, 58
Boyarin, Daniel, 6 n10
Boyarin, Jonathan, 2 n3
Boyle, Elizabeth, 66, 74, 86
Brightman, Thomas, 122 &n3, 137
Bruns, Gerald, 6 n10

Campbell, Lily B., 31 n1, 32, 52 n11
Canticles *see* Song of Songs
carnality, 6, 18, 19, 22, 23, 25, 26, 28, 29, 31, 33, 37, 39–42, 47, 50–6, 63, 72–4, 78, 80–1, 86, 87, 90, 91, 99, 100–1, 103, 105–9, 116 n11, 118, 119, 121, 124–5, 127, 128, 135, 139, 140, 145, 149–50, 155, 157, 158, 160
Castiglione, Baldassare 98 n3
Cavalcanti, Guido, 20–3, 25, 26, 29, 65, 70–2, 140–5
Cavanaugh, Sister Francis Camilla 32, 47 n9, 57 n15
Chaucer, Geoffrey, 19 &n21, 28, 29, 31, 54, 56, 160
Church
  Anglican, 34
  Protestant, 11, 33, 34, 40, 41, 45, 47, 67, 100, 101, 103, 105, 117, 118, 120, 149, 160
  Roman Catholic, 46, 47, 50, 60
Clarkson, Laurence, 123–5, 129–33, 135, 136, 139, 140, 145, 147, 152, 155, 157, 160
closure, 1, 10–12, 18, 19, 33, 52, 65, 66, 83, 85 n13, 87, 158
Cohn, Norman, 120 n1, 127–8 n11
Contini, Gianfranco, 21, 22 n26, 144
Coppe, Abiezer, 123, 125–7, 131–40, 145, 147–50, 152–5, 157–8, 160
Coverdale, Miles, 33 n1, 43, 52 n11, 53 n12
coyness, 54, 55, 93, 108, 109, 137
cuneiform, 12, 13 n16, 15

Dante Alighieri, 20, 21, 23–9, 65, 72, 80, 140, 144
Davis, J. C., 120–21 n1
DeNeef, A. Leigh, 67, 74 n10, 75, 82
Derrida, Jacques, 3 &n5
desire, 16, 17, 19, 21, 23, 25, 28, 37, 40, 42, 43, 51, 66, 71–3, 78–81, 91–4, 96, 101, 104, 105, 108–10, 114, 116, 122, 123, 130, 136, 144, 149 n15, 150, 155, 157, 158
di Giunta, Bernardo, 70 &n4, 141
diachronic development, 1, 2, 144
doctrine, 18, 25, 33, 35, 36, 39, 41, 45, 47,

Index

56, 60, 98 n3, 102, 117, 124, 128, 133, 146, 152, 158
dolce stil nuovo, 21, 140–1
donna angelicata, 22, 24, 71, 74, 141, 144
Donne, John, 32, 57, 59–60, 65, 94, 103, 105–6, 115
Dronke, Peter, 20, 22 n27
Dubrow, Heather, 91
Dumuzi, 13, 14, 99
Dunlop, Alexander, 68

Eco, Umberto, 29
Eden, 25, 63, 80, 117, 137, 147, 148, 159
Edward VI, 32, 34, 35, 37, 40
Ein-Gedi (En-gaddi), 48, 49
Engammare, Max, 20, 32, 52 n11
eros, 71, 119, 148–52
Etienne, Robert (Stephanus) 43, 48–50, 63
Eve, 62, 109 n7, 119, 140, 145–53, 155–9

Faur, José, 4–5 n7, 11
Fisch, Harold, 150–1 n17
Fixler, Michael, 122 n4, 138 n15
Fletcher, Giles, 113 n10, 116 n11, 117
Fletcher, Phineas, 116 n11, 117
Fowler, Alastair, 57 n16, 148 n12
Fox, George, 128
Fox, Michael V., 16, 17
Frazer, Sir James, 90 n1
Friedman, Jerome, 120 n1

gardens, 20, 29, 54, 63, 64, 75, 80, 94, 141, 143, 144, 150
Geller, Mark J., 15 n.17
Geneva [Bible], 43, 53 n12, 92
Gibbs, Donna, 74 n10, 82
Goodblatt, David, 7 n11
Great Bible, 33 &n2, 34, 39–42, 46–9, 52 n11, 53 n12, 92
Gresham, Stephen, 31 n1, 32
Grossman, Marshall, 1 n1, 34
Guibbory, Achsah, 147 n10, 151 n18
Guinizelli, Guido, 143, 144

Hamilton, A. C., 91, 98 n3
Handelman, Susan, 3 n5
Hardison, O. B., Jr., 21 n23, 71
Harrison, Robert P., 21 n25, 22 n27
Hawes, Clement, 121 n1, 128 n11, 132 n12, 155
Hebrew, 3, 4, 6 n10, 8, 11, 16–18, 23, 24, 32, 33, 39, 40, 42–3, 46, 48, 63, 66, 86, 89, 95, 118, 124, 137, 138, 151 nn17 and 18
Henry VIII, 34, 35, 40
Herbert, George, 32, 47, 48, 57, 60, 62
Hester, M. Thomas, 68–9, 85 n13
Hill, Christopher, 120 n1, 128 n11, 132 n12, 145, 146 &n9
Holstun, James, 121 n1, 128 n11, 155
Homes, Nathanael, 118, 119, 122 & n4, 137–8
humanism, 86, 144
Hunter, William B., 101 n3, 113 n10, 116 n11

imagery
   agricultural, 36
   apocalyptic, 2
   body, 47, 55, 80, 85
   breast, 17, 39–41, 48, 53, 55, 75–7, 79–81, 136
   carnal, 39, 73, 74, 118
   coal, 97
   contrastive, 45
   conventional, 85 n13
   darkness, 47
   dawn, 143–4
   domestic, 10
   epithalamic, 67
   erotic, 36, 75
   fish, 50
   flower, 76
   food, 75, 111
   horse, 95, 96
   jewelry, 53
   light, 69
   nature, 44, 58
   negative, 47
   night, 46
   olfactory, 75
   pastoral, 37
   place, 49
   sexual, 52, 71, 93, 106, 110, 113, 135, 136, 148, 150
   silver, 73
   violent, 11, 92, 97, 114–15
   woman as flower, 76
Inanna, 13 &n16, 14, 99
intertextuality, 4, 6 n10, 22, 24, 28, 31, 62, 65, 66, 69, 72, 73, 86, 99, 100, 140, 141, 143, 146
Italian, 20, 22, 24–6, 69, 140–5

171

Index

Jesus, 7–11, 42, 90, 108, 113 n10, 153, 157
Jews, 45, 90, 122, 127, 137–9, 155
Johnson, William C., 67, 68, 74 n10, 78, 80–3
Josephus, 49
Judaism, 6 n10, 10, 11, 136, 137

Kalmin, Richard, 7 n11
Kaske, R. E., 28, 29,
Kaske, Carol, 67, 68, 82, 85 n13
Kasten, David S., 32 n1
Katz, David S., 122 n4, 138 n15
Keach, William, 91, 98
Kermode, Frank, 63 n18, 64
Kerrigan, John, 58
King, John N., 32, 33 n2, 67, 82
kisses, 41, 42, 93, 98, 135, 155, 158, 160
Kraemer, David, 3 n4
Kramer, Samuel N., 12 n15, 13 &n16, 17

Lachs, Samuel T., 18 n20
Lambert, W. G., 12 n15, 15 n17
Leick, Gwendolyn, 14–15, 17
Lever, J. W., 91
Lewalski, Barbara K., 101, 102
libertinism, 125, 127, 133, 134, 135
Littledale, Richard F., 20, 45
Lord, Albert B., 2 &n2, 10
Low, Anthony, 68, 149 n14
Lucianus Samosatensis, 89
Luther, Martin, 11, 41

Marlowe, Christopher, 109
Marot, Clément, 55 &n14, 69, 77
Martz, Louis, 82
Marvell, Andrew, 31, 32, 57, 62–5, 109 &n7, 137
Matter, E. Ann, 20
McColley, Diane K., 148 n12
Mesopotamia, 12, 16, 17, 42
Middle Ages, 8, 20, 21, 29, 54
midrash, 2, 3, 5, 6 & n10, 8–11
Milton, John, 32, 57–8 n16, 62, 63, 65, 88, 99, 100, 101 n3, 109 &nn 7 and 8, 116–9, 140–59, 160; *Paradise Lost*, 57, 62, 65, 99, 100, 109 n7, 116 n12, 119, 140, 145–59; Sonnet 5, 140–44
Morton, A. L., 120 n1, 122, 128, 129
Moses, 4–6, 11, 133
Muggleton, Lodowick, 132–3;
  Muggletonians, 130, 133

myth, 2, 5, 10, 11, 13 n16, 22, 23, 80, 88–92, 95, 97, 99, 104, 137, 141, 145

Neusner, Jacob, 10 n14
New Testament, 2, 6–10, 42, 108, 112, 119
nudity, 77, 147

Ong, Walter J., 2, 3 n4
orality, 1–8, 10–12, 15, 17–19, 22, 24, 25, 27, 29, 31–4, 37, 38, 40, 43, 44, 50, 54, 56, 61, 69, 76, 78, 80, 87, 91, 92, 103, 118, 119, 121, 123, 124, 127, 139, 140, 150–2, 160
Origen, 18–20, 25, 33, 56, 100, 105, 107, 118, 119
Ovid, 88, 90, 91, 99 ; *Ovide Moralisé*, 90, 91

Padelford, Frederick M., 100 n1, 103, 104, 110, 116 n12
Palliser, D. M., 34
parable, 2, 8–11, 19
Parry, Milman, 1, 2 n2, 10
Partridge, Eric, 96
Perkins, William, 102
Petrarch, Francesco, 93, 140, 142, 144
polysemy, 3, 6, 15 n17, 30, 31
Poole, Matthew, 108
Pope, Marvin H., 12 n15, 16 n18, 17 n19, 39, 43 n7
Pound, Ezra, 70 &n6, 72
Prescott, Anne L., 67
prostitution, temple, 89–90
Puritans, 116, 120–22, 124

Rabbinic discourse, 2–11, 18–19, 31
Ranters, 19, 65, 88, 119, 120–39, 140, 145–50, 152–8, 160
Ranters Declaration, The, 129
Ranter's Religion, The, 130
Rogers, Richard, 102
Rosenblatt, Jason, 150–1 n17
roses, 93, 116 n11, 143, 144
Roulston, Gilbert, 123 n5, 128, 147
Russell, Rinaldina, 141 n1, 143

Salmon, Joseph, 122–4, 130–1
Sandys, George, 88, 89, 92
Satan, 146–52, 156, 157
Scheper, George, 67, 118

172

Index

secrecy, 121, 123, 125–7, 131, 134, 138, 139, 160
Sefati, Yitschak, 12–14, 17
sexuality, 2, 12, 13, 15–17, 23, 29, 31, 33, 39, 40–2, 47, 48, 50–4, 56, 60, 65, 67, 69, 71, 72, 76–80, 86, 88, 89, 91, 93, 95, 96–8, 100–1, 103–10, 113–19, 120–1, 127–39, 143–52, 155, 157, 158, 160
Shakespeare, William, 32, 38, 55 n14, 57–9, 65, 88–99, 109 n7, 120, 140, 160; *Venus and Adonis*, 65, 88–99, 140
Shawcross, John T., 141 n4, 143 n8, 144–5
Sidney, Sir Philip, 31 &n1
Smith, Hallett, 57–8
Smith, Nigel, 121 n1, 122 n2, 125–7, 130–8, 152–8
Solomon, 13 n16, 16, 25, 28, 32, 36, 41, 54, 67, 73, 111, 112, 121, 132, 133, 135, 148, 149, 152
Song of Solomon *see* Song of Songs
Song of Songs (references to specific verses in parentheses): 16 n18 (1.1), 17 (8.1–3), 17 n19 (8.6), 21–2 n 26 (3.6, 6.9[10], 8.5), 25 (4.8), 28 (6.10, 8.6), 32 (2.17), 33 n2 (6.8), 36 (3.7–8, 7.11–12), 37 (1.3), 39 (1.2), 41 &n6 (1.4), 42–4 (2.11–14), 44–7 (3.1–4), 47 (2.6), 47–50 (1.12–14), 50–52 (5.4–6), 52–6 (7.2–10 [AV 7.1–9]), 59 (1.7), 61 (1.15), 62–3 (5.1), 71–3 (6.10), 73–4 (5.11, 14–15), 75–8 (4.10–16), 78–9 (2.10–13), 81 (4.1–3), 83 (3.1–4), 84 (6.8), 93 (1.2), 94 (5.10–13, 6.1–3), 95 (1.9–11), 97 (4.4, 8.6–7), 112 (4.1–6), 113 n10 (2.8–9, 4.1–5, 5.10–16, 6. 4–10, 7. 1–9), 114 (8.6), 116 n11 (5.2–8), 118 (5.4), 132 (4.7), 134 (2.10–13, 2.17, 5.2), 135 (1.2), 136 (1.13), 138 (5.4), 141 (6.10), 148–9 &n12 (2.10–13, 7.11–12), 152 (2.10, 4.7).
Spenser, Edmund, 21 n23, 32, 57, 65, 66–87, 88, 100–1, 103–5, 108, 116–20, 140, 141, 160; *Amoretti*, 21 n23, 57, 66–87, 101, 108, 116–17, 141; *Anacreontics*, 68–9, 85–6; *Epithalamion*, 66, 68, 71, 82–3, 85–6
spirituality, 7, 18, 19, 21–24, 27, 28, 31, 33, 35–37, 39–42, 44, 45, 47, 50–2, 54–7, 60–5, 67–9, 72, 73, 77–82, 84, 85, 99, 101–10, 113, 115–17, 119, 121, 122, 124–7, 129–36, 139–41, 143–6, 148–55, 157, 160
Stern, David, 8, 11
Stewart, Stanley, 32, 52 n11, 63 n18
Sumer, 12–17, 29, 31, 65, 94, 99
Synagogue, 4, 45
synchronic pattern, 1, 4, 12, 19, 29, 31, 151 n18

Talmud, 3 n4, 5–8
Tanna DeBe Eliyyahu, 8–11
Tasso, Torquato, 69 &nn2 and 3, 70, 142
textuality, 1–6, 10–12, 19, 24, 33, 37–8, 40, 56, 69, 80, 91–2, 121, 144, 151 n17, 160
Thompson, Charlotte, 67
Todd, H. J., 148 n12
Turner, James G., 120 n1, 123 n7, 146, 149 n13

Urbach, Ephraim, 8

Valency, Maurice, 21 &n24, 141, 142

Walton, Isaak, 60
Whitchurche, Edwarde, 33 n2
Wilcher, Robert, 63 n18
Williams, Gordon, 96
Wimsatt, James I., 28, 29, 54 &n13, 56
Winstanley, Gerrard, 129, 131
women, 14, 89, 103–8, 114, 115, 117, 129–33, 136, 139, 153–5
Wyatt, Sir Thomas, 57 n15, 143 n5

Zumthor, Paul, 24